CONS[barcode: D0932854]

EQUAL PROTECTION OF THE LAWS

by

LOUIS MICHAEL SEIDMAN
Professor of Law
Georgetown University Law Center

TURNING POINT SERIES®

New York, New York
FOUNDATION PRESS
2003

THOMSON
—————★———— ™
WEST

Turning Point Series is a registered trademark used herein under license.

COPYRIGHT © 2003 By FOUNDATION PRESS

          395 Hudson Street
          New York, NY 10014
          Phone Toll Free 1–877–888–1330
          Fax (212) 367–6799
          fdpress.com

TURNING POINT SERIES

CIVIL PROCEDURE

Civil Procedure: Class Actions by Linda S. Mullenix, University of Texas (Available 2003)

Civil Procedure: Economics of Civil Procedure by Robert G. Bone, Boston University (Available December 2002)

Civil Procedure: Preclusion in Civil Actions by David L. Shapiro, Harvard University (2001)

Civil Procedure: Jury Process by Nancy S. Marder, Illinois Institute of Technology (Available 2003)

Civil Procedure: Territorial Jurisdiction and Venue by Kevin M. Clermont, Cornell (1999)

CONSTITUTIONAL LAW

Constitutional Law: Equal Protection by Louis M. Seidman, Georgetown University (2002)

Constitutional Law: Religion Clause by Daniel O. Conkle, Indiana University, Bloomington (Available 2003)

CRIMINAL LAW

Criminal Law: Model Penal Code by Markus D. Dubber, State University of New York, Buffalo (2002)

Criminal Law: Habeas Corpus by Larry W. Yackle, Boston University (Available 2003)

INTERNATIONAL LAW

International Law: United States Foreign Relations Law by Phillip R. Trimble, UCLA (2002)

LEGISLATION

Legislation: Statutory Interpretation: Twenty Questions by Kent R. Greenawalt, Columbia University (1999)

PROPERTY

Property: Takings by David Dana, Northwestern University and Thomas Merrill, Northwestern University (2002)

CORPORATE/SECURITIES

Securities Law: Insider Trading by Stephen Bainbridge, UCLA (1999)

TORTS

Torts: Proximate Cause by Joseph A. Page, Georgetown University (Available December 2002)

For Jessica and Andrew

*

Acknowledgments

I could not have written this book without the intellectual stimulation that has come from over a quarter century of contact with my colleagues at the Georgetown University Law Center. I am especially grateful to my friend, Girardeau Spann, who read and provided helpful comments on a substantial portion of the manuscript. I am also in debt to a wonderful research assistant, Graeme Smyth, who checked sources, cleaned up my prose, and provided much needed intellectual and emotional support, and to Anna Selden, who did outstanding work to help prepare the manuscript for publication.

*

About the Author

———

Louis Michael Seidman has taught constitutional law at Georgetown University Law Center for more than a quarter century. He has been a visiting professor at Harvard Law School, University of Virginia Law School, and New York University Law School. He is coauthor of a leading casebook on constitutional law and author of *Our Unsettled Constitution: A New Defense of Constitutionalism and Judicial Review.*

*

TABLE OF CONTENTS

ACKNOWLEDGMENTS ------------------------------------ VII
ABOUT THE AUTHOR------------------------------------ IX

CHAPTER ONE WHAT IS EQUALITY AND WHY
    SHOULD WE CARE? ------------------------------ 1
The Problem of Sameness and Difference-------- 3
Rational Equality ----------------------------------- 5
Ethical Equality ------------------------------------- 7
Why Should We Care about Equality?------------ 10
The Political Valence of Equality ----------------- 14

CHAPTER TWO AN OVERVIEW OF THE EQUAL
    PROTECTION CLAUSE ---------------------------- 18
The Origins of Equal Protection ------------------ 19
The Basic Structure of Equal Protection Re-
    view--- 23
A Summary --- 36

CHAPTER THREE LOW LEVEL SCRUTINY ---------- 39
An Example --- 39
Identifying the Classification --------------------- 41
Choosing the Standard of Review ----------------- 46
Identifying the Legislative Purpose -------------- 52
Examining the Nexus------------------------------- 66

CHAPTER FOUR RACE–SPECIFIC CLASSIFICA-
    TIONS THAT DISADVANTAGE RACIAL MINOR-
    ITIES -- 74
The Nature of Heightened Scrutiny for Race–
    Specific Classifications--------------------------- 76
The Actual Status of Race–Based Classifica-
    tions -- 79
What's Wrong with Racial Classifications? ----- 85

TABLE OF CONTENTS

CHAPTER FIVE NON–RACE–SPECIFIC CLASSIFICA-
TIONS THAT DISADVANTAGE RACIAL MINOR-
ITIES 95
Rational Basis Review for Non–Race–Specific
Classifications 96
Improperly Motivated Classifications 103
Limitations on Review for Improper Motive 110
A Summary 119

CHAPTER SIX RACE–SPECIFIC CLASSIFICATIONS
THAT ARE FACIALLY NEUTRAL 120
Separate but Equal 122
The Struggle against Jim Crow 128
Brown 135
Enforcing *Brown* 139
Modern Examples of Strict Scrutiny for Race–
Specific but Facially Neutral Statutes 146

CHAPTER SEVEN RACE–SPECIFIC CLASSIFICA-
TIONS THAT BENEFIT RACIAL MINORITIES 157
Washington v. Davis, Racial Integration, and
Affirmative Action 158
The Modern Law of Affirmative Action 166
Two Unanswered Questions 174
A Normative Appraisal 179

CHAPTER EIGHT GENDER DISCRIMINATION 186
Heightened Scrutiny for Gender–Specific Class-
ifications 188
Should There Be Heightened Scrutiny for
Gender–Specific Classifications? 195
Formal versus Interventionist Equality 201
Examples 207
Affirmative Action 214

TABLE OF CONTENTS

CHAPTER NINE THE BOUNDARIES OF EQUALITY   219
Gay Men and Lesbians   220
Noncitizens   229
Poor People   236
The Future of Suspect Classification Analysis   244

CHAPTER TEN EQUAL PROTECTION AND FUNDA-
    MENTAL RIGHTS   248
An Example, Two Problems, and a Proposed
    Solution   248
The Right to Vote   257
Vote Dilution   264
Access to Judicial Process   277
Travel   279
The End of Substantive Equal Protection?   285

TABLE OF CASES   291
INDEX   297

Constitutional Law:
Equal Protection of the Laws

*

CHAPTER ONE

WHAT IS EQUALITY AND WHY SHOULD WE CARE?

Although the concept of equality is central to modern American constitutional culture, concern about equal treatment long predates enactment of the equal protection clause. For several thousand years, philosophers have written about the importance of equality. They have argued that equal treatment reflects a fundamental postulate grounded in both rationality and fairness.

If two entities are alike, then treating them differently is irrational. Suppose, for example, that an investor owns two identical shares of common stock, in the XYZ company. The investor might be willing to sell one share, two shares, or neither share, but it would be very strange indeed if she cared whether she sold share A or share B. Most people would say that because the shares are fungible, it is irrational to distinguish between them.

When we are talking about human beings, rather than shares of stock, the equality norm reflects an ethical ideal as well as standard of rationality. Suppose that two high school students get the same score on a multiple choice examination. A teacher

1

who gave the two students different grades would have some explaining to do. By virtue of their status as human beings, we might say, both students are of equal moral status. Equality of moral status, in turn, entails equality of treatment. It follows that because the two students have gotten the same score, they ought to get the same grade.

Yet despite the foundational status of the equality norm, it is easy to generate hypothetical situations where the norm produces results that seem perverse. Suppose that two codefendants are wrongfully charged with murder. After the first has been convicted and executed, the innocence of both is established. Does it make sense to execute the second?

Suppose that a boat with eleven people on it is sinking. If the life raft will hold only ten, does it make sense to insist that all eleven go down with the ship?

Suppose that A and B are married. Would we think it morally admirable if A treated C, D, and E with precisely the same love and devotion that A gave to B?

How can it be that the basic requirements of rationality and fairness can also be used to generate results that seem manifestly irrational and unfair? In order to answer this question, we need to examine more closely what the equality requirement amounts to.

The Problem of Sameness and Difference

The first step toward understanding the equality norm is to realize that the unadorned requirements of rationality and fairness do not get us very far.

One problem is that sometimes the demands of rationality and fairness conflict. Suppose that A and B both apply for the same job. A is an extremely hard worker, but B is lazy. However, B's innate ability means that he will do the job better than A. If we are committed to rewarding people according to moral worthiness, we might give the job to A, but if we are interested in maximizing output, B should get the job.

Moreover, even when the demands of rational and ethical equality don't conflict, each considered individually is problematic. Consider first rationality. It is easy to imagine situations where even apparently straightforward requirements of rationality do not yield determinate outcomes. The hypothetical concerning the sale of different shares of stock illustrates the problem. If the shares were purchased at different times, the choice of which share to sell might have important tax consequences. It might then make sense to care which share was sold. Or perhaps one share, given to the investor at birth by her grandparent, has sentimental value that the other share lacks.

Similarly, one can imagine circumstances under which it would not violate fairness norms to give two students with the same test score different grades. Perhaps one of the students is a freshman, who, given the student's age and experience, has performed far better than a senior with an identical raw score.

These examples illustrate two important points about equality. First, despite appearances, two entities are never identical. If one looks hard enough, one can always find differences between them. The two shares of stock may seem the same, but, on closer examination, there are many differences between them.

Second, equality is not the same thing as identity. Sometimes, equality requires that we treat two things the same even though they are not identical. For example, the answers provided by two students who receive the same scores on a multiple choice exam may not be identical. Yet although the students may have answered different questions correctly or incorrectly, the exams may be of equal merit, and the students may therefore deserve the same grade.

In the case of two different exams with the same score, the equality norm requires similar treatment despite nonidentity. On other occasions, though, nonidentity seems to require *different* treatment if equality is to be respected. For example, under most circumstances, it would violate the equality norm if a teacher gave the same grade to two students with different scores.

So how do we know when equality requires the same treatment and when it requires different treatment? Because equality is different from identity, and because no two entities can ever be completely identical, equality analysis encourages us to formulate analogies. Even though A and B are not identical, we can say that A is *like* B and therefore should be treated like B. One might say, for example, that a bank employee who embezzles $100,000 is *like* a bank robber who takes the same amount of money at gunpoint and that both criminals should receive the same sentence.

Of course, the problem with analogies is that they focus our attention on similarities, when we might also focus on differences. The robber and embezzler are also different in many respects. We therefore need some method for determining when to focus on similarities and when to focus on differences.

Rational Equality

Thinking about equality in terms of means-ends rationality may help us derive such a method. On this view, similarities are important only if they are *relevant* to a goal that we are trying to accomplish. Indeed, without the specification of such a goal, the equality requirement has no content. For example, two separate shares of stock are similar and dissimilar in an infinite variety of ways. The only way to know whether they are analogous—whether they are *relevantly* similar—is by specifying some end. If an investor values the shares according to their worth in the market, there is no reason to treat them differently. If the investor attaches an idiosyncratic value to one share but not the other, there may be powerful reasons for different treatment.

It is important to see that the equality requirement itself does not restrict the universe of ends
necessary to give the requirement content, at least
so long as it is considered an aspect of rationality.
This fact has led some critics of the requirement to
insist that it is "empty." It is, after all, always
possible to imagine some end that will make different treatment rational and that will therefore de-
feat the analogy between two entities. Given one set
of ends (for example, discouraging theft of property), distinctions between robbers and embezzlers
appear discriminatory, but given another (for example, discouraging the use of violence) such distinctions might appear entirely sensible.

Equality critics have used this fact to argue that
equality really amounts to no more than a requirement that we follow whatever rule we have already
specified. If the rule is "anyone who unlawfully
appropriates $100,000 shall be sentenced to 10
years imprisonment" then a sentence of less than
10 years for the embezzler will appear unequal. But
we might then just as well say "obey the rule."
Saying that we should "obey the rule equally" adds
nothing to the analysis. And, of course, if the rule
is "a ten year sentence for armed robbers, but a
five year sentence for embezzlers," then there is
nothing unequal about a lesser sentence for the
embezzler. Indeed, we might say that a particular
embezzler given a ten year sentence was treated
unequally.

Although this argument has some force, it is also
easy to overstate. Saying that equality is empty

without a specification of ends is merely saying that equality is an aspect of means-ends rationality, which is our starting point. True, rationality itself does not limit the universe of ends, and therefore neither does equality, when it is conceived of as an adjunct to rationality. Still, the equality requirement might be useful in forcing us to examine whether we in fact want to achieve the ends that would make the distinction rational. For example, once it is pointed out that embezzlers and armed robbers are receiving different sentences, we are forced to confront the question whether we mean to deter violence or theft. It is wrong, therefore, to reduce equality to the requirement that any rule we formulate must be obeyed. Equality analysis also makes us think about whether we want the rule in the first place.

Ethical Equality

Perhaps the complaint about the "emptiness" of equality is really a complaint about reducing equality to means-ends rationality. Consider, for example, a rule that provides that men but not women are entitled to an academic scholarship. Equality, conceived of as means-ends rationality, forces us to confront the question whether this distinction really advances any end that we wish to pursue. A person so confronted might conclude that the distinction is irrational and abolish it. But it is also possible that someone might come away from this analysis still convinced that the rule makes sense. For someone who believes that men are simply more deserving than women, it is perfectly rational to grant the scholarship solely to men.

Conceiving of equality as reflecting an ethical requirement might limit the domain of ends, thereby preventing us from hypothesizing certain kinds of ends even though the existence of these ends would make a distinction rational. We might say, for example, that even though a rule providing for male-only scholarships rationally promotes the end of advantaging men, this end itself is inconsistent with the equal moral status of all persons and is therefore impermissible. Focusing on equality as an ethical norm brings to the forefront an important aspect of equal protection that we have so far ignored. The history of equality in the United States has not been about shares of stock and high school exam grades. Rather, it has been about groups that have been—or at least have perceived themselves to be—oppressed. When equality most matters, we are not dealing with isolated cases of injustice or irrationality, but with systematic subjugation. This kind of subjugation is not just a mistake—a failure to think through the relationship of means to ends—but an exercise of power. One might suppose, therefore, that the ethical version of equality would be useful in explaining what is wrong with such subjugation and in identifying it when it occurs.

Unfortunately, though, ethical equality is also problematic. Consider, for example, the debate over abortion. Some abortion opponents have argued that pro-choice advocates dehumanize fetuses in much the way that pro-slavery advocates dehumanized African Americans.[1] They claim that the equal moral status of all human beings means that we should analogize the unborn to the born and treat both equally, just as we must treat persons equally despite differences in skin color. Pretending that fetuses are not human beings reflects the same sort of ethical blindness that made slavery possible.

Understandably, arguments of this sort infuriate believers in abortion choice, as well as some defenders of racial equality. African Americans are nothing like fetuses, they will claim. African Americans are appropriate rights bearers, whereas fetuses are not. For these advocates, it is the comparison between African Americans and fetuses that reflects ethical blindness.

It should be apparent that equality analysis cannot settle this argument. On the contrary, equality analysis presupposes that the argument has already been settled. If the unborn are "like" the born, in the same way that African Americans are "like" people of other races, then the argument makes sense; if they are not, then it doesn't. But now we again confront the fact that the born and unborn are both alike and different. Treating equality as an ethical norm requires us to specify the ethical relevance of the similarities and differences. And once we have done this, the equality norm is left with no work to do.

1. *See, e.g.* John T. Noonan, Jr., *The Root and Branch of* Roe v. Wade, 63 Neb. L. Rev. 668 (1984).

But although equality rhetoric cannot settle this argument, it might serve to sharpen it. Just as rational equality encourages us to think about whether we really wish to achieve certain ends, so too, ethical equality brings out into the open questions about the ethical relevance of difference. One might ultimately reject the analogy between the born and unborn, or between abortion and slavery, but when an abortion opponent claims that the two are analogous, an abortion supporter is confronted with the necessity of explaining why she thinks that they are different. True, this argument will be rooted in some sort of substantive ethical theory that is not, itself, premised on equality. But although equality itself cannot provide such a theory, it can serve as a goad that forces us to develop it.

Why Should We Care about Equality?

The preceding discussion suggests that it may be a mistake to think of the equality norm as settling arguments. It cannot do that, because, in its rationality form, it presupposes a set of ends that may be disputed and, in its ethical form, it presupposes an ethical theory that it cannot supply. Still, equality discourse may be valuable to the extent that it sharpens arguments and allows us to see what is really at stake. On this view, the problem is not with the equality norm per se, but with equality as a *legal and constitutional* requirement. Most theories of constitutional law assume that constitutional text and norms are supposed to settle legal disputes. For reasons we have already explored, constitution-

al text and norms embodying the equality requirement may be unable to accomplish this goal.

We will return to this difficulty in the chapters
that follow. First, though, it is important to see that
even the more modest goals of equality discourse
can be achieved only if we care about equality in the
first place. But it is not at all clear that we should
care. There are good reasons why we might find the
equal treatment norm unattractive. First, equality
privileges horizontal equity over vertical justice.
Second, equality privileges the universal over the
particular.

To see the first problem, imagine a society where
there are two types of people—the blues and the
greens. Imagine further that the distinction between these two groups is entirely arbitrary and is
wholly unrelated to any ethically or instrumentally
relevant characteristic. Any distinction between the
two is therefore both irrational and unfair. Now
suppose that this society has enacted a law providing that only blue people are eligible for publicly
funded abortions.

I have tried to construct this hypothetical carefully so as to make this difference of treatment un-
controversially unequal. Yet it is far from clear that
we would want to remedy the inequality. Imagine
first that I am an opponent of all abortion funding.
Of course, I would prefer a world in which no one
received it, but this stance has nothing to do with
my commitment to equality; it is instead an entail-
ment of my substantive opposition to the funding.

Equality does real work only if it would cause me to favor a world where both blues and greens receive the funding to one where only blues receive it. But how attractive is this? Surely many opponents of abortion funding would oppose a shift to more such funding.

Similarly, a proponent of funding would favor the elimination of the wholly arbitrary exemptions for greens. But would such a proponent really favor a world where blues and greens alike are unjustly denied the funds to one where at least the blues are treated justly?

This hypothetical suggests that when equality comes into conflict with norms of substantive justice, many people prefer substantive justice (and it is worth emphasizing again that equality does real work only when it requires a result we would not reach if we were applying only the norms of substantive justice).

Of course, not everyone will have the same intuition about the hypothetical. Some people might indeed insist that it is better for all people to be treated unjustly than for some to be treated unjustly while others are not. Similarly, some people might believe that we would, in some sense, be better off in a society where everyone had less, but pretty much the same, than in one where even the poorest had more, but the rich had much more. For these people, equality has an intrinsic value that cannot be reduced to, and should not be subordinated to, substantive claims of justice. Still, for those who have different intuitions, the claims for equality are bound to be problematic.

Moreover, even those who believe that equality is an intrinsic good are likely to be troubled by a second problem. The equality norm is public regarding and universalist in the sense that it pushes us toward valuing the welfare of every member of the community equally. Taken alone, this emphasis seems attractive. The difficulty is that communities themselves are inevitably formed against a backdrop of the exclusion of those who are not community members and therefore not entitled to equal treatment. The problem for equality is how to justify this exclusion.

For example, few Americans believe that United States economic policy should treat the welfare of Canadians in just the way that it treats the welfare of its own citizens. Here, the community boundary, and the exclusion it entails, is relatively uncontroversial. But what are we to make of a Massachusetts law that treats its own citizens better than citizens of New Hampshire, or a United States law that privileges the welfare of people alive today as against future generations?

These problems are difficult because the impulse toward the universal but disinterested beneficence, which the equality norm embodies, runs up against the idea of particularistic, more intimate relationships, with which the norm is in tension. No one supposes that parents should treat their own children in just the same way that they treat the children of strangers. The ability to maintain authentic connection with others—surely an important part of our status as human beings—seems to require the maintenance of special relationships that, in turn, entail unequal treatment of those who are not special. This fact demonstrates that equality has a dark underside: The norm of equal regard for those within a community is always defined against the backdrop of others, who are excluded from the community. Indeed, it is this backdrop of otherness that makes the moral obligation of equality within a community special and valuable.

The Political Valence of Equality

The preceding discussion suggests not only that the equality norm can be controversial, but also that it has a political valence. But the political implications of equality are complex and contradictory.

Sometimes, equality rhetoric tends to promote social change and bring into question distributions created by the private sphere. The reasons for this effect stem from the very nature of equality analysis. As we have already seen, rational equality encourages reconsideration of our underlying goals, and ethical equality encourages reconsideration of our empathic boundaries. Although the equality requirement itself cannot force change, it can at least open up the possibility for change. Application of the norm makes us think about whether we really want to pursue a previously unquestioned goal, and about whether we can really justify a preexisting difference in treatment.

Moreover, to the extent that government intervention is the primary engine of redistribution, equality rhetoric can promote change by making such redistribution seem more acceptable. For reasons addressed above, the culture of equality pushes us toward a public, universalist stance that emphasizes disinterested beneficence at the expense of special relationships. To the extent that government is the home for public values, and to the extent that fear of government amounts to fear of the overriding of private special relationships, widespread acceptance of the equality norm advances the case for government redistribution.

The mechanics of equality analysis also tend to promote government intervention into the private sphere. Consider again our example of the blues and the greens. Conventional constitutional doctrine makes clear that the state is not required to provide any funding at all for abortion services. Nonetheless, if the state provides such funding for the blues, but not the greens, it has violated the equality norm. In theory, the state might remedy this violation by denying funding to both groups, but often it will be politically or practically difficult to take away a benefit already granted to some. The result will be an extension of government benefits to those not previously entitled to them. Hence, political liberals have often attempted to evade the essentially libertarian thrust of American constitutional doctrine by relying on arguments drawn from equality.

Yet, although equality analysis has the potential to undermine the status quo, it also has a countervailing tendency to reinforce it. This tendency stems from equality's commitment to analogical reasoning. Equality claims get off the ground once it is demonstrated that two entities are *like* each other, but treated differently. Of course, as we have already seen, any two entities are both alike and different in an infinite number of respects. Whether the entities *seem* alike is therefore a matter of social construction, rather than a fact about the world. It follows that the scope of socially available analogies can reflect and reinforce, as well as destabilize, the existing distribution of social power.

For example, the first Justice John Harlan, writing in defense of the equality of African Americans at the end of the nineteenth century, found it necessary to make clear that they were nothing like "Chinamen."[2] More than a half century later, his grandson, also a Supreme Court Justice, wrote in defense of married couples who wish to use contraception, but felt called upon to insist that they were nothing like gay couples.[3] And when the Supreme Court got around to providing some constitutional protection for gay Americans, it found it necessary to insist that they were nothing like people who practiced polygamy.[4]

2. *See* Plessy v. Ferguson, 163 U.S. 537, 561 (1896) (Harlan, J., dissenting).

3. *See* Poe v. Ullman, 367 U.S. 497, 552–53 (1961) (Harlan, J., dissenting).

4. *See* Romer v. Evans, 517 U.S. 620, 633 (1996).

These examples do no more than illustrate a point already discussed—that equality is about both sameness and difference and that equality analysis presupposes an intermediate range between the two. If no two things were relevantly similar, then the equality norm could never be violated, yet if everything were like everything else, then the norm would have no meaning. Because equality both destabilizes and reinforces our sense of difference and otherness, it can both promote social change and make the existing distribution of power seem natural and inevitable.

CHAPTER TWO

AN OVERVIEW OF THE EQUAL
PROTECTION CLAUSE

So far, our discussion of equality has been on a high level of abstraction. As we have seen, when the equality norm is viewed in this way, it raises more questions than it answers. But of course equality is about more than abstract philosophical discussions. It is also an important *legal* principle, regularly enforced by courts. Courts do not have the luxury of simply raising questions. The parties to the actual cases that judges decide want answers. In part for this reason, courts rarely resort to abstract philosophical arguments when addressing specific legal issues. Instead, the philosophical arguments are usually mediated through a complex body of constitutional text, history, and doctrine that transform a fundamentally indeterminate set of ideas into a tool that can provide concrete legal answers. The rest of this book consists of an effort to describe how courts have used this tool. This description, in turn, raises a persistent and troubling question: Have judicial efforts to implement the equality norm successfully captured, or merely distorted, the norm itself.

The Origins of Equal Protection

Although several provisions in the Constitution mandate equal treatment under a variety of circumstances, most cases concerning equality arise under the equal protection clause of the fourteenth amendment. The clause provides: "nor shall any State . . . deny to any person within its jurisdiction the equal protection of the laws."

This language states a very broad requirement, but its inclusion in the Constitution arose out of a particular set of historical circumstances. In the immediate wake of the Civil War, Congress enacted the thirteenth amendment, abolishing slavery and freeing African Americans throughout the South. Much to the chagrin of the Radical Republicans then controlling Congress, the formal bonds of slavery were quickly replaced by "Black Codes," which deprived the freedmen of many of their newly granted civil rights, like the right to enter contracts, to testify in court, or to move from place to place.

The Reconstruction Congress was deeply concerned that the fruits of the northern victory in the bloodiest war in American history might be slipping away. It responded with a number of measures, the most important of which, for our purposes, being the Civil Rights Act of 1866.[1] This Act provided that "all persons born in the United States and not subject to any foreign power, excluding Indians not taxed" were citizens of the United States and were

1. 14 Stat. 27.

granted the same right to make and enforce contracts, sue, give evidence, acquire property and "to full and equal benefit of all laws and proceedings for the security of person and property as enjoyed by white citizens." Moreover, all citizens were to be "subject to like punishment, pains, and penalties, and to none other, any law, statute, ordinance, regulation or custom to the contrary notwithstanding."

The authors of the Act claimed that Congress had the constitutional power to enact the provision under section 2 of the thirteenth amendment, which authorized Congress to enforce the abolition of slavery with "appropriate legislation." President Andrew Johnson vetoed the measure in part because he believed that the Act exceeded the federal government's constitutional authority and, although his veto was overridden, doubt remained about whether the Supreme Court would uphold the Act.

The immediate impetus for the fourteenth amendment was the desire to provide a firm constitutional basis for Congress' power to enact the 1866 Act. Early versions of the amendment, drafted by the Joint Committee on Reconstruction, would have done no more than authorize congressional action and would have tied the new rights to rights already granted in the original Constitution. For example, the provision originally adopted by the Joint Committee on Reconstruction provided:

The Congress shall have power to make all laws which shall be necessary and proper to secure to citizens of each state all privileges and immunities of citizens in the several states (Art. IV, Sec. 2); and to all persons in the several States equal protection in the rights of life, liberty and property (5th Amendment).[2]

Eventually, however, this language was changed to make the amendment self-executing. Instead of merely granting power for Congress to act, the newly drafted amendment provided that all persons were entitled to "equal protection of the laws." Section 5 of the amendment was then added, granting to Congress the authority to "enforce" this self-executing requirement "with appropriate legislation." Moreover, the references to the "life, liberty, and property" guarantees of the fifth amendment and the privileges and immunities clause of article IV were removed. These were replaced by separate guarantees against state infringement of "due process" with respect to life, liberty, and property and of the privileges and immunities of United States citizens.

This legislative history leaves a number of interpretive puzzles in its wake. First, it is unclear whom the framers meant to protect. As noted above, there is no doubt that the original proposal was directed primarily at ensuring the freedom of African Americans and seemed designed to grant to them the same rights already granted to white Americans by the original Constitution. However, the Reconstruction Congress also seems to have

2. Quoted in William E. Nelson, The Fourteenth Amendment: From Political Principle to Judicial Doctrine 50 (1988).

made a conscious choice to expand the scope of its concern. As finally adopted, the amendment makes no reference to race and grants a new equality right in sweeping and ambiguous terms that are not tethered to rights granted by the rest of the Constitution. This history leaves unclear the extent to which the new right was meant to be interpreted in light of the particular problems facing African Americans.

This question is linked to a second problem: what institution was going to do the protecting. Specifically, did the framers mean to grant to courts broad authority to interpret the "equal protection" command? There is no doubt that the revised language was intended to give the courts *some* authority. The author of the changes, Representative Hotchkiss of New York, made clear that he intended to broaden the scope of the amendment from a mere grant of authority to Congress to a constitutional command that would be effective even in the absence of congressional action. His purpose was to make certain that courts would enforce the right even if the Republicans lost control of Congress. Still, as a leading historian of the fourteenth amendment concludes, "Hotchkiss, like nearly all others who participated in the adoption of the amendment, expected that 'laws of Congress' would be the primary instrument 'for the enforcement of these rights'."[3] The extent to which the courts might serve as secondary enforcers was left ambiguous.

3. *Id.* at 55.

Finally, the third puzzle concerns what sorts of rights would be protected. The framers seem to have distinguished between "civil," "political," and "social" rights—a distinction that is unfamiliar to us today. There is no doubt that they wished to guarantee the "civil" rights of newly freed slaves. These were the sorts of rights denied by the Black Codes—the right to form contracts, to own property, to move from place to place, and to testify in court. The principal "political" right was the right to vote. Here, the framers seem to have been divided—a division made irrelevant (at least with regard to race-based classifications) by the passage in 1870 of the fifteenth amendment, which prohibited the denial or abridgment of the right to vote "on account of race, color, or previous condition of servitude." Finally there were "social" rights, by which the framers apparently meant equality in social intercourse with whites. Racist assumptions about the inherent inferiority of African Americans were widespread in mid-nineteenth century America, and most of the framers who spoke on the issue disclaimed any intent to create "social" equality.

As explained below, each of these interpretive puzzles has had an important effect on the modern structure of equal protection review.

The Basic Structure of Equal Protection Review

The Court's first occasion to consider these questions came in the Slaughter–House Cases,[4] decided

4. 83 U.S. (16 Wall.) 36 (1872).

five years after passage of the equal protection
clause. In a 5–4 decision the Court rejected a constitutional challenge to a Louisiana statute that granted exclusive rights to a particular corporation to
engage in the slaughtering business in New Orleans. Justice Miller devoted most of his opinion to
disposing of objections to the statute grounded in
the privileges and immunities and due process
clauses of the fourteenth amendment. In the course
of doing so, however, he made clear that the expan-
sive language of the equal protection clause would
be narrowly read in light of the particular historical
experience that gave rise to it. The Court emphasized that in the immediate wake of the Civil War

[Blacks] were in some States forbidden to appear
in the towns in any other character than menial
servants. They were required to reside on and
cultivate the soil without the right to purchase or
own it. They were excluded from many occupa-
tions of gain, and were not permitted to give
testimony in the courts in any case where a white
man was a party. It was said that their lives were
at the mercy of bad men, either because the laws
for their protection were insufficient or were not
enforced.[5]

In light of this history, the Court thought that it
was

not difficult to give a meaning to [the equal
protection] clause. The existence of laws in the
States where the newly emancipated negroes re-

5. *Id.* at 70.

sided, which discriminated with gross injustice and hardship against them as a class, was the evil to be remedied by this clause, and by it such laws are forbidden.

> If, however, the States did not conform their laws to its requirements, then ... Congress was authorized to enforce it by suitable legislation. We doubt very much whether any action of a State not directed by way of discrimination against the negroes as a class, or on account of their race, will ever be held to come within the purview of this provision. It is so clearly a provision for that race and that emergency, that a strong case would be necessary for its application to any other.[6]

As this language makes clear, the Court's initial answer to the first and second questions was that the clause was primarily (perhaps even exclusively) intended to remedy the problems faced by African Americans and that the primary (if not exclusive) source of that remedy was to be Congress. Moreover, the Court's description of the hardships faced by African Americans suggests that its answer to the third question was that the clause was designed to protect civil rights. As we will see, the modern court continues to be influenced by the *Slaughter–House* Court's answer to the first question, although the doctrine has also moved beyond that answer in some important respects. In contrast, the Court has completely rejected the *Slaughter–House* Court's answer to the second question. Over a cen-

6. *Id.* at 81.

tury after it was first asked, the Court's answer to the third question remains ambiguous and contested.

Consider first the view that the Amendment is designed primarily for the protection of African Americans. Some modern doctrine incorporates this limitation. On the one hand, the Court has been extremely skeptical of statutes that facially discriminate against African Americans. For example, seven years after the *Slaughter–House* decision, the Court was confronted with a West Virginia statute that excluded African Americans from jury service. The Court held that the statute violated the equal protection requirement. It interpreted the requirement as

> declaring that the law in the States shall be the same for the black as for the white; that all persons, whether colored or white, shall stand equal before the laws of the States, and, in regard to the colored race, for whose protection the amendment was primarily designed, that no discrimination shall be made against them by law because of their color[.] The words of the amendment, it is true, are prohibitory, but they contain a necessary implication of a positive immunity, or right, most valuable to the colored race,—the right to exemption from unfriendly legislation against them distinctively as colored,—exemption from legal discriminations, implying inferiority in civil society, lessening the security of their enjoyment of the rights which others enjoy, and dis-

criminations which are steps towards reducing them to the condition of a subject race.[7]

In more recent years, the Court has refined this test, holding that laws that classify people on the basis of race are "suspect" and subject to "strict scrutiny." This scrutiny is said to entail a requirement that a law containing a racial classification be in support of a "compelling" governmental end and that the means be "narrowly tailored" so as to accomplish this end. The Court has usually (but not quite always) invalidated such laws.

On the other hand, when classifications are not based upon race, the Court usually applies what is sometimes called "low level" scrutiny. This scrutiny entails a "rational relationship" test. The Court has formulated and applied this test in different ways, but, in general, it has said that the law need be supported by only a "legitimate" state purpose and that the classification need only be "rationally related" to the achievement of that purpose. For example, in Williamson v. Lee Optical,[8] the Court was faced with a statute that made it unlawful for any person not a licensed optometrist or ophthalmologist to fit lenses to a face or to duplicate or replace lenses into frames except on a written prescription of an ophthalmologist or optometrist. Opticians claimed that this statute violated their rights under the equal protection clause, but the Court disagreed:

7. Strauder v. West Virginia, 100 U.S. 303, 307–08 (1879).
8. 348 U.S. 483 (1955).

The problem of legislative classification is a perennial one, admitting of no doctrinaire definition. Evils in the same field may be of different dimensions and proportions, requiring different remedies. Or so the legislature may think. Or the reform may take one step at a time, addressing itself to the phase of the problem which seems most acute to the legislative mind. The legislature may select one phase of one field and apply a remedy there, neglecting the others. The prohibition of the Equal Protection Clause goes no further than the invidious discrimination. We cannot say that the point has been reached here.[9]

The Court has nonetheless departed from the notion that the equal protection clause is restricted to the protection of African Americans in three respects. First, it has adopted a principle which it has labeled "consistency," requiring that *all* racial classifications, even those intended to favor rather than harm African Americans, should be strictly scrutinized.[10] Although this scrutiny need not always be fatal, the Court has exhibited considerable skepticism toward "affirmative action" measures arguably intended to accomplish the very purposes the equal protection clause was meant to serve. Even here, however, remnants of the original *Slaughter–House* approach remain. Thus, the Court continues to assert that the remedying of specific acts of discrimination against African Americans is

9. *Id.* at 489.

10. *See* Adarand Constructors, Inc. v. Pena, 515 U.S. 200 (1995).

a "compelling" governmental purpose which might support affirmative action statutes that are "narrowly tailored."[11] Moreover, it has claimed that strict scrutiny for such measures is appropriate in part because "[a]bsent searching judicial inquiry into the justification for [affirmative action statutes], there is simply no way of determining what classifications are 'benign' or 'remedial' and what classifications are in fact motivated by illegitimate notions of racial inferiority."[12]

Second, the Court has expanded the categories triggering strict scrutiny beyond race. For example, statutes disadvantaging noncitizens,[13] nonmarital children,[14] and, most prominently, women,[15] have been subject to some form of heightened scrutiny, albeit not always as "strict" as that accorded racial classifications. And although the Court has claimed

11. *See* Id.

12. City of Richmond v. J.A. Croson Co., 488 U.S. 469, 493 (1989).

13. *See, e.g.,* Graham v. Richardson, 403 U.S. 365 (1971); Sugarman v. Dougall, 413 U.S. 634 (1973); In re Griffiths, 413 U.S. 717 (1973); Nyquist v. Mauclet, 432 U.S. 1 (1977); Bernal v. Fainter, 467 U.S. 216 (1984). *But cf.* Mathews v. Diaz, 426 U.S. 67 (1976); Foley v. Connelie, 435 U.S. 291 (1978); Ambach v. Norwick, 441 U.S. 68 (1979); Cabell v. Chavez–Salido, 454 U.S. 432 (1982).

14. *See, e.g.,* Levy v. Louisiana, 391 U.S. 68 (1968); Glona v. American Guarantee & Liability Insurance Co., 391 U.S. 73 (1968); Weber v. Aetna Casualty & Surety Co., 406 U.S. 164 (1972); Gomez v. Perez, 409 U.S. 535 (1973). *But cf.* Mathews v. Lucas, 427 U.S. 495 (1976); Lalli v. Lalli, 439 U.S. 259 (1978).

15. *See, e.g.,* Craig v. Boren, 429 U.S. 190 (1976); United States v. Virginia, 518 U.S. 515 (1996).

that it is applying no more than ordinary rational basis review, it has on occasion subjected statutes discriminating against the mentally disabled[16] and gay men and lesbians[17] to something that looks like more than ordinary low-level scrutiny. Here, as well, remnants of the *Slaughter–House* approach are nonetheless apparent. Much of the discussion of which other groups are deserving of special attention has focused on whether these other groups are relevantly "like" African Americans and, so, entitled to similar treatment. For example, Justice William Brennan's influential plurality opinion in Frontiero v. Richardson,[18] first arguing for strict scrutiny of gender classifications, contains a lengthy discussion comparing the history of discrimination against African Americans and women.

Third, the Court has departed from the *Slaughter–House* approach by occasionally heightening the level of scrutiny in response to the interest affected by a classification, rather than to the group discriminated against. Again, this approach contains some echoes of the framers' concerns, especially when one recalls that enactment of the fourteenth amendment was originally triggered by concern for particular civil and political rights. However, the modern court may have gone beyond the original understanding both by expanding the sorts of rights that trigger heightened scrutiny and by insisting on such scrutiny even when the classification itself was not

16. *See* City of Cleburne v. Cleburne Living Center, 473 U.S. 432 (1985).

17. *See* Romer v. Evans, 517 U.S. 620 (1996).

18. 411 U.S. 677 (1973).

along racial or other suspect lines. For example, in Skinner v. Oklahoma,[19] the Court was confronted with a criminal statute that subjected some, but not all, felons to sterilization. In an opinion by Justice William Douglas, the Court did not question an earlier holding that there was no substantive right to avoid forced sterilization. But although the right was not directly protected by the Constitution, it was nonetheless "one of the basic civil rights of man"[20] and "fundamental to the very existence and survival of the race."[21] For this reason, the Court held, discrimination in access to the right was especially suspect. "[S]trict scrutiny of the classification which a State makes in a sterilization law is essential, lest unwittingly, or otherwise, invidious discriminations are made against groups or types of individuals in violation of the constitutional guaranty of just and equal laws."[22] In other cases, the Court has added the right to vote,[23] the right to travel,[24] and, in some circumstances, the right to access to the judicial process[25] to the list of "fundamental rights" triggering heightened scrutiny.

19. 316 U.S. 535 (1942).

20. *Id.* at 541.

21. *Id.*

22. *Id.*

23. *See, e.g.,* Harper v. Virginia State Board of Elections, 383 U.S. 663 (1966); Kramer v. Union Free School Dist., 395 U.S. 621 (1969); Reynolds v. Sims, 377 U.S. 533 (1964).

24. *See, e.g.,* Shapiro v. Thompson, 394 U.S. 618 (1969); Zobel v. Williams, 457 U.S. 55 (1982); Hooper v. Bernalillo County Assessor, 472 U.S. 612 (1985).

25. *See, e.g.,* Griffin v. Illinois, 351 U.S. 12 (1956); Douglas v. California, 372 U.S. 353 (1963); M.L.B. v. S.L.J. 519 U.S. 102 (1996).

As we have seen, the *Slaughter–House* case also expressed a view about the second interpretive puzzle posed by the equal protection clause—the extent to which the clause was meant to add to judicial, as opposed to legislative, power. In keeping with the legislative history of the clause, the Court suggested that Congress was vested with primary enforcement authority, with the courts serving a back-up role. However, the modern court has almost completely reversed this understanding.

Two strands of doctrine bear on the problem. First, the Court has complemented its "consistency" requirement with a requirement of "congruence" which it has defined as requiring the same level of equal protection review for federal and state statutes.[26] This requirement is difficult to explain. As we have already seen, the fourteenth amendment was originally intended to expand, rather than contract, congressional power. Moreover, by its terms, and in keeping with this general purpose, the equal protection clause applies only to the states and imposes no limitations on the federal government. The Court has avoided the textual embarrassment by reading into the fifth amendment due process clause, which applies to the federal government, an equal protection component.[27] This solution creates its own textual difficulties, however, since there is also a due process clause in the

26. *See* Adarand Constructors, Inc. v. Pena, 515 U.S. 200 (1995).

27. *See, e.g.,* Bolling v. Sharpe, 347 U.S. 497 (1954).

fourteenth amendment and, if "due process" really means "equal protection," this renders the fourteenth amendment equal protection clause redundant. The second strand of doctrine involves the Court's construction of the affirmative grant of power to enforce the equal protection clause contained in section 5 of the fourteenth amendment. As we have seen, this affirmative grant to Congress was originally thought to be at the heart of the amendment, with judicial enforcement playing a secondary role. Contrary to the framers' expectations, the modern court has reversed this understanding. It has sharply limited the ability of Congress to exercise its section five power, while giving primacy to its own interpretation of the clause. For example, in United States v. Morrison,[28] Chief Justice William Rehnquist, writing for the majority, held that Congress's section five power was insufficient to support the Violence Against Women Act, which provided a federal civil remedy for gender-based violence. In this and other cases, the Court has insisted on its own interpretation of the equal protection clause, permitting congressional intervention only as an adjunct to judicial enforcement.

What about the framers' distinction between civil and political rights on the one hand and social rights on the other? In 1896, the Supreme Court decided Plessy v. Ferguson,[29] which upheld a Louisiana statute providing for "equal but separate [railroad] accommodations for the white and colored

28. 529 U.S. 598 (2000).

29. 163 U.S. 537 (1896).

races.''[30] The Court relied in part on the argument that association between the races was a social, rather than a civil or political right:

> The object of the [fourteenth] amendment was undoubtedly to enforce the absolute equality of the two races before the law, but, in the nature of things, it could not have been intended to abolish distinctions based upon color, or to enforce social, as distinguished from political, equality, or a commingling of the two races upon terms unsatisfactory to either. Laws permitting, and even requiring, their separation, in places where they are liable to be brought into contact do not necessarily imply the inferiority of either race to the other, and have been generally, if not universally, recognized as within the competency of the state legislatures in the exercise of their police power.[31]

Plessy was effectively overruled in 1954 when the Court held school segregation unconstitutional in Brown v. Board of Education.[32] *Brown* can be read as a repudiation of the distinction between social rights on the one hand and political and civil rights on the other. Thus, the Court emphasized that segregated education was not simply a matter of social interaction. Rather, education

> is required in the performance of our most basic public responsibilities, even service in the armed forces. It is the very foundation of good citizenship. Today it is a principal instrument in awak-

30. *Id.* at 540.

31. *Id.* at 544.

32. 347 U.S. 483 (1954).

ening the child to cultural values, in preparing him for later professional training, and in helping him to adjust normally to his environment.[33]

It followed that "[s]uch an opportunity, where the state has undertaken to provide it, is a right which must be made available to all on equal terms."[34]

However, despite *Brown*'s importance to modern equal protection law, significant aspects of the old social-civil-political trichotomy survive. In particular, the Court continues to insist on some form of governmental action to trigger an equal protection violation. Thus, private discrimination is coded as "social," and therefore involving freedom of association, in contrast to public discrimination, coded as "civil" or "political" and therefore interfering with freedom. For a brief period during the mid-twentieth century, it appeared that this distinction might be on the verge of collapsing. For example, in Shelley v. Kraemer,[35] the Court held unconstitutional judicial enforcement of private racially discriminatory covenants that prevented African Americans from purchasing or occupying homes. Similarly, in the wake of *Brown*, some of the Court's decisions might have been read as mandating desegregation even when the segregation was the product of private housing or enrollment choices.[36] In more re-

33. *Id.* at 493.

34. *Id.*

35. 334 U.S. 1 (1948).

36. *See, e.g.,* Green v. County School Board, 391 U.S. 430 (1968); Swann v. Charlotte–Mecklenburg Board of Education, 402 U.S. 1 (1971).

cent years, however, the Court has veered sharply away from this approach and suggested that, far from being constitutionally vulnerable, private, "social" choices enjoy constitutional protection. For example, in Boy Scouts of America v. Dale,[37] the Court invalidated a state statute that had the effect of preventing the Boy Scouts from dismissing a gay scoutmaster.

Relatedly, the Court has insisted that statutes or government policies having a disproportionate racial impact, but that do not discriminate on their face and do not have the purpose of disadvantaging a suspect class, are subject to only low level scrutiny. For example, in Washington v. Davis,[38] the Court upheld a District of Columbia test for police officers despite the fact that a disproportionately large number of African Americans failed the test. The Court's reasoning rested in part upon the idea that because the statute was facially "neutral," its disproportionate impact was attributable to the private "social" sphere, rather than the public sphere of civil and political rights.

A Summary

Modern equal protection doctrine is a complex amalgam of insights drawn from the text of the fourteenth amendment, the history from which it arose, and a set of modern preoccupations often at variance with that text and history. As we shall see, this mixture often produces confusing and contesta-

37.   530 U.S. 640 (2000).

38.   426 U.S. 229 (1976).

ble outcomes. However, the formal structure of equal protection review can be stated quite simply:

When a court is faced with an equal protection problem, it must first identify the classes of people affected by the statute. Which group of people is advantaged by the statute and which group is disadvantaged? The Court must then ask whether this classification is subject to some sort of heightened scrutiny. Laws or government policies are subjected to such scrutiny when they facially discriminate along suspect lines like race or gender. However, a facially neutral statute does not trigger such scrutiny solely because it has a discriminatory impact on a protected group. Facially neutral laws face heightened review only when they are motivated by the desire to harm the group disadvantaged by them. Even if a law or government policy does not discriminate along suspect lines, it may nonetheless be subject to heightened scrutiny when the law impinges on a "fundamental right" like the right to vote, to travel, to bear children, and to access to judicial processes. Heightened scrutiny involves close judicial oversight over the importance of the end the government is pursuing and the fit between that end and use of the challenged classification. This scrutiny usually, but not always, results in invalidation of the law or policy.

Laws and policies not subject to heightened scrutiny are said to be accorded "low level" review. In these cases, the end need not be "compelling" but only "permissible" and the means need not be "narrowly tailored" but only "rationally related" to the end. This sort of scrutiny usually, but not always, results in validation of the law or policy.

As this summary demonstrates, the basic structure of equal protection jurisprudence is reasonably straightforward. However, the Court's elaborations on this structure are complex and controversial. The chapters that follow explore the complexity and the controversy.

CHAPTER THREE

LOW LEVEL SCRUTINY

As the previous chapter makes clear, statutes and government policies that do not discriminate along "suspect" lines and do not impinge upon "fundamental" rights are subject to low level scrutiny, which usually results in upholding the statute or policy.

An Example

What does such scrutiny amount to? New York City Transit Authority v. Beazer[1] provides a useful illustration of the way in which courts actually apply this test. Beazer challenged the constitutionality of a New York City Transit Authority (TA) policy of refusing to employ persons who used methadone, a synthetic narcotic that, when taken orally, blocks the effect of heroin. Beazer claimed that the law violated the equal protection clause because there was no sound basis for discriminating between the class of individuals using methadone and the class of individuals who did not use the drug. The District Court found as a matter of fact that "there are substantial numbers of methadone users who are just as employable as other members of the general population and that normal personnel-

1. 440 U.S. 568 (1979).

screening procedures—at least if augmented by some method of obtaining information from the staffs of methadone programs—would enable TA to identify the unqualified applicants on an individual basis."[2] Accordingly, the District Court held that a blanket exclusion of all methadone users violated the equal protection clause.

In an opinion written by Justice John Paul Stevens, the Supreme Court reversed this judgment:

At its simplest, the District Court's conclusion was that TA's rule is broader than necessary to exclude those methadone users who are not actually qualified to work for TA. We may assume not only that this conclusion is correct but also that it is probably unwise for a large employer like TA to rely on a general rule instead of individualized consideration of every job applicant. But these assumptions concern matters of personnel policy that do not implicate the principle safeguarded by the Equal Protection Clause. As the District Court recognized, the special classification created by TA's rule serves the general objectives of safety and efficiency.... Under these circumstances it is of no constitutional significance that the degree of rationality is not as great with respect to certain ill-defined subparts of the classification as it is with respect to the classification as a whole.[3]

2. *Id.* at 577.
3. *Id.* at 592–93.

At first, this reasoning seems puzzling. If it is indeed true that some methadone users are as employable as nonusers, why is the distinction between these two groups rational? Why, precisely, is the putative irrationality of "subparts of the classification" insignificant if Beazer, himself, belongs to a subpart that is unfairly treated? How is the TA's objective of running a safe and efficient transit system advanced by refusing to hire those methadone users who will be safe and efficient workers?

In order to answer these questions, it is necessary to examine more closely the mechanics of equal protection review. As we saw in the last chapter, these mechanics typically involve four separate steps. First, some group of people must be identified that is treated "unequally" under the statute or policy in question. Put differently, we must identify two classes of people, one of which is treated worse than the other. Once this is accomplished, the second step is to identify the level of scrutiny to be applied to this classification. The third step is to assign a purpose or goal for the statute. The final step is to use the chosen level of scrutiny to examine the nexus between the classification and the goal. The rest of this chapter uses the facts of *Beazer* to describe each of these steps.

Identifying the Classification

In order for there to be an equal protection classification, there must be two groups of people, one of which is treated worse than the other. But which groups should we compare? The groups we choose can make a big difference in how the case is decided. For example, on the facts of *Beazer*, if we compare all methadone users to all nonusers, it is quite possible that as a class, users are statistically more likely to cause accidents than non-users. On the other hand, if we compare users who have successfully completed three years of treatment to nonusers who are chronic alcoholics, the outcome might be very different.

In general, the Court has insisted that the groups to be compared are those formed by the policy itself. Thus, the TA policy distinguishes between all methadone users and all nonusers, not between long-time methadone users and alcoholics. Therefore, the constitutionality of the statute depends upon whether the distinction between users and nonusers is permissible.

This general rule is subject to an important qualification: Sometimes, a government policy is deliberately gerrymandered with the purpose of singling out a group that is not described on the face of the statute. Suppose, for example, that the officials formulating the TA policy knew that virtually all potential employees who used methadone lived within certain neighborhoods. If the policy disqualified individuals living within those neighborhoods, and the policy was established *so that* methadone users would be excluded, then a court would treat the policy as if it facially excluded methadone users. (This qualification is discussed at greater length in Chapter Five).

Why are plaintiffs challenging government action stuck with classifications formed by the statute and not permitted to choose classifications of their own? At least part of the reason stems from the theory of ethical equality. Recall from Chapter One that this theory treats equality as an outgrowth of the claim that every individual has to equal regard and respect. A classification that facially disadvantages a class might be taken to express disrespect for members of that class in a way that the unintentional impact of the policy does not. Moreover, the Court's approach also makes some sense from the perspective of rational equality. Rational equality grounds the equality norm in the observation that sometimes different treatment of two entities does not serve our ends. But often, it will serve the ends of government to create classifications that have an unfair impact on some subgroups. Indeed, if plaintiffs could choose their own classifications, virtually no statute or policy could survive equal protection scrutiny. Consider, for example, a statute that restricts driver's licenses to individuals over the age of 16. An opponent of this statute could always define some class 15 year old applicants who are safer drivers than some class of 17 year old applicants. (Perhaps the class of 15 year old applicants who are outstanding students are safer drivers than 17 year old applicants who have criminal convictions). If statutes were unconstitutional for this reason, all of government would be paralyzed.

It does not follow, however, that unfairness to classes of individuals not defined by the government action is irrelevant to the analysis. As we shall see when we get to the examination of the nexus between means and ends, this unfairness may influence our judgment about whether the statutory classification is, overall, a fair one. For now, the important point is that it is this classification, rather than other classifications we might imagine, that must be evaluated.

Before we turn to that evaluation, one further complication must be introduced: In order to make out an equal protection violation, there must *be* a classification. This means that a mere mistake, or *mis*classification, does not give rise to an equal protection violation. Suppose, for example, that Beazer was qualified for a TA job, but the TA failed to hire him because it lost his application. To be sure, he would have reason to complain, but the reason would not be grounded in the equal protection clause. The equal protection clause does prohibit some classifications even when there is only one person in the disadvantaged class.[4] Thus, if a government official deliberately threw out Beazer's application because he did not want him to get the job, Beazer could justly invoke the equal protection clause even if he were the only one so treated. However, as the Court has put the point, "mere errors of judgment by officials will not support a claim of discrimination. There must be something more—something which in effect amounts to an

4. *See, e.g.,* Village of Willowbrook v. Olech, 528 U.S. 562 (2000).

intentional violation of the essential principle of practical uniformity."[5] When the government merely makes a mistake, it has, once again, not demonstrated the kind of disrespect that it shows when it deliberately excludes a class of people from a benefit. Moreover, in an important sense, it has not really created a classification at all. The classification is formed by the government's policy, not by the misapplication of the policy in a particular case.

Suppose that a government agency makes a mistake and then deliberately fails to correct it? This deliberate failure does create a classification: an official government policy divides people into the class of individuals victimized by a mistake and those not so victimized. It does not follow that this division necessarily constitutes an equal protection violation, however. The government might have a good reason for discriminating between these two groups. Suppose, for example, that the government mistakenly gave one person extra social security benefits to which the person was not entitled. It does not follow from this single mistake that thousands of other recipients must now get the extra benefit. Of course, the government could remedy the equal protection problem by recouping the benefits wrongly provided, but it might be rational for the government to conclude that this remedy would impose a special hardship on the individual who, perhaps, had already spent the money.

5. Sunday Lake Iron Co. v. Wakefield Tp., 247 U.S. 350, 353 (1918).

Choosing the Standard of Review

As the social security example illustrates, the mere fact that a classification treats some people worse than others does not make out an equal protection violation. Once we have identified the classification, the next step is to choose the standard under which the classification is to be judged. Classifications like the one challenged in *Beazer* are typically referred to as "ordinary social and economic legislation" and subject to "low level" or "rational basis" review. The Supreme Court has used a variety of verbal formulations to capture this test. It has said that the classifications are valid if "rationally related to a legitimate state interest,"[6] and invalid only if "the classification rests on grounds wholly irrelevant to the achievement of the State's objective."[7] Classifications "[do] not violate the Equal Protection clause merely because [they] are imperfect,"[8] but "the classification must be reasonable, not arbitrary, and must rest upon some ground of difference having a fair and substantial relation to the object of the legislation, so that all persons similarly circumstanced shall be treated alike."[9]

If some of this language were taken literally, virtually any legislative classification would satisfy the equal protection clause. It would be surprising if

6. City of New Orleans v. Dukes, 427 U.S. 297, 303 (1976).

7. McGowan v. Maryland, 366 U.S. 420, 425 (1961).

8. Dandridge v. Williams, 397 U.S. 471, 485 (1970).

9. F.S. Royster Guano Co. v. Commonwealth of Virginia, 253 U.S. 412, 415 (1920).

government officials often acted in ways that were completely beyond the bounds of rationality. And, indeed, invocation of low level scrutiny almost always does lead to upholding the challenged policy, although, as we shall see, there are important exceptions. Thus, in *Beazer* itself, the court was prepared to concede that the TA policy was unwise, but nonetheless had little trouble upholding its constitutionality.

Does low level scrutiny of this sort abdicate the court's responsibility to enforce the equal protection clause? One could fairly ask why it matters whether government officials have been "rational" if they have in fact treated two groups of people unequally. If methadone workers are in fact equally qualified for transit jobs, shouldn't they have an equal opportunity to have the jobs, even if some people hold the rational, but mistaken belief that they are not qualified?

There are no fully satisfactory answers to these questions, but we can at least understand the impetus behind low level scrutiny if we distinguish between issues about the substantive requirements of the equal protection clause and issues about the institution best able to enforce those requirements. The first question is whether the TA policy violates the clause. The second question is what to do when there is reasonable disagreement about the answer to the first question. A judge might say, for example, that she believes that the TA policy violates the equal protection clause, but that, nonetheless, the TA itself should have the last word about this issue.

Put differently, the equal protection clause might be "underenforced" by courts. Even though it substantively requires certain results, the final judgment as to the results it requires might be left to the political branches, at least so long as political actors behave "rationally."

Of course, merely stating that this allocation of power is possible does not make the case that it is desirable. There are some obvious reasons why it might seem undesirable. After all, if the equal protection clause is intended to impose restrictions on government bodies like the TA, it hardly seems sensible to allow the TA to decide for itself the scope of those restrictions.

A standard answer to this argument is to invoke democracy. On this view, whenever courts upset political decisions, they are interfering with democratic outcomes, which is taken to be presumptively problematic. There are several weaknesses in this argument, however. One might start by wondering just how democratically responsive a bureaucracy like the TA really is. Its employment rules are hardly the subject of constant democratic deliberation—especially when the rules disadvantage a group lacking much political power, like recovering drug addicts. As we shall see in Chapter Four, a substantial body of equal protection doctrine has grown up around the argument that political decisions are not necessarily democratic in cases where "discrete and insular minorities" are disadvantaged by government classifications.

Some defenses of rational basis review are premised on the assumption that, aside from occasional malfunctioning (like discrimination against discrete and insular minorities), political processes work fairly well. By forming coalitions with others, groups are generally able to prevent legislation that imposes grievous loss. True, any legislative scheme produces political winners and losers, but, because most Americans have multiple political identities, these tend to balance out over time. Thus, it is wrong to suppose that just because one statute imposes costs on farmers, they have been denied equal treatment. A second statute might grant them special benefits. And even if some groups rarely or never are political winners, members of these groups may also be members of other, overlapping, groups that are winners.

This optimistic view of the political process is controversial, however. An alternative view argues that there is no reason to suppose that things work out fairly, even over time. This view holds that the political process is vulnerable to systematic capture by special interests, who are able to use public power to direct resources to themselves at the expense of disorganized and diffuse majorities. A person holding this more pessimistic view might be more troubled by low level review of statutes that seem to amount to no more than mere wealth transfers.

In any event, there is a more basic problem with an argument for rational basis review that is premised on respect for political decisionmaking. Constitutional provisions are usually assumed to limit the scope of this decision making. For example, if a court invalidates a statute that prohibits the practice of a minority religion, it is hardly fair to criticize that result because it is undemocratic. As Justice Robert Jackson wrote many years ago,

> The very purpose of a Bill of Rights was to withdraw certain subjects from the vicissitudes of political controversy, to place them beyond the reach of majorities and officials and to establish them as legal principles to be applied by the courts. One's right to life, liberty, and property, to free speech, a free press, freedom of worship and assembly, and other fundamental rights may not be submitted to vote; they depend on the outcome of no elections.[10]

Presumably one's right to equal protection stands on no lesser footing.

Perhaps a more satisfactory defense of rational basis review rests on the incapacity of courts, rather than on special deference owed to political decision-makers. Recall that the framers' original intent was to empower the legislative, rather than the judicial branch, to enforce the requirements of equal protection. One can think of some good reasons for this choice. Even a pessimist about the political process might have qualms about the ability of judges to correct the problem. It will often be unclear whether a particular piece of legislation unfairly transfers wealth away from politically disadvantaged groups,

10. West Virginia State Board of Educ. v. Barnette, 319 U.S. 624, 638 (1943).

or whether it serves an authentic public purpose. Moreover, as the previous analysis indicates, the unfairness of any statutory scheme depends not just on that scheme alone, but on a global view of the way in which all statutes impact on the group in question. Even if the TA's policy disadvantages methadone users, perhaps they have been compensated for their loss by an increased appropriation for drug treatment programs. One might fairly doubt the ability of judges, who are restricted to deciding the individual cases that come before them, to accurately map and respond to these complex interactions.

Moreover, as we shall see, resolution of an equal protection claim almost always requires a value judgment that, by its nature, is not resolvable through resort to constitutional text or history. In *Beazer*, for example, the TA was faced with a judgment about whether to use scarce resources to make more individualized judgments about the employability of individual methadone users. More fine textured judgments would be fairer to individual workers and might even produce a better work force. On the other hand, the resources spent making these judgments could be used to refurbish trains, improve service, or even to provide more and better drug treatment programs. It is simply fanciful to suppose that tools of legal analysis are useful to resolve this dilemma.

Of course, this problem alone does not differentiate equal protection cases from a host of other constitutional issues regularly resolved by courts despite the fact that text and history are indeterminate. If equal protection is special, it is because these value judgments are more often linked to factual states of affairs that are contingent and ephemeral. Thus, the wisdom of a particular hiring policy depends not just on judgments about how resources should be allocated, but also on empirical judgments that will be different at different times and in different places. Government programs might therefore be constitutional in some places, but not others, or might be unconstitutional for a period and then become constitutional. Decentralized political decision makers can take empirical differences into account, but were the Supreme Court to do so, it would draw attention to the contingency and impermanence of constitutional law. And although some might believe that this attention would be a good thing, it would create considerable discomfort for judges whose self-image revolves around their supposed role as the defenders of enduring principles.

Identifying the Legislative Purpose

Recall that rational equality requires that the means we choose be efficacious in advancing our ends. Having identified the classification (the means) and settled on a level of scrutiny, the next step in the analysis is to identify the end we are trying to achieve.

This problem is more complex than it might at first appear. Individuals have purposes or ends, but collective institutions do not. To be sure, their members have purposes, but these purposes may not be the same. Perhaps one member of the TA wants to exclude methadone users because he thinks that they are unsafe workers, a second wants to exclude them because she thinks that their treatment will require them to miss work too often, a third has an irrational prejudice against methadone users, a fourth wants to exclude them because he fears bad publicity if they are hired, and a fifth has no intention at all, but merely goes along with the majority. How are we to sort out the TA's collective purpose? Moreover, even if all persons voting for the policy have the same purpose, how are courts to go about discovering what it is?

For reasons like this, the Supreme Court has often been reluctant to investigate issues of legislative purpose. In the context of low level scrutiny, the Court has sometimes held that so long as *any* imaginable purpose might be inferred from the government action itself, the action must be upheld. For example, in U.S. R.R. Retirement Bd. v. Fritz,[11] there was considerable evidence that Congress had simply misunderstood the impact on various groups of railroad workers of changes in the railroad retirement system. Nonetheless, the Supreme Court sustained the changes against equal protection attack, observing that "[w]here, as here, there are plausible reasons for Congress' action, our inquiry is at an end. It is, of course, 'constitutionally irrelevant whether this reasoning in fact underlay the legislative decision' because this Court has never insisted

11. 449 U.S. 166 (1980).

that a legislative body articulate its reasons for enacting a statute."[12]

This approach to legislative purpose solves one problem, but only at the expense of creating another. It will always be possible to reason backwards from a government action and imagine a purpose that might support it. All government actions accomplish something, and, if unconstrained by what actually motivated the action, one can always assert that the action's purpose was to do what was in fact done. The upshot is that if the *Fritz* formulation is taken literally, no government action could ever violate the equal protection clause. For example, one might infer from the TA's decision in *Beazer* that its purpose was to discourage methadone use. Surely, the classification advances this purpose and, therefore, the hiring policy satisfies the demands of equal protection

There are two escape routes from this conclusion: One might argue that the equal protection clause itself outlaws certain purposes. On this view, for example, a TA rule that excludes women from employment advances the goal of benefitting men, but this purpose is, itself, unconstitutional. The second possibility is to reject the *Fritz* formulation and hold government actors to the purpose they actually have, rather than to some hypothetical purpose. On this view, if the TA's real purpose is to hire safe and efficient workers, its classification must be judged by whether it advances this purpose, rather than whether it advances other purposes that it might

12. *Id.* at 179.

have had. The Supreme Court has flirted with each of these approaches, but it has not unambiguously embraced either of them.

Consider first an approach that treats certain government purposes as illegitimate. The Court first articulated this idea in U.S. Department of Agriculture v. Moreno.[13] An amendment to the statute establishing the food stamp program provided that households were ineligible to participate in the program if they contained any individual who was unrelated to any other individual. The Court assumed arguendo that this provision was rationally related to the purpose of excluding "hippies" and "hippie communes" from participation in the program. Despite this rational relationship, it invalidated the amendment because "if the constitutional conception of 'equal protection of the laws' means anything, it must at the very least mean that a bare congressional desire to harm a politically unpopular group cannot constitute a legitimate governmental interest."[14]

In City of Cleburne v. Cleburne Living Center,[15] the Court used a similar approach in invalidating the decision of a city not to permit operation of a group home for the mentally retarded in a particular location. A wide variety of other structures were permitted in the same location, including hospitals, sanitariums, nursing homes, and homes for convalescents and the aged. The City Council justified its

13. 413 U.S. 528 (1973).

14. *Id.* at 534.

15. 473 U.S. 432 (1985).

different treatment of these facilities in part on the ground that a majority of home owners near the facility had a "negative attitude" toward a home for the mentally retarded and some elderly residents feared the retarded. But the Court held that

> mere negative attitudes, or fears, unsubstantiated by factors which are properly cognizable in a zoning proceeding, are not permissible bases for treating a home for the mentally retarded differently from apartment houses, multiple dwellings, and the like. It is plain that the electorate as a whole ... could not order city action violative of the Equal Protection Clause, and the City may not avoid the strictures of that Clause by deferring to the wishes or objections of some fraction of the body politic.[16]

There is a powerful argument for the position that the Court articulates in *Moreno* and *Cleburne*. If mere "negative attitudes" or a "desire to harm a politically unpopular group" were sufficient to sustain a challenged statute, the equal protection guarantee would be stripped of its meaning. The prohibition on purposes of this sort has its roots in the ethical, rather than the rational, conception of equality. The core insight is that every individual is entitled to equal regard, and that mere dislike of certain individuals is therefore an insufficient basis for government action that disadvantages them.

But as strong as this intuition is, it remains exceedingly difficult to provide it with determinate

16. *Id.* at 448.

content. The difficulty is that there will usually be some reason why a particular group is subject to negative attitudes, and that reason will take the case out of the forbidden category. Consider, for example, a zoning ordinance that prohibits the erection of high-rise apartment buildings in a certain area. Are "mere negative attitudes" toward such buildings a sufficient reason to ban them? Of course, it is one thing to oppose certain kinds of buildings on aesthetic grounds, and quite another to oppose certain kinds of people. Indeed, if opposition to high-rise apartments stemmed from dislike or fear of the people who lived in them, perhaps an equal protection challenge to the exclusion would prevail.

But now consider a congressional program that subsidizes farmers, but not factory workers. Congress might enact such a program because it believes that the farm lifestyle is wholesome in a way that the factory lifestyle is not. But if this conclusion is "rational," then why can't Congress similarly conclude that a "middle class" lifestyle is preferable to a "hippie" lifestyle?

The problem is neatly posed by Romer v. Evans,[17] where the Court considered an equal protection challenge to an amendment to the Colorado constitution prohibiting local governments from enacting antidiscrimination measures protecting "homosexual, lesbian, or bisexual orientation, conduct, practices or relationships." Citing *Moreno*, the Court invalidated the amendment.

17. 517 U.S. 620 (1996).

[L]aws of the kind now before us raise the inevitable inference that the disadvantage imposed is born of animosity toward the class of persons affected.... Even laws enacted for broad and ambitious purposes often can be explained by reference to legitimate public policies which justify the incidental disadvantages they impose on certain persons. Amendment 2, however, in making a general announcement that gays and lesbians shall not have any particular protections from the law, inflicts on them immediate, continuing, and real injuries that outrun and belie any legitimate justifications that may be claimed for it.[18]

Writing in dissent, Justice Antonin Scalia mounted a powerful attack against the Court's reasoning.

The Court's opinion contains grim, disapproving hints that Coloradans have been guilty of "animus" or "animosity" toward homosexuality, as though that has been established as un-American. Of course it is our moral heritage that one should not hate any human being or class of human beings. But I had thought that one could consider certain conduct reprehensible—murder, for example, or polygamy, or cruelty to animals—and could exhibit even "animus" toward such conduct. Surely that is the only sort of "animus" at issue here: moral disapproval of homosexual conduct....[19]

18. *Id.* at 634–35.

19. *Id.* at 644.

The dispute between the majority and Justice Scalia does no more than demonstrate what we have already seen: in order to have content, ethical equality must be supplemented by an ethical theory that it cannot itself supply. If homosexuality is like heterosexuality, then Colorado's discrimination is indeed unwarranted. If homosexuality is like cruelty to animals, then the discrimination is entirely acceptable.

One might respond that the Colorado amendment is distinguishable from a ban on cruelty to animals because it discriminates merely on the basis of status (homosexual "orientation"), and not conduct (specific acts of animal cruelty). There is surely a difference between action that is chosen and mere status.

But this distinction only partially resolves the difficulty. First, it opens up the vexed and contentious question whether homosexual "orientation" is indeed an unchosen trait. Even if it is, the *Romer* majority made no distinction between the Colorado amendment's treatment of homosexual "orientation" and its treatment of homosexual "conduct, practices, and relationships." It is easy to see why the Court was unconcerned with this distinction. To be sure, homosexual "conduct, practices, and relationships" are chosen in some sense, but the choice is obviously influenced by homosexual status, which, by hypothesis, is not chosen. Defenders of gay rights can justly claim that the amendment puts homosexuals to a hard choice that heterosexuals need not make, and that the choice is hard for homosexuals because of their unchosen status. Finally, the law regularly makes distinctions based on characteristics that are not, in a meaningful sense, chosen. An individual who, despite her best very efforts, is unable to score high enough on a Scholastic Aptitude Test does not have a very strong equal protection claim when she is rejected by a state university. And how many factory workers have a meaningful choice to go off and become farmers?

The upshot is that one's reaction to *Romer* will inevitably turn on one's views about the morality of homosexuality. Justice Scalia argues that, faced with this moral disagreement, the Court should defer to the political process. The desire to defer is understandable because it is hard to ground such a judgment in constitutional text. Nonetheless, Scalia's position is vulnerable to an important counter-argument. Presumably, Justice Scalia does not mean to rob the equal protection clause of all content. As we saw in Chapter Two, the framers of the clause apparently intended that courts enforce its terms at least occasionally. But if the Court must defer to the political process whenever the validity of a classification turns on a contestable moral judgment, no classification will ever be struck down. Defenders of the classification can always justify it on the basis of a bare desire to disadvantage the group that is in fact disadvantaged, and this claim can be refuted only by resort to the sort of moral judgment that Justice Scalia insists courts should withhold.

One might attempt to escape from this conclusion by abandoning ethical equality entirely. One could read the equal protection requirement as imposing only those limitations derived from rational equality. On this view, classifications are indeed valid if they serve the purpose of simply disadvantaging the group discriminated against. However, the equal protection clause might nonetheless have some bite if the Court were to reject the dicta in *Fritz* and judge the statute by the legislature's actual purpose, rather than on the basis of some hypothetical purpose. Suppose, for example, that Colorado was motivated not by moral disapproval of homosexuality, but by the belief that the failure to discourage homosexuality might lead to a higher incidence of child abuse. The amendment might then be invalidated if a court concluded that, as an empirical matter, this belief was simply irrational.

Despite the clarity of the *Fritz* dicta, the Supreme Court has been ambivalent about actual purpose review. Ironically, Chief Justice William Rehnquist, the author of *Fritz*, has been at the forefront of the Justices who have argued that the actual purpose of the legislature is crucial when deciding whether a facially neutral statute that disadvantages racial minorities should be strictly scrutinized.[20] Moreover, other Justices have disagreed with Rehnquist and embraced actual purpose review in the context of low level scrutiny. For example, on the same day

20. *See, e.g.*, Hunter v. Underwood, 471 U.S. 222 (1985) (Rehnquist, J.); Jefferson v. Hackney, 406 U.S. 535 (1972) (Rehnquist, J.).

that *Fritz* was decided, Justice William Brennan, writing for the Court in Minnesota v. Clover Leaf Creamery Co.,[21] observed that "[i]n equal protection analysis, this Court will assume that the objectives articulated by the legislature are actual purposes of the statute, unless an examination of the circumstances forces us to conclude that they 'could not have been the goal of the legislation.' "[22] Similarly, in Nordlinger v. Hahn,[23] Justice Harry Blackmun, writing for the Court, observed that "the Equal Protection Clause does not demand for purposes of rational basis review that a legislature or governing decisionmaker actually articulate at any time the purpose or rationale supporting its classification. Nevertheless, this Court's review does require that a purpose may conceivably or 'may reasonably have been the purpose and policy' of the relevant governmental decisionmaker."[24] Yet only a year later, Justice Clarence Thomas, writing for the Court in F.C.C. v. Beach Communications, Inc.[25] observed that "because we never require a legislature to articulate its reasons for enacting a statute, it is entirely irrelevant for constitutional purposes whether the conceived reason for the challenged distinction actually motivated the legislature."[26]

21. 449 U.S. 456 (1981).
22. *Id.* at 463.
23. 505 U.S. 1 (1992).
24. *Id.* at 15–16.
25. 508 U.S. 307 (1993).
26. *Id.* at 315.

Given this confusion, it is appropriate to ask whether the Court *should* judge statutes by the actual purpose of the legislature. An argument against doing so is that legislative purpose is simply irrelevant. What we care about is what a statute *does*, not what its authors *hoped that it would do*. If a statute in fact advances a permissible purpose, then it hardly matters that it was meant to advance some other purpose. This point is dramatically illustrated by some seeming anomalies produced by actual purpose review. A legislature that, acting with a "bad" purpose, enacts a law might reenact the very same law the day after it is struck down so long as its drafters are now thinking the "right" thoughts. Or a legislature in one state might act constitutionally when, acting with the "right" purpose, it enacts an statute identical to an unconstitutional statute passed by the legislature of an adjoining state whose lawmakers were thinking the "wrong" thoughts.

On the other hand, there is a sense in which actual purpose review actually demonstrates judicial deference toward legislative judgments. Suppose that the legislature enacted a statute in order to achieve objective X. Suppose further that the statute does not in fact achieve objective X, but does achieve objective Y. A court faced with a challenge to the statute has no way to know whether the legislature in fact wanted to achieve objective Y or would have enacted the statute if it thought that only objective Y would be achieved. Invalidating the statute because it fails to achieve its actual purpose can be thought of as a kind of remand to the legislature. If the legislature wants to achieve objective Y, it can do so by simply reenacting the same statute. If it decides that this is not an objective it wishes to pursue, the court's invalidation of the statute gives it a chance to say so.

Even if this theory is defensible, it might be thought that the epistemic problems in discovering the legislature's actual purpose strongly counsels against this sort of review. As Chief Justice Rehnquist has written, "litigants who wish to succeed in invalidating a law [under this theory must] have a certain schizophrenia . . .: They must first convince this Court that the legislature had a particular purpose in mind in enacting the law, and then convince it that the law was not at all suited to the accomplishment of that purpose."[27]

This problem may be less serious than first meets the eye. "Schizophrenia" is hardly necessary if the statute itself, or its legislative history, makes plain that the legislature intended a purpose that the statute does not serve. In part for this reason, some Justices and commentators have suggested that legislatures should be encouraged to provide a statement of purposes for the legislation they enact. For example, Justice Lewis Powell, dissenting in Schweiker v. Wilson,[28] wrote:

When a legitimate purpose for a statute appears in the legislative history or is implicit in the

27. Trimble v. Gordon, 430 U.S. 762, 783 (1977) (dissenting opinion).

28. 450 U.S. 221 (1981).

statutory scheme itself, a court has some assurance that the legislature has made a conscious policy choice. Our democratic system requires that legislation intended to serve a discernible purpose receive the most respectful deference....

> In my view, the Court should receive with some skepticism *post hoc* hypotheses about legislative purpose, unsupported by the legislative history. When no indication of legislative purpose appears other than the current position of [an executive officer] the Court should require that the classification bear a "fair and substantial relation" to the asserted purpose. This marginally more demanding scrutiny indirectly would test the plausibility of the tendered purpose, and preserve equal protection review as something more than "a mere tautological recognition of the fact that Congress did what it intended to do."[29]

An odd feature of Justice Powell's approach is that it reserves "more demanding" scrutiny for the cases where it is least practicable. In cases where the statute's purpose "appears in the legislative history or is implicit in the statutory scheme itself," it is relatively easy to judge the statute against this purpose. In contrast, when there is "no indication of legislative purpose," the Court is reduced to the "schizophrenia" that Justice Rehnquist complains about. If it is to invalidate the statute, it must

29. *Id.* at 244–45.

imagine a purpose that the statute self-evidently fails to serve.

Perhaps for this reason, Justice Brennan's approach to the problem would have reversed Justice Powell's approach. Brennan argued that "[w]here Congress has expressly stated the purpose of a piece of legislation, but where the challenged classification is either irrelevant to or counter to that purpose, we must view any *post hoc* justifications proffered by Government attorneys with skepticism."[30] But this approach, too, presents problems. Enhanced review in cases where Congress makes its purpose clear provides the legislature with an incentive to leave its purpose unclear. Hence, Brennan's suggestion risks aggravating, rather than solving, the epistemic problem.

Examining the Nexus

Suppose that we have overcome the difficulties outlined in the last section and determined the statute's purpose. The last stage of the analysis is to evaluate the nexus between the means (i.e., the classification) and that purpose. What sort of nexus is required?

Suppose, for example, that in *Beazer*, the TA's purpose is to run a safe and efficient transit system. Must its hiring policy be sustained if the policy promotes this objective to some minimal extent? If a rational person would think that it does so? Suppose the policy promotes the objective to some ex-

30. U.S. R.R. Retirement Bd. v. Fritz, 449 U.S. 166, 188 (1980) (Brennan, J., dissenting).

tent, but an alternative policy, that imposed fewer costs, would do more to promote the objective?

One might imagine, at least hypothetically, a classification that perfectly matches the specified end. For example, we could imagine a world where every methadone user is an inefficient worker and every nonuser is an efficient worker. Even in this (clearly unrealistic) world, there might be doubts about the classification. Perhaps methadone users pose only a small additional risk, but the denial of employment to them will be devastating. Even a classification perfectly tailored to the government end might be "irrational" in the sense that the benefits of the classification are not worth the cost.

In the real world, however, virtually all classifications are much more imprecise. They typically suffer from two separate defects: overinclusion and underinclusion. A classification is overinclusive if it includes people who need not be included in order to accomplish the government's ends. For example, the classification in *Beazer* is almost certainly overinclusive because, as the District Court pointed out, some methadone users are safe workers.

Classifications are underinclusive if they fail to include some people who should be included to accomplish the government's ends. The classification in *Beazer* is almost certainly underinclusive as well: there are, after all, many inefficient workers who are not methadone users.

Consider first the problem of overinclusion. Virtually every statute creates some overinclusion. Not all people under the age of 16 are unsafe drivers. It does not follow, however, that we should be unconcerned about overinclusion. Suppose, for example, that the TA required all its workers to have perfect, uncorrected vision. Perhaps as a class people with such vision cause slightly fewer accidents than people who wear glasses, yet surely the classification is troubling. There are many TA jobs (e.g., selling subway tokens) for which perfect vision is irrelevant and many others for which its relevance is marginal at best. It seems likely that the cost of the exclusion greatly exceeds the benefits.

In this and other cases of overinclusion, the issue comes down to comparing judgments that are more or less individualized. A general, overinclusive rule eliminates some people we want to exclude, but only at the cost of also eliminating some we want to include. If we make the rule narrower, we can eliminate more false positives, but only at the risk of either tolerating more false negatives or of incurring additional administrative costs to separate the false positives from the false negatives. For example, the TA might substitute a rule excluding only those methadone users who have not completed three years of treatment for the "no methadone rule." This approach would allow some more "good" workers to get jobs, but, arguably, only at the expense of also allowing more "bad" workers to secure employment. Alternatively, the TA might abandon a rule-based approach and do an individual investigation of each employee. This approach might eliminate both false positives and false negatives, but only at the cost of a far more expensive hiring procedure.

Underinclusion poses a similar set of dilemmas. Suppose, for example, that methadone users are, as a class, marginally less efficient workers than non-users. Suppose further that another class of potential workers—perhaps applicants who have previously been discharged for misconduct—are much less efficient workers. If the TA hires previously discharged workers, do methadone users have a just complaint?

Viewed from one perspective, it is hard to see why underinclusion is a problem. Why should methadone users have grounds to object because another group is favorably treated? If both methadone use and previous discharge are correlated with bad work performance, then the sensible remedy would seem to be exclusion of both groups, but the exclusion of a broader class of workers does nothing to improve the lot of methadone users.

Perhaps motivated by concerns such as this, the Court has sometimes suggested that the legislature may proceed "one step at a time," and that it is constitutionally unobjectionable to solve part of a problem without solving all of it.[31]

On the other hand, if the TA were put to the choice of excluding both groups or neither, perhaps it would exclude neither. Viewed from this perspective, invalidation on underinclusion grounds, like

31. *See, e.g.,* Williamson v. Lee Optical, 348 U.S. 483, 489 (1955).

invalidation under actual purpose review, paradoxically respects legislative judgments. The point was perhaps best made by Justice Robert Jackson in a concurring opinion in Railway Express Agency v. New York:

> The burden should rest heavily upon one who would persuade us to use the due process clause to strike down a substantive law.... Invalidation of a statute ... on due process grounds leaves ungoverned and ungovernable conduct which many people find objectionable.

Invocation of the equal protection clause, on the other hand, does not disable any governmental body from dealing with the subject at hand. It merely means that the prohibition or regulation must have a broader impact. I regard it as a salutary doctrine that [governments] must exercise their powers so as not to discriminate between their inhabitants except upon some reasonable differentiation fairly related to the object of regulation.... [T]here is no more effective practical guaranty against arbitrary and unreasonable government than to require that the principles of law which officials would impose upon a minority must be imposed generally. Conversely, nothing opens the door to arbitrary action so effectively as to allow those officials to pick and choose only a few to whom they will apply legislation and thus to escape the political retribution that might be visited upon them if larger numbers were affected.[32]

Even if Justice Jackson is correct and underinclusion is an appropriate ground for invalidating a statute, how underinclusive must the law be to trigger invalidation? All statutes are, to some degree, underinclusive. It is always possible to imagine a group not covered by a statute that poses the same problem as covered groups. One might try to limit the scope of underinclusion review by saying that underinclusion should lead to invalidation only when the disadvantaged group causes *less* of the problem than a group that is not disadvantaged. This formulation covers over serious ambiguities, however. Suppose, for example, that applicants suffering from epilepsy are more likely to be inefficient workers than methadone users. It might nonetheless make sense to exclude the latter, but not the former, if the administrative costs of identifying the latter are smaller.

Moreover, there is nothing that makes it illegitimate for the legislature to pursue ancillary purposes. For example, the TA might modify its primary purpose of having an efficient workforce when it comes into conflict with giving people what they deserve. If the TA thought that methadone users were in part responsible for their plight, but that people suffering from epilepsy were not, it might sensibly exclude the former but not the latter even though methadone users were more efficient workers than epileptics.

32. 336 U.S. 106, 112–13 (1949) (Jackson, J., concurring).

As the above analysis makes clear, an actual investigation of the nexus between the classification and the purpose of a statute is exceedingly complex. It is made more complex still when one takes account of the inevitable empirical uncertainties which we have so far assumed away. It is unlikely that there are sound social science data about many of the judgments that a hiring agency like the TA or other government actors must make. Often, government officials, like the rest of us, act on hunch or conventional wisdom that may or may not withstand careful empirical scrutiny. If one were really systematic about the matter, the costs and the benefits of such scrutiny must, themselves, be factored into the overall analysis. Moreover, as already noted, it is not possible to weigh costs and benefits of a particular classification without a bridging discourse of value that the constitutional text does not supply.

No doubt because of these complications, the Court rarely actually performs this analysis in anything like the detail set forth here. Instead, its general approach is simply to posit a purpose for the challenged governmental program, to observe that a rational person might suppose that under some conceivable set of facts the classification advances that purpose, and to summarily dismiss the constitutional challenge.

On rare occasions the Court goes beyond this, as *Cleburne*, *Moreno*, and *Romer* illustrate. The Court has been less than forthcoming in explaining the circumstances under which low level scrutiny is more than pro forma, but examination of the sorts of statutes that have actually been invalidated suggests that the Court's primary concern is with ethical equality. When the Court is dealing with gay men and lesbians, with the mentally retarded, or with "hippies," its concern is probably not just about means and ends, but about a disrespect for, or undervaluing the welfare of, certain unpopular groups. In contrast, most laws dealing with "ordinary social and economic legislation" do not involve this kind of undervaluation. These laws may be stupid, or they may be the product of a squalid interest group deal, but they generally are not the product of, and do not convey, a disregard of the common humanity of the legislative losers. Cases like *Romer*, *Cleburne*, and *Moreno* are anomalous within low level scrutiny jurisprudence precisely because their real doctrinal home is elsewhere. The Court has developed a complex body of doctrine that deals with concerns for ethical equality through the use of enhanced scrutiny. The next chapter begins the process of explicating this doctrine.

CHAPTER FOUR

RACE-SPECIFIC CLASSIFICATIONS THAT DISADVANTAGE RACIAL MINORITIES

If low level scrutiny were all that equal protection amounted to, equal protection jurisprudence would not much matter. As the previous chapter indicates, courts rarely invalidate government programs when utilizing this test. Equal protection jurisprudence does matter because courts have developed a complex set of doctrines that sometimes result in heightened scrutiny.

Heightened review falls into two broad categories. On some occasions, courts are suspicious of the classification itself. For example, classifications that differentiate on a racial basis are said to be suspect. On others, they are concerned about the interest affected by the classification. For example, differential treatment of two groups with regard to the right to vote is subject to heightened scrutiny. This chapter, and Chapters Five through Nine concern the first category of cases. Chapter Ten addresses the second category.

The paradigm case for suspect classifications is a statute or government policy that discriminates on the basis of race. The conventional wisdom is that policies of this kind are subject to the most rigid scrutiny and almost always invalidated. Given the history of the equal protection clause, outlined in Chapter Two, the special status of racial classifications is hardly surprising. It turns out, however, that the doctrine is quite a bit more complicated than the conventional wisdom suggests.

A word of caution is necessary about the discussion that follows. The American encounter with racial difference is often portrayed as a conflict between whites and African Americans. In fact, this portrayal reflects an unfortunate effacement of both historical memory and current reality. A variety of racial groups have encountered discrimination. For example, statutes in many states prohibited Asian Americans from owning real property and Asian Americans were subjected to widespread violence and abuse. Latinos were often forced to attend segregated schools and have faced generations of job and housing discrimination. The systematic destruction of the lives and culture of American Indians forms an important part of our history.

Despite these facts, it remains true that much of the legal struggle over racial discrimination has been dominated by the special problems faced by African Americans. For that reason, most of the cases discussed below concern problems of black-white interaction. For the most part, the cases have not yet addressed the extent to which the African American experience is the same or different from the experiences of other racial groups and, to the extent that the experience is different, whether the legal treatment of other groups should differ as well.

The Supreme Court has distinguished between four kinds of racial classifications, with different rules applying to each category. This chapter addresses the problem posed by race-specific classifications that disadvantage racial minorities. The chapters that follow deal with non-race-specific classifications disadvantaging racial minorities, race-specific classifications that are facially neutral, and race-specific classifications that benefit racial minorities.

The Nature of Heightened Scrutiny for Race–Specific Classifications

Race-specific classifications that disadvantage racial minorities involve statutes that distinguish facially on the basis of race in a way that treats a racial minority worse than another group. Suppose for example a city passed an ordinance permitting individuals to secure a driver's license at age 16, except for African Americans, who are required to wait until their eighteenth birthday. The classification is race-specific (because on the face of the statute it distinguishes between African Americans and other racial groups) and disadvantages a racial minority (because African Americans must wait longer to obtain driver's licenses than members of other racial groups).

In all likelihood, there is simply no basis at all for such a distinction. However, in order to illustrate the doctrinal point, let us suppose that there is some empirical support for the proposition that young African Americans tend to have more traffic accidents than young members of other racial groups. An analogous classification based on grounds other than race with similar empirical support would almost certainly be upheld. For example, most courts would have little difficulty with an ordinance that denied licenses to young people who failed to maintain passing school grades, or who used drugs, or who had poor vision. All of these classifications are no doubt both under-and overinclusive, but, as we have seen, imperfect fit is hardly disqualifying when the court engages in low level review.

Race is different. If there is any principle of equal protection law that is uncontroversial, it is that classifications of this sort deserve "strict scrutiny." What does this strict scrutiny consist of? According to standard doctrine, a court confronted with such a classification would insist not just upon a rational relationship between means and ends, but also that the means be "narrowly tailored" to accomplish the ends. Thus, a mere statistical correlation between race and safe driving would be insufficient. Instead, a defender of the statute would have to demonstrate that the classification was "necessary, and not merely rationally related, to the accomplishment" of the state's goal.[1] Moreover, even if this first test were satisfied, the classification would still fail unless the government interest it advanced was not

1. McLaughlin v. Florida, 379 U.S. 184, 196 (1964).

merely legitimate or permissible, but "compelling."[2]

As with rational basis review, the formal test imposed by strict scrutiny obscures some ambiguities. Suppose, for example, that the accident level could be reduced to a similar extent by a race-blind test that was extremely expensive to administer or was very overinclusive. Or suppose that a race-neutral classification would reduce the accident level somewhat, but not quite as much as the racial classification. Simply saying that the classification is "necessary" or that it must be "narrowly tailored" does not make clear whether a race-specific test would be permissible in these situations.

As a practical matter, this ambiguity may make little difference because of the second branch of the test. Even if the racial classification is "necessary" and "narrowly tailored," it is impermissible unless it serves a "compelling" state interest. Unfortunately, however, the courts have not been very illuminating as to what counts as a "compelling" government interest or as to what standards should be used in evaluating the weight of various interests. For example, it seems obvious that establishing standards for driver's permits does not rank with, say, protection against nuclear war or terrorist attack. If this is the relevant comparison, then the interest in auto safety is surely not "compelling." On the other hand, one might recharacterize the government interest as the saving of human life, which is surely threatened by unsafe driving

2. *See, e.g.,* City of Richmond v. J.A. Croson Co., 488 U.S. 469 (1989).

and which begins to sound pretty compelling as compared to a host of other governmental functions.

The Actual Status of Race–Based Classifications

This analysis, which takes the stated test literally, may seem deeply beside the point. As a sociological fact, if not a logical deduction, we can be certain that a court would invalidate the hypothetical licensing statute, whatever the precise formulation of the test it used to do so. This fact, in turn, has led some commentators to claim that racial classifications that disadvantage racial minorities are simply per se impermissible.

The reality is a bit more complicated. If one looks beyond the Supreme Court's official position, it turns out that the actual status of race-specific classifications disadvantaging racial minorities is contested and uncertain. True, if our hypothetical licensing statute were somehow enacted in the current social environment, there is little doubt that a court would invalidate it. But it is also true that no jurisdiction in America today would enact such a statute, and that if it did so, the surrounding social context would be so different from our current state of affairs that a court's treatment of the classification would actually be quite unpredictable. In contrast, there are—today—race-specific classifications disadvantaging racial minorities in use, and it is far from clear that courts stand ready to invalidate these actual statutes and programs.

The deviation between the official story and the actual status of such classifications begins more than a half century ago with Korematsu v. United States.[3] This case is conventionally treated as providing the doctrinal origins of the strict scrutiny test for race-specific classifications. In fact, the case arguably did not involve a racial classification, the court did not apply strict scrutiny, and the classification was not invalidated.

At issue in *Korematsu* was an order of a military commander, issued at the height of World War II, mandating the exclusion of Americans of Japanese descent from the West Coast. Pursuant to the order, thousands of loyal Japanese–American citizens were forced to leave their homes, lose their businesses, and live for years in "relocation camps" located in the interior of the country. Korematsu was convicted for disobeying the order by remaining in his home, and challenged the conviction on equal protection grounds.

The Supreme Court, with Justice Hugo Black writing for the majority, upheld the conviction. Justice Black began his analysis by announcing the heightened level of scrutiny for race-specific classifications:

> It should be noted, to begin with, that all legal restrictions which curtail the civil rights of a single racial group are immediately suspect. That is not to say that all such restrictions are unconstitutional. It is to say that courts must subject

3.   323 U.S. 214 (1944).

them to the most rigid scrutiny. Pressing public necessity may sometimes justify the existence of such restrictions; racial antagonism never can.[4]

There are several problems with this passage. First, it is not clear that Korematsu was singled out because of his race. On its face, the military order applied to Americans of Japanese descent rather than to members of a racial group. This fact, in turn, raises a difficulty at the core of Court's analysis. The term "race" has no clear scientific meaning. Whether particular characteristics demarcate a "race" depends upon when and where one asks the question.

Second, the Court does not seem to have engaged in anything like the "rigid scrutiny" it promised. Of course, victory in World War II was a compelling government interest but the Court did little to inquire into whether the exclusion of Japanese Americans was "necessary" to that end. Most modern commentators agree that if the Court had in fact engaged in the rigid scrutiny it supposedly required, it would have discovered that the risk of Japanese American sabotage was wildly overstated by military officials. Instead of a searching inquiry into this question, the Court simply deferred to the judgment of these officials.

Finally, there is substantial evidence that "racial antagonism" played a considerable role in the decision to uproot the Japanese American population. Animus toward Japanese Americans was wide-

4. *Id.* at 216.

spread in the western United States, and had been for years. The exclusion order was issued in a political atmosphere dominated by hatred and fear of the Japanese in the wake of the Japanese attack on Pearl Harbor. There was virtually no hard evidence to support the suspicion that Japanese Americans were disloyal. It is also noteworthy that no one proposed similar measures directed against German or Italian Americans despite evidence that some members of these groups supported the Axis powers.

Today, *Korematsu* is almost universally regarded as a tragic mistake. A generation after the decision, a United States District Court overturned Korematsu's conviction, and Congress enacted legislation providing for partial restitution for Japanese Americans forced to leave their homes. The case has come to stand for something close to the opposite of its actual holding. Most people now seem to agree, at least in the abstract, that even when racial classifications seem justified in the heat of the moment, on calmer reflection they virtually always turn out to be immoral and unconstitutional.

It is surprising, therefore, that despite the near unanimous condemnation of the result in *Korematsu*, the government continues to rely on similar classifications in a variety of settings. Perhaps the most salient and troubling examples arise in the context of law enforcement. Following the bombing of the World Trade Center, there have been persistent reports that security officials have used "racial profiling" when screening airline passengers. The

Supreme Court has yet to speak on this issue, but there is nothing like a social consensus that racial profiling is wrong in this setting. There is more agreement about the impropriety of including race as part of a "drug-courier" profile, and there has been widespread outrage at police who stop individuals for committing the "crime" of "Driving While Black." Yet some courts have permitted the use of race as part of such a drug-courier profile,[5] and the Supreme Court itself has approved the selective referral of motorists at immigration checkpoints to secondary inspection areas based in part on "apparent Mexican ancestry."[6] Moreover, virtually no one objects to the use of race in a more particularized fashion. If a crime victim describes the perpetrator as African American, few courts would hold that the Constitution was violated by the failure of police to stop whites who otherwise fit the description.

Another context in which racial classifications sometimes go unchallenged is family law. In Palmore v. Sidoti,[7] the Supreme Court took a strong stand against the use of such classifications to resolve a child custody dispute. Palmore and Sidoti (who were both white) were married and had a young daughter. When the couple divorced, the trial court awarded custody of the child to the wife, but when the wife remarried an African American, the court determined that the "best interest of the

5. *See, e.g.,* United States v. Weaver, 966 F.2d 391 (8th Cir.1992).

6. U.S. v. Martinez–Fuerte, 428 U.S. 543, 563 (1976).

7. 466 U.S. 429 (1984).

child" required that custody be granted to the father. The court found that "despite the strides that have been made in bettering relations between the races in this country, it is inevitable that [the child] will, if allowed to remain in her present situation [suffer] from the social stigmatization that is sure to come."[8]

In a strongly worded opinion by Chief Justice Warren Burger, a unanimous Supreme Court reversed. Even though it acknowledged that the state's interest in the well-being of the child was "of the highest order"[9] and that the child might indeed be "subject to a variety of pressures and stresses"[10] if she lived in a mixed-race home, the Court held that the use of race was impermissible.

Given the result in *Sidoti*, one might suppose that race is simply not a permissible factor in family law decisions. In fact, some courts have upheld the use of race as a factor in adoption decisions.[11] More

8. *Id.* at 431.

9. *Id.* at 422.

10. *Id.*

11. Congress has responded by making it a civil rights violation for

A person or government that is involved in adoption or foster care placements [to] delay or deny the placement of a child for adoption or into foster care, on the basis of race, color, or national origin of the adoptive or foster parent, or the child involved.

42 U.S.C. § 1996(b)(1)(B). *See also* 42 U.S.C. § 671(a)(18)(B) (withholding federal funds for agencies that engage in similar practice). The statute does not appear to prohibit the use of race as a factor in choosing between equally qualified adoptive par-

striking is the almost universal assumption that the Constitution permits the state to facilitate the racial choice of prospective adoptive parents with respect to the child they wish to adopt.

Perhaps decisions of this sort are too personal and intimate to be subject to constitutional scrutiny, but other sorts of decisions, which plainly are not personal or intimate, also seem to be outside the strictures of the prohibition on the use of race. For example, elected officials regularly take race and ethnicity into account in making political appointments, and the Supreme Court has intimated that "judicial oversight of [such] appointments may interfere with the ability of an elected official to respond to the mandate of his constituency."[12] Many people would not object to a racial classification in casting particular roles in a state-funded theater production. Some have even suggested that racial classifications are appropriate in the education setting where, for example, the allegedly special problems of African–American males might be addressed.

What's Wrong with Racial Classifications?

All of this suggests that the ban on racial classifications disadvantaging racial minorities is more porous than is commonly supposed. But if courts are not, in fact, using strict scrutiny in all these cases,

ents when the use does not "delay or deny the placement of a child."

12. Mayor of City of Philadelphia v. Educational Equality League, 415 U.S. 605, 615 (1974).

how can we differentiate between permissible and impermissible uses of race?

One way to approach this question is to ask why we have strict scrutiny for racial classifications in the first place. Once we articulate the reasons for opposition to racial classifications, we can then examine whether these reasons are implicated in the various contexts discussed above.

Commentators and jurists have offered a variety of theories explaining the special problem posed by racial classifications, but no consensus on the subject has developed. Perhaps the most sophisticated theory is derived from the most famous footnote in constitutional law—footnote 4 in United States v. Carolene Products.[13] Written at the historical moment when the Supreme Court was moving away from the hostility to redistributive legislation that marked the *Lochner* era, Justice Harlan Stone's opinion in *Carolene Products* argued that such legislation should be subject to only minimal judicial scrutiny. In footnote 4, however, he suggested that a more stringent standard of review might apply to statutes "directed at particular religious or national or racial minorities." Stricter review was required because "prejudice against discrete and insular minorities may be a special condition, which tends seriously to curtail the operation of those political processes ordinarily to be relied upon to protect minorities."

Over forty years after *Carolene Products*, Professor John Hart Ely provided a sophisticated and

13.   304 U.S. 144, 153 (1938).

immensely influential book-length gloss on footnote 4.[14] Deeply troubled by decisions like Roe v. Wade, which seemed to rest upon contestable value judgments formulated by unelected judges, Ely argued that the central commitment of the Constitution was to fair procedures by which the political branches would resolve value disputes. The role of the courts was not to displace these value judgments, but rather to police the process so as to insure that it was democratic—to "reenforce representation," in Ely's words.

Ely identified a number of pathologies that might infect the political process. For our purposes, the most interesting was the risk that "discrete and insular minorities" might be prevented by prejudice from forming coalitions with other groups. In a pluralist democracy, most minorities can protect themselves by bargaining with other minorities so as to block legislation that is grievously harmful to them. In the case of a few minorities however, "a system of 'mutual defense pacts' [would] prove recurrently unavailing."[15] On Ely's view, judicial protection of these minorities is not premised on any substantive value judgment, but rather on the need to correct for this defect so as to make the process truly democratic.

Ely's systematization of the *Carolene Products* footnote has played a significant role in modern thought about racial classifications, but it has also

14. *See* John Hart Ely, Democracy and Distrust: A Theory of Judicial Review (1980).

15. *Id.* at 151.

been subject to important criticism. Three problems are especially troubling. First, it is not apparent how, without making the very sort of value judgments that Ely wishes to avoid, we can separate out groups that are disadvantaged by prejudice from groups disadvantaged by substantive disagreement with the positions they support. As Professor Laurence Tribe famously argued, Ely's theory provides no basis for distinguishing between homosexuals and exhibitionists.[16]

Second, modern public choice theory suggests that Ely may have underestimated the extent to which discrete and insular minorities can protect themselves within the political process. Indeed, in some respects well-organized minorities may be at an advantage over diffuse and unorganized majorities. Minority groups, sharing a common culture, physical location, or network of institutions, will find it easier to organize and overcome "free-rider" problems than widely dispersed majorities. These problems exist when individual interests are so diffuse that each individual would prefer to benefit from, or "free ride" on, the efforts of others, rather than to let others benefit from, or "free ride" on, the efforts that they themselves have expended.

Finally, Ely's theory does not capture the intuition most of us share about the evils of racially discriminatory laws. Many people believe that these laws would be unacceptable even if enacted through

16. Laurence H. Tribe, *The Puzzling Persistence of Process–Based Constitutional Theories,* 89 Yale L. J. 1063, 1076 (1980).

a fair process, but Ely's theory lacks the resources to respond to the moral objection to such laws.

A different approach to the problem embraces a frankly substantive view of racial classifications. Advocates of this view claim that opposition to such classifications reflects a fundamental moral postulate, rather than a process defect. On this view, it is simply wrong to differentiate between individuals based upon skin color.

Today, belief in this postulate is widely shared (at least in the abstract), but there are nonetheless real problems with grounding constitutional doctrine on this belief. When we move from abstract sentiment to particular cases, the postulate turns out to be insufficient to do the work that needs to be done. To be sure, if *everyone* believed that racial classifications were *always* wrong, there would be no difficulty, but if this were true, we would not need strict scrutiny to enforce the prohibition because these classifications would never be adopted. As the examples discussed above illustrate, at least some people believe that racial classifications sometimes are morally permissible. Once this disagreement emerges, the naked assertion of the postulate will not resolve the argument. Moreover, if we abandon the absolutist position, some further elaboration of the reasons why racial classifications are wrong will be necessary to differentiate between cases where they should be permitted and cases where they should be prohibited.

A closely related argument against racial classifications is rooted in rational, rather than ethical, equality. The strong version of the argument is that race is never relevant to any legitimate government objective. Of course, if the strong version were correct, there would be no need for strict scrutiny of racial classifications; low level scrutiny would be sufficient to invalidate them. Moreover, the strong version is almost certainly incorrect. For a variety of historical and cultural reasons, race is sometimes a salient characteristic in twenty-first century America. For example, race correlates (albeit imperfectly) with attitudes toward the criminal justice system, especially in racially charged situations, such as cases involving putative police misconduct directed against racial minorities. A racial classification (even one that resulted in the substitution of some white for black jurors) might therefore be relevant to the legitimate government interest of providing for juries that represent a fair cross-section of the community.

A weaker version of the argument is more plausible. On this view, racial classifications *rarely* advance legitimate government interests, and there is a risk that race prejudice will cause us to overestimate the extent to which race is a useful proxy for other characteristics. Moreover, even when it is otherwise rational for government to use race, this use encourages people to think in racial terms more generally, thereby aggravating the risk of prejudicial stereotyping. If one accepted this view, one might support strict scrutiny for racial classifications so as to weed out cases where seemingly rational use of race is in fact either the product of or conducive to race prejudice.

In order to be plausible, this argument must be supplemented with the empirical assertion that judges are likely to be more sensitive to race prejudice than other government officials—an assertion that is at least contestable, as *Korematsu* demonstrates. Moreover, even if the argument makes sense as a matter of policy, more work needs to be done to ground it in the Constitution.

A common response to the latter problem is to point to the special role concern about race prejudice played in the framing of the equal protection clause. As explained in Chapter Two, the clause was written to deal with the pressing and special difficulties faced by African Americans in the immediate wake of emancipation. Even though the prediction of the *Slaughter-House* Court that the clause would never be applied outside the race context has turned out to be wrong, it is entirely appropriate that the clause has special bite when applied to laws that are unfriendly to African Americans.

A purely historical approach does not adequately account for current doctrine, however. As outlined above, the framers of the fourteenth amendment were concerned primarily with "civil" rights. It is much less clear that they disfavored racial classifications that dealt with "social" rights. Although widely discredited, perhaps this distinction retains some vestigial force and explains the modern tolerance for racial classifications in the adoption context. Still, a purely historical focus cannot explain which spheres of life under modern conditions should be considered "social" as opposed to "civil."

A related problem arises because the modern status of African Americans is very different from their position in the wake of the Civil War. As discussed above, the framers were concerned about a particular set of disabilities suffered by African Americans: they were not permitted to testify in court, to own land, to move from one place to another, or to inherit property. This history provides an available set of analogies that might be of some help in reasoning about modern problems. Perhaps, for example, nineteenth century restrictions on movement could be analogized to modern police harassment of African American motorists. Still, there is no denying that modern race discrimination is importantly different from the nineteenth century version, and arguments drawn from the concerns of the Reconstruction Congress are therefore bound to be contestable.

One might, of course, express the intentions of the Reconstruction Congress on a higher level of generality. The framers of the fourteenth amendment were concerned about the subjugation of African Americans. Or more broadly still, they were concerned about the subjugation of any racial, national, or ethnic group. The particular disabilities suffered by African Americans in the mid-nineteenth century might then be seen as no more than examples of a broader problem that remains with us still, albeit in a different form. On this view, racial classifications should be invalidated when, but only when, they contribute to this subjugation under modern conditions.

There is much that is appealing in this way of thinking about the equal protection clause, but it, too, presents difficulties. Two objections are particularly important. First, there is widespread disagreement about which government policies contribute to subjugation, or, indeed, about whether subjugation is taking place. This disagreement might not be worrisome if one were confident in the ability of judges to resolve it in a wise and sensitive fashion. The argument therefore brings us back to the necessity for an empirical evaluation about how judges are likely to behave—an evaluation that will, inevitably, be influenced by the very substantive disagreement about subjugation that we began with.

A second problem emerges even among those who agree that racial subjugation continues to exist and that courts are the best institution to remedy the situation. Even on these assumptions, it is far from clear that racial classifications are the primary contributor to subjugation. As already noted, in the modern period, it is highly unlikely that a jurisdiction would enact the sort of overtly racist classifications that concerned the framers of the equal protection clause. What is arguably much more common is legislative indifference to the problems faced by minorities and classifications that are facially neutral but have a disproportionate impact on minority groups.

Consider, for example, the problem of jury selection in a racially charged case. In Strauder v. West Virginia,[17] decided in 1879, the Court struck down a racial classification that disqualified African Americans from sitting on juries. In the nineteenth century context, the court was surely correct that a racial classification with respect to jury service was "unfriendly" to the "colored race" and implied their "inferiority in civil society."[18] It is not clear, however, that the elimination of racial classifications solves these difficulties. Today, of course, no jurisdiction employs an explicit racial classification in jury selection. But how are we to react when by chance, or by the unintended operation of facially neutral jury selection criteria, no African American is selected to serve on a jury deciding the fate of white police officers charged with brutality directed against a black suspect? Might not the *failure* to utilize a racial classification so as to ensure some African American representation on the jury contribute to black subjugation?

As this example illustrates, race-specific classifications are not the only, and perhaps not the most important government actions that affect the status of racial minorities. The next chapter focuses on classifications that are not race specific, but that nonetheless disadvantage racial minorities.

17. 100 U.S. (10 Otto) 303 (1879).
18. *Id.* at 308.

CHAPTER FIVE

NON-RACE-SPECIFIC CLASSIFICATIONS THAT DISADVANTAGE RACIAL MINORITIES

Chapter Four discussed a hypothetical statute that allowed applicants of other races to obtain a driver's license at age 16, but prohibited African Americans from obtaining a license until age 18. Under standard doctrine, this statute would be strictly scrutinized and invalidated. Suppose, instead, that a jurisdiction provided that a 16 year old of any race could obtain a license, but only if the applicant was enrolled in school. As we saw in Chapter Three, a court would apply low level scrutiny to this statute and it would almost certainly be upheld, even if there were no good empirical studies demonstrating that enrollment in school has anything to do with driving safety. Now suppose that the school enrollment requirement not only does not correlate with driver safety but also does correlate with race. Imagine that the practical effect of the requirement is to disqualify a large number of African American potential drivers, but virtually no white drivers.

This classification is similar to the outright prohibition of young African American drivers in the sense that it disadvantages a racial minority. It is different from the outright prohibition in the sense that it is not facially race-specific. Should a court invalidate the classification?

Rational Basis Review for Non–Race–Specific Classifications

The Supreme Court's first systematic treatment of this question appears in Washington v. Davis.[1] The District of Columbia Metropolitan Police Department administered a qualifying test to applicants for positions as police officers. The test purported to measure verbal ability, vocabulary, and reading comprehension. Plaintiffs, a group of unsuccessful African American applicants, established two facts about the test. First, a higher percentage of African Americans than of whites failed the test. Second, the test had not been validated so as to demonstrate that it related to subsequent job performance.

Despite these showings, the Supreme Court, in an opinion by Justice Byron White, held that the classification should be subject only to low level review, and that it easily survived this scrutiny.

> [W]e have not held that a law, neutral on its face and serving ends otherwise within the power of government to pursue, is invalid under the Equal Protection Clause simply because it may affect a greater proportion of one race than of another. Disproportionate impact is not irrelevant, but it is not the sole touchstone of an invidious racial

1.   426 U.S. 229 (1976).

discrimination forbidden by the Constitution. Standing alone, it does not trigger the rule, that racial classifications are to be subjected to the strictest scrutiny and are justifiable only by the weightiest of considerations.[2]

The Court advanced three arguments to support this conclusion. First, the Court's prior precedent did not mandate heightened scrutiny premised simply on a showing of disproportionate racial impact. For example, the Court pointed to Strauder v. West Virginia,[3] where the Court had invalidated a rule that automatically excluded African Americans from juries, but had also noted that juries need not necessarily statistically reflect the racial composition of the community.

Second, the Court thought that mere discriminatory impact did not deny any particular African American equal protection:

> Respondents, as Negroes, could no more successfully claim that the test denied them equal protection than could white applicants who also failed. The conclusion would not be different in the face of proof that more Negroes than whites had been disqualified by [the test]. That other Negroes also failed to score well would, alone, not demonstrate that respondents individually were being denied equal protection of the laws by the application of an otherwise valid qualifying test being administered to prospective police recruits.[4]

2. *Id.* at 242.

3. 100 U.S. (10 Otto) 303 (1879).

4. Washington v. Davis, 426 U.S. 229, 246 (1976).

Finally, the Court argued that

A rule that a statute designed to serve neutral ends is nevertheless invalid, absent compelling justification, if in practice it benefits or burdens one race more than another would be far-reaching and would raise serious questions about, and perhaps invalidate, a whole range of tax, welfare, public service, regulatory, and licensing statutes that may be more burdensome to the poor and to the average black than to the more affluent white.[5]

Washington v. Davis has been intensely controversial, but the result is supported by a powerful intuition: Giving all applicants the same test and treating them the same way based upon their score on that test epitomizes equal treatment. Indeed, if the *Washington* plaintiff had been successful in his challenge, the court would, in effect, be mandating unequal treatment. Test scores would then have to be adjusted in some way so as to improve the performance of African Americans vis à vis their non-African American competitors for the same position. This differential treatment would treat racial groups unequally, since two applicants with the same score would be treated differently because of their respective races. Perhaps "affirmative action" of this sort is constitutionally *permissible*—a subject discussed in Chapter Seven—but it would be ironic if the equal protection clause made this sort of departure from equality constitutionally *mandatory*.

5. *Id.* at 248.

This position undoubtedly has force, but there are also powerful arguments on the other side. Four interlocking arguments raise serious questions about *Washington*. First, the *Washington* Court seemed remarkably uninterested in the source of the disparity in test scores. Of course, a racist would have little doubt why African American candidates performed more poorly than white candidates. The disparity is more troubling for those of us who do not believe in innate racial superiority. People who are not racists must at least entertain the possibility that test outcomes are the predictable result of past or present government and societal discrimination. In the case of a District of Columbia exam testing verbal and writing skills, this possibility is especially salient given the fact that for years African Americans attended inferior schools that were segregated by law. If the disparity is indeed linked to this, or other, government action, one might suppose that the equal protection clause mandates, or at least permits, a government remedy.

Moreover, even if differential test results are not caused by anything the government has done, they are surely caused by things the government has failed to do. We can imagine a wide variety of programs the government might have instituted that would lead to better verbal skills among African American police applicants. Washington v. Davis rests on a more general conception of constitutional law that treats government *action* as problematic and raising constitutional concerns, while government *failure to act* is treated as a natural state of affairs, leaving a presumptively free private sphere intact.

A different conception might cause us to worry more about private forces that produce unequal outcomes and impose a duty upon government to attempt to counteract these forces. In this regard, the passage quoted above, pointing out the range of government statutes that would come under question if the plaintiff had prevailed, is especially troubling. The Court seems to count this fact as an argument against the plaintiff's position. But for it to so count, one would have to begin with the view that an equal protection doctrine that challenged the overall justice of current arrangements is presumptively incorrect. In other words, *Washington* is arguably influenced by a strong presumption that government intervention is unnecessary because current distributions are, for the most part, natural, just, and, therefore, constitutional.

A second, closely related argument focuses on the choice of ends. Recall that in its standard form, equal protection analysis takes the end as given and asks whether the means—the classification—is sufficiently related to the end. Thus, the *Washington* Court started by taking as given the end of producing a police department with a particular level of verbal skill. The only question was whether the test was sufficiently related to the achievement of this end.

Unfortunately, this analysis ignores the possibility that race prejudice might be reflected in the choice of ends as well as means. If the end is not racially neutral, then even neutral means will not guarantee equality. And there are reasons to question whether the end in *Washington* was racially neutral. The test that the police department administered produced one racial outcome, but a test given in "ebonics" or "black English" would doubtless produce a different outcome. Similarly, a test measuring knowledge of local neighborhoods or ability to deal with the local populace might produce very different outcomes from a test of verbal proficiency.

A third problem is that even if the ends are in some sense neutral, the choice of ends may nonetheless reflect differential racial concern. Perhaps verbal proficiency really is an important qualification for working as a police officer. Still, it is at least possible that government officials, faced with a test that disqualified a high percentage of white applicants, would decide that this end need not be pursued quite so vigorously. (Remember that there was no empirical data linking high scores on the test to good performance as a police officer.) If there is a lower level of concern about the welfare of African American applicants, government officials might be more ready to endorse a program that leads to larger losses for people in this category. We can only speculate about whether this differential concern is at work in *Washington*, but the Court's test does nothing to address the problem.

Finally, *Washington* raises troubling questions about whether we should think of equality in terms of inputs or outputs. The Court assumes without much discussion that our concern is with inputs. Since everyone takes the same test, the equal protection clause is satisfied even if the test produces racially differential outcomes.

There is a version of ethical equality that supports this approach. If we start with the postulate that every human being is intrinsically equal, then equality of treatment (the same test) seems to follow. Similarly, there is an argument from rational equality that supports an approach focusing on inputs. So long as the test is rationally related to a legitimate state goal, there is no reason why it should not be used.

But there are also versions of ethical and rational equality that cut in the opposite direction. From the ethical point of view, one might doubt the extent to which performance on the test is linked to factors over which applicants have control. If ethical equality requires that we give people "what they deserve" on an equal basis, the test may be "unfair" in the sense that it penalizes people for traits for which they have no responsibility. Imagine, for example, that a university gave the same written entrance examination to blind and sighted applicants. Even though both applicants take the same examination, many people might believe that giving blind applicants a written test denies them equal treatment.

From the standpoint of rational equality, even if the means (the police test) is linked to a legitimate end (a verbally proficient force), one might reach different conclusions if one looked at the problem more globally. It is not as if African Americans do disproportionately poorly on this particular test but, elsewhere in society, are at or above average on scales of power, wealth, and well-being. One might wonder about the long-term stability of a society where a readily identifiable subgroup systematically fails not just a single test, but test after test, especially when the tests are usually designed by people who are not members of this subgroup. Even if one concedes arguendo that each of these tests, taken individually, is "fair," (a proposition that is deeply contestable), when taken together, they are bound to breed resentment and unrest. Hence, if one takes as a primary end the maintenance of a community premised on consent, some control for equality of outputs may be a reasonable—even necessary—means.

Improperly Motivated Classifications

Whatever the merits of *Washington*, the case, standing alone, need not have had a major impact on equal protection law. *Washington* left intact prior doctrine suggesting that even non-race specific government actions should be strictly scrutinized if they were motivated by race. Moreover, as Justice John Paul Stevens pointed out in a concurring opinion,[6] some of these cases suggested that it was appropriate for courts to infer an improper motiva-

6. *Id.* at 252 (Stevens, J., concurring).

tion from the effect of the statute. Thus, even though a disproportionate effect does not, itself, trigger heightened scrutiny, it might form the basis of an inference of improper motivation, which would lead to high level review.

The cases that establish heightened scrutiny for improperly motivated classifications fall into two categories: discriminatory enactment and discriminatory administration.

The Court dealt with discriminatory enactment in Gomillion v. Lightfoot.[7] The City of Tuskegee Alabama altered city boundaries from a square to what the Court characterized as an "uncouth twenty-eight sided figure."[8] The effect of this change was to place virtually all African Americans outside the city limits. The Supreme Court held that it was permissible to infer from these facts that "the legislation is solely concerned with segregating white and colored voters by fencing Negro citizens out of town so as to deprive them of their pre-existing municipal vote."[9] On these facts, the Court held, the redrawing of the boundary line was unconstitutional.

The leading case concerning discriminatory administration is Yick Wo v. Hopkins.[10] Yick Wo was convicted of violating a statute prohibiting the operation of a laundry not located in a brick or stone

7.   364 U.S. 339 (1960).

8.   *Id.* at 340.

9.   *Id.* at 341.

10.   118 U.S. 356 (1886).

building without the consent of the board of supervisors. He demonstrated that virtually all Chinese nationals who sought consent were turned down, while virtually all requests by whites were granted. Although the Court did not find that the statute itself was motivated by a discriminatory intent, it nonetheless reversed the conviction:

[T]he facts shown establish an administration directed so exclusively against a particular class of persons as to warrant and require the conclusion that, whatever may have been the intent of the ordinances as adopted, they are applied by the public authorities charged with their administration, and thus representing the State itself, with a mind so unequal and oppressive as to amount to a practical denial by the State of ... equal protection of the laws .... [11]

Similarly, the Supreme Court has consistently held that facially neutral jury-selection statutes are insufficient to shield criminal convictions from reversal when the statutes are administered in a discriminatory fashion. It has also stood ready to infer discriminatory administration from statistical inferences based upon the number of African Americans who actually serve on juries.

Perhaps more controversial has been the Court's extension of this principle to the motivation of prosecutors and defense attorneys exercising "peremptory challenges" to jurors. In many jurisdictions, the prosecution and defense each has the

11. *Id.* at 373.

right to disqualify a certain number of jurors without giving a reason. In Swain v. Alabama,[12] the Court rejected an equal protection attack on the use of these challenges to remove African Americans from juries, holding that unless there was a practice of removing them systematically in case after case, it was in the nature of a peremptory challenge that the prosecutor could act without having to account for his reasons. However, in Batson v. Kentucky,[13] decided twenty-one years later, the Court overruled *Swain* and brought the law of peremptory challenges into line with other cases concerning discriminatory administration:

> Although a prosecutor ordinarily is entitled to exercise peremptory challenges "for any reason at all, as long as that reason is related to his view concerning the outcome" of the case to be tried, the Equal Protection Clause forbids the prosecutor to challenge potential jurors solely on account of their race or on the assumption that black jurors as a group will be unable impartially to consider the State's case against a black defendant.[14]

It is easy to see how cases like *Gomillion*, *Yick Wo*, and *Batson* might have been used to limit the force of *Washington*. True, after *Washington*, a statute was not subject to strict scrutiny just because of its disproportionate racial effects. However, such a statute would be subject to strict scrutiny if it was

12.   380 U.S. 202 (1965).

13.   476 U.S. 79 (1986).

14.   *Id.* at 79–80.

motivated by animus toward a racial minority. Moreover, as an evidentiary matter, a court might infer such animus from the disproportionate racial effect. Courts might therefore have used the improper motivation cases to get to the same place via a different route.

Should discriminatory motivation trigger strict scrutiny? On the facts of cases like *Gomillion* and *Yick Wo*, the argument for strict scrutiny seems compelling. In *Gomillion*, the legislature might have passed a statute simply providing that no African American could be a lawful resident of Tuskegee. Instead of directly accomplishing this goal, the legislature indirectly accomplished virtually the same thing by deliberately drawing the boundaries so as to exclude African Americans. It is hard to see why the form of words used to achieve the same goal should make a constitutional difference. Similarly, in *Yick Wo*, there is no doubt that a statute precluding Chinese Americans from operating laundries would be unconstitutional. Why should the government be allowed to accomplish the same end by enacting a neutral statute but then administering it in a way that effectively outlawed these establishments?

When one moves away from blatant cases like *Gomillion* and *Yick Wo*, however, the use of illegitimate purpose to heighten the level of scrutiny becomes more problematic. One difficulty, which we have already encountered, is epistemological: How is one to know what a collective body "intends?" In *Gomillion* and *Yick Wo*, the intent may be obvious, but many cases will be more subtle. Consider, for example, the hypothetical statute discussed at the beginning of this chapter. Perhaps a city councilman favors restricting 16 year old drivers to students enrolled in school because she thinks that these drivers are safer, but it is also certainly possible that she favors this result because she knows that it will keep African Americans off the road. If legislators are smart enough to avoid giving blatantly racist speeches when they enact legislation such as this, courts will have a hard time uncovering impermissible motivation.

United States v. Armstrong[15] demonstrates these practical difficulties. The defendant, an African American, was charged with conspiring to distribute "crack" cocaine. He brought a *Yick Wo* challenge to his conviction, alleging that the government was not prosecuting persons violating this law who were not African Americans. In order to support this challenge, he sought discovery of prosecution records concerning the races of people charged with this offense. The court of appeals granted his request, but the Supreme Court reversed. The Court held that before discovery was appropriate, the defendant must first show that persons of other races who had committed the offense were not prosecuted—the very requirement that the defendant hoped to meet by the discovery of prosecutorial records.

Moreover, even when discriminatory intent is uncovered, it sometimes remains mysterious why it should matter. Consider, for example, Hunter v.

15.   517 U.S. 456 (1996).

Underwood.[16] A constitutional provision adopted by Alabama in 1901 prevented any person from voting if the person had committed a crime of moral turpitude. There was unmistakable evidence in the legislative record indicating that the provision was motivated, at least in part, by the desire to disfranchise African Americans. On the other hand, there was no evidence that the current legislature had this intent, or, indeed, that the classification had a current disproportionate impact on African Americans. Writing for the *Hunter* Court in 1985, Justice Rehnquist held that the statute was unconstitutional because of the intent of its framers several generations earlier. But why should what legislators thought then affect the validity of the statute now? Presumably, the Alabama legislature could have responded to *Hunter* by promptly reenacting the statute if only legislators asserted (and perhaps even believed) that they had nonracial reasons for doing so.

Similarly, dissenting Justices have mounted a powerful argument against *Batson*. True, *Swain* allowed prosecutors to challenge African American jurors when they thought that this would be helpful to their case, but prosecutors could also challenge white jurors for the same strategic reasons. And in cases where prosecutors challenged African Americans, defense attorneys had the same power and same motivation for challenging whites. How, then, do these challenges treat African Americans unequally? To be sure, the *Swain* rule might have had

16. 471 U.S. 222 (1985).

a disproportionate *effect*—at least in jurisdictions where the initial jury pool is disproportionately white. Remember, though, that *Washington* establishes that disproportionate effect, standing alone, does not raise the level of scrutiny.

Limitations on Review for Improper Motive

Perhaps because of these difficulties, the Supreme Court has sharply limited improper motive review. The upshot of these limitations is that the *Washington* barrier to strict scrutiny remains quite high.

The Court has erected three significant obstacles to the use of improper motivation to raise the level of review.

First, and perhaps most significant, is the Court's definition of the kind of motive that is impermissible. The initial case establishing this definition involved gender, rather than race discrimination, but as we shall see, the Court has applied the definition to race cases as well. In Personnel Administrator v. Feeney,[17] the Court considered a challenge to a Massachusetts law providing that all veterans who qualified for state civil service positions must be hired ahead of qualifying nonveterans. The statute had a severe, and entirely predictable, impact on the ability of women to secure these jobs. In nonetheless upholding the statute, the Court conceded that this result was intended in the sense that the legislature enacting the provision knew that it would have a disproportionately adverse effect on

17.   442 U.S. 256 (1979).

women. But, the Court held, this was not the kind of intent that raised the level of scrutiny.

> "[D]iscriminatory purpose," ... implies more than intent as volition or intent as awareness of consequences. It implies that the decisionmaker ... selected or reaffirmed a particular course of action at least in part "because of," not merely "in spite of," its adverse effects upon an identifiable group. Yet, nothing in the record demonstrates that this preference for veterans was originally devised or subsequently re-enacted because it would accomplish the collateral goal of keeping women in a stereotypic and predefined place in the Massachusetts Civil Service.[18]

Put differently, the *Feeney* test seems to mean that governmental officials have an illegitimate purpose only when they act with the deliberate aim of harming the affected group. If taken literally, this definition excludes two important categories of cases. First, many classifications will be enacted not because government officials act with the sadistic desire of diminishing the welfare of minority groups, but because they associate membership in these groups with an evil they wish to control. Suppose, for example, that a legislator thinks that African American teenagers are more likely to be unsafe drivers than teenagers of other races and knows that more African Americans than whites are high school dropouts. If such a legislator voted for a requirement that only teenagers who attend school are eligible to receive a license, she would be

18. *Id.* at 279.

doing so not " 'because of' ... its adverse affects upon an identifiable group,"[19] but rather "because of" her interest in auto safety.

Perhaps the *Feeney* court did not mean to exclude this sort of case from heightened scrutiny. It is at least possible to read the "because of" language to refer to the instrumental use of race as well as the blatant desire to harm racial minorities. A second class of cases cannot be so easily dismissed, however. Often, discrimination will take the form of the sort of selective indifference discussed above. The risk here is not that government officials will set out to harm racial minorities, and not even that they will make instrumental generalizations about them, but rather that they will care less about harm to these groups that is the byproduct of pursuing other independent objectives. Thus, we can assume that the Massachusetts legislature was motivated by the desire to help veterans, rather than the desire to harm women. It may even be true that the legislature was not motivated by some stereotypical notion of how women would perform in government jobs. Still, the Court might have asked whether the legislature would have been as eager to help veterans if doing so had imposed comparable harm on men. If the answer to this question is "no," then there is an important sense in which the legislature denied women equality, even though the statute was enacted "in spite of" rather than "because of" its effect on women.

19. *Id.*

The impact of the *Feeney* definition on cases alleging racial discrimination is dramatically illustrated by McCleskey v. Kemp.[20] The defendant, an African American, was convicted of murdering a white victim and sentenced to death. He claimed that the system of capital punishment in Georgia (where he was convicted) was racially biased. In support of this claim, he produced a statistical study based on over two thousand murder cases occurring in Georgia. After attempting to account for intervening variables, the study concluded that defendants charged with killing white victims were 4.3 times more likely to receive a death sentence than defendants who killed blacks. Although the findings were less dramatic, the study also concluded that African American defendants were significantly more likely to be executed than white defendants.

Despite these statistics, the Court rejected the defendant's claim that the legislature adopted and maintained the death penalty for discriminatory reasons.

> For this claim to prevail, McCleskey would have to prove that the Georgia Legislature enacted or maintained the death penalty statute *because of* an anticipated racially discriminatory effect.... There is no evidence ... that the Georgia Legislature enacted the capital punishment statute to further a racially discriminatory purpose.[21]

20. 481 U.S. 279 (1987).

21. *Id.* at 298.

The Court thus treats as irrelevant the possibility that the legislature might not have adopted capital punishment but for its undervaluation of the welfare of African Americans. Put differently, it is at least possible that the legislature might have enacted the death penalty *because of* its belief that capital punishment deterred murder, but would not have pursued this goal so vigorously if the victims of such punishment had been disproportionately white rather than black. The Court's unwillingness to treat this possibility as drawing the statute into question is in tension with the conception of ethical equality that insists on equal valuation of every person's welfare.

A second obstacle for someone who wants to advance a discriminatory purpose claim is the methods of proof that the Court has permitted. As previously discussed, some of the Court's cases have suggested that it might be appropriate to infer discriminatory purpose from an otherwise unexplained discriminatory effect. Taken to its limit, this approach would collapse the practical distinction between a purpose and an effect test.

However, in Village of Arlington Heights v. Metropolitan Housing Development Corp.,[22] the Court substantially limited the extent to which a party might rely on the inference of purpose from effect. The plaintiffs brought an equal protection challenge to the Village's refusal to rezone a parcel of land so as to permit the construction of low-and moderate-income housing. Plaintiffs claimed that the level of

22.   429 U.S. 252 (1977).

scrutiny ought to be heightened because the decision was motivated by racial considerations. They asked the court to infer such discrimination from the fact that the adverse decision had a disproportionate impact on African Americans. Writing for the Court, Justice Lewis Powell held that the plaintiffs "simply failed to carry their burden of proving that discriminatory purpose was a motivating factor in the Village's decision."[23] In the course of so holding, the Court sharply narrowed the ability of a litigant to rely on impact alone in order to meet the burden of proof:

Determining whether invidious discriminatory purpose was a motivating factor demands a sensitive inquiry into such circumstantial and direct evidence of intent as may be available. The impact of the official action ... may provide an important starting point. Sometimes a clear pattern, unexplainable on grounds other than race, emerges from the effect of the state action even when the governing legislation appears neutral on its face. The evidentiary inquiry is then relatively easy. But such cases are rare. Absent a pattern as stark as that in Gomillion or Yick Wo, impact alone is not determinative, and the Court must look to other evidence.[24]

In some ways, *Arlington Heights* was an especially unfavorable case for the use of impact evidence because the plaintiffs challenged a single decision. Statistical evidence concerning the effect of govern-

23. *Id.* at 270.
24. *Id.* at 266.

ment action will be more persuasive in cases where government officials make recurring decisions that are subject to sophisticated statistical analysis. As already noted, for example, the Court has approved inference of purpose from effect in the context of jury selection, where regression analysis of recurring decisions can demonstrate a racial motivation.

But, as already noted, in *McCleskey,* the Court rejected just such an analysis in the context of the death penalty. McCleskey's statistical study purported to demonstrate that, over the range of cases, race determined who lived and who died in Georgia. But the Court, again per Justice Powell, rejected the challenge, holding that "McCleskey must prove that the decisionmakers in *his* case acted with discriminatory purpose."[25] The Court distinguished the jury cases as follows:

> [T]he nature of the capital sentencing decision, and the relationship of the statistics to that decision, are fundamentally different from the corresponding elements in the venire-selection ... cases. Most importantly, each particular decision to impose the death penalty is made by a petit jury selected from a properly constituted venire. Each jury is unique in its composition, and the Constitution requires that its decision rest on consideration of innumerable factors that vary according to the characteristics of the individual defendant and the facts of the particular capital offense. Thus, the application of an inference drawn from the general statistics to a specific

25.   481 U.S. at 292.

decision in a trial and sentencing simply is not comparable to the application of an inference drawn from general statistics to a specific venire-selection....[26]

Of course, the very claim McCleskey made was that capital punishment decisions were *not* made on the basis of "innumerable factors," but rather on the basis of race. Whatever the force of this claim, the upshot of the case is that it is now very difficult to make out a claim of discriminatory motivation even in recurring cases so long as the decision seems to take into account a wide variety of factors.

Still a third limitation on improper purpose review is the requirement that the person challenging the statute demonstrate a causal link between the illicit purpose and the discriminatory effect. The requirement is illustrated by two cases, Palmer v. Thompson[27] and Mt. Healthy City School District Board of Education v. Doyle.[28]

In *Palmer*, a case decided five years before *Washington*, a city council was confronted with an order to desegregate a municipal swimming pool, but decided to close the pool instead. Plaintiffs challenged this decision, claiming that the decision to close the pool was racially motivated. In a decision by Justice Hugo Black, the Court rejected this claim. In language that seems in tension with the Court's subsequent *Washington* holding, Justice Black disap-

26. *Id.* at 294–95.
27. 403 U.S. 217 (1971).
28. 429 U.S. 274 (1977).

proved the notion that "a legislative act may violate equal protection solely because of the motivations of the men who voted for it."[29]

The *Washington* Court might have simply overruled *Palmer*, but, instead, it chose to explain the case on the ground that closing the pool extended "identical treatment to both whites and Negroes."[30] When the two cases are taken together, they seem to hold that even if a classification is the result of a discriminatory intent, it may nonetheless be valid if it does not have a discriminatory effect. Put differently, when a classification is not race specific, both effect and intent are necessary to raise the level of scrutiny.

Mt. Healthy goes still further by holding that even when both intent and effect are present, there must be a causal link between the two. (Although Mt. Healthy arose in the free speech context, its holding seems to apply to equal protection cases as well.) The plaintiff was not rehired as a teacher by a public school because of conduct protected by the first amendment. In an opinion by Justice William Rehnquist, the Court held that even though the firing was improperly motivated, he was not necessarily entitled to reinstatement. Here, unlike *Palmer*, there was both an improper motive (the firing was in retaliation for first amendment activity) and an improper effect (the firing itself). Nonetheless, the Court said that the school district should have been given the chance to establish by a preponder-

29.   403 U.S. at 224.

30.   Washington v. Davis, 426 U.S. 229, 243 (1976).

ance of the evidence that "it would have reached the same decision as to [Doyle's] reemployment even in the absence of the protected conduct."[31] Had the district made such a showing, the improper motivation would not have been the "but-for" cause of the firing, and plaintiff would therefore not be entitled to relief.

A Summary

The doctrine covered above is quite complex, so a summary is in order. Mere disproportionate impact produced by a classification that does not explicitly divide people according to race is insufficient to raise the level of scrutiny. However, if the disproportionate impact is the result of a discriminatory purpose, the classification is treated as if it were race specific and will be invalidated unless it is narrowly tailored to serve a compelling state interest. The mental state that serves to heighten the level of scrutiny is a purpose to *cause* the disproportionate impact and not merely to achieve some other end *in spite of* that impact. The impact itself may be some evidence of such a purpose, but it will rarely be sufficient by itself. Moreover, heightened scrutiny is appropriate only when the purpose causes the impact.

31. Mt. Healthy City School Dist. Bd. of Educ. v. Doyle, 429 U.S. 274, 287 (1977).

CHAPTER SIX

RACE-SPECIFIC CLASSIFICATIONS THAT ARE FACIALLY NEUTRAL

We have seen that statutes that facially classify people according to race and treat some racial groups worse than others are strictly scrutinized. On the other hand, if a statute is non-race specific, disproportionate effect on a racial group does not trigger strict scrutiny. This chapter concerns statutes that are race-specific, in the sense that they classify people based upon their race, but that, at least facially, treat racial groups equally.

Loving v. Virginia[1] provides a good example of such a statute. Virginia law made it a criminal offense for "any white person [to] intermarry with a colored person, or any colored person [to] intermarry with a white person."[2] In a unanimous decision written the Chief Justice Earl Warren, the Court invalidated the statute.

Today, few would quarrel with the result in *Loving*, but the case fits uneasily with the doctrine outlined so far. Recall that the first step in equal protection analysis is to identify the class that is disadvantaged on the face of the statute. Here, the

1. 388 U.S. 1 (1967).

2. *Id.* at 4.

class consists of whites who want to marry African Americans and African Americans who want to marry whites. There is no doubt that this class of people is treated unequally when compared to whites who want to marry whites and African Americans who want to marry African Americans. The difficulty, though, is that the disadvantaged class has both white and African American members. Indeed, since every black/white couple wishing to marry consists of one African American and one white, the disadvantaged class necessarily includes an equal number of whites and African Americans.

Since the classification is facially race neutral, the doctrinal frame outlined above might suggest that it should be subject to only low level scrutiny and upheld if it has a rational basis. Instead, the *Loving* Court held that "mere 'equal application' of a statute containing racial classifications is [not] enough to remove the classifications from the Fourteenth Amendment's proscription of all invidious racial discrimination,"[3] and that it must be subject to "the most rigid scrutiny" because the statute "rest[ed] solely upon distinctions drawn according to race."[4] In other words, even though the statute is facially neutral, the fact that it draws a distinction based upon race subjects it to heightened review.

What is the basis for heightened scrutiny of statutes, like that invalidated in *Loving*, that are race specific but facially neutral? The Court's encounter with this question involved it in the most dramatic

3. *Id.* at 8.
4. *Id.* at 10.

and celebrated struggle in American constitutional history.

Separate but Equal

The story begins in 1896 with the Court's infamous decision in Plessy v. Ferguson.[5] The case concerned an equal protection challenge to a Louisiana statute, enacted six years earlier, requiring railroad companies to provide "equal but separate accommodations for the white and colored races," with the qualification that "nothing in this act shall be construed as applying to nurses attending children of the other race."[6] In an opinion by Justice Henry Brown, over Justice John Marshall Harlan's lone dissent, the Court upheld the statute. The Court held, in effect, that a facially neutral race-specific statute should be treated in the same way as a statute that was not race-specific.

Justice Brown made several arguments in favor of the statute. First, he relied upon the distinction between social and political equality. Although the fourteenth amendment "was undoubtedly [intended] to enforce the absolute equality of the two races before the law," it was not meant to abolish racial distinctions or to "enforce social, as distinguished from political, equality or a commingling of the two races upon terms unsatisfactory to either."[7]

Second, the Court argued that separation of the races did not impose on African Americans a badge

5. 163 U.S. 537 (1896).

6. *Id.* at 540–41.

7. *Id.* at 433.

of inferiority. "If this be so, it is not by reason of anything found in the act, but solely because the colored race chooses to put that construction upon it."[8]

Third, the Court argued that unlike other requirements that one might imagine (like requiring separate compartments for people belonging to different nationalities, or requiring blacks and whites to walk on different sides of the street), this regulation was "reasonable" and was "enacted in good faith for the promotion of the public good, and not for the annoyance or oppression of a particular class."[9]

Finally, in a passage that seemed to ignore the fact that the statute prevented willing individuals from racial intermixing, the Court objected to "the enforced commingling of the two races." In the Court's view

If the two races are to meet upon terms of social equality, it must be the result of natural affinities, a mutual appreciate of each other's merits, and a voluntary consent of individuals. . . . Legislation is powerless to eradicate racial instincts, or to abolish distinctions based upon physical differences, and the attempt to do so can only result in accentuating the difficulties of the present situation. If the civil and political rights of both races be equal, one cannot be inferior to the other civilly or politically. If one race be

8. *Id.* at 551.

9. *Id.* at 550.

inferior to the other socially, the constitution of the United States cannot put them upon the same plane.[10]

In his dissenting opinion, Justice Harlan prophetically warned that in time, the decision would "prove to be quite as pernicious as the decision made by this tribunal in the Dred Scott Case."[11] He pointed out that "[e]very one knows that the statute in question had its origin in the purpose, not so much to exclude white persons from railroad cars occupied by blacks, as to exclude colored people from coaches occupied by or assigned to white persons."[12] And, in a often quoted passage, he wrote the following:

> The white race deems itself to be the dominant race in this country. And so it is, in prestige, in achievements, in education, in wealth, and in power. So, I doubt not, it will continue to be for all time, if it remains true to its great heritage, and holds fast to the principles of constitutional liberty. But in view of the constitution, in the eye of the law, there is in this country no superior, dominant, ruling class of citizens. There is no caste here. Our constitution is color-blind, and neither knows nor tolerates classes among citizens. In respect of civil rights, all citizens are equal before the law. The humblest is the peer of the most powerful. The law regards man as man, and takes no account of his surroundings or of his

10. *Id.* at 551–52.

11. *Id.* at 559 (Harlan, J., dissenting).

12. *Id.* at 556 (Harlan, J., dissenting).

color when his civil rights are guaranteed by the supreme law of the land are involved.[13]

There are two ways to think about *Plessy*. Imagine first that one approached the decision as the proverbial person from Mars, entirely ignorant of anything about the social context in which the case was decided. As a matter of abstract logic, there is nothing extraordinary about Justice Brown's reasoning. It is easy to think of settings in which there might be good reason for the separation of two identifiable groups and in which this separation does not imply the inferiority of either.

Consider, for example, Board of Education v. Grumet.[14] Parents who were Satmar Hasedim (practitioners of an especially strict form of Judaism) complained that some of their children, who attended regular public schools, suffered from "panic, fear and trauma ... in leaving their own community and being with people whose ways were so different."[15] In response to these complaints, the state enacted a statute setting up a special school district for these children. Although the Supreme Court held that the statute violated the first amendment's establishment clause, not even opponents of the statute suggested that the separation of these children under these circumstances implied their inferiority or deprived them of basic civil rights.

13. *Id.* at 559 (Harlan, J., dissenting).

14. 512 U.S. 687 (1994).

15. *Id.* at 692.

If *Plessy* had been decided in the same social setting as *Grumet*, the *Plessy* Court's argument would make some sense. To be sure, the Court's rhetoric about "enforced commingling" and social intercourse based upon "voluntary consent," seems puzzling given the fact that the statute in question prevented people who wished to engage in interracial contact from doing so. Still, if one thinks about the problem purely as a matter of abstract logic, Louisiana's position is not altogether unreasonable. On this view, the state was faced with a practical problem: It would be very difficult to satisfy both those who wanted segregated accommodations and those who wanted integrated accommodations. Faced with a choice between the two, the state made a decision that, it thought, would satisfy the majority. One might wish that individuals were more willing to have social contact with people of different races or cultures, but state recognition of a desire not to engage in such social intercourse might be seen as an aspect of personal freedom.

Of course, the trouble with this defense of *Plessy* is that it completely ignores the social context and actual effect of this recognition. If one thinks about the Court's reasoning in terms of its social location, rather than as a matter of abstract logic, a very different picture emerges. As historians of the period have demonstrated,[16] segregated facilities did not just happen, and the state governments did not require segregation to serve the mutual convenience

16. *See, e.g.,* Joel Williamson, The Crucible of Race 109–17 (1984).

of blacks and whites. Instead, Jim Crow statutes, which first became prevalent during the late nineteenth century, were a deliberate and effective exercise of power by whites over blacks. Their motivation was to remind African Americans on a daily basis of their subservient position by regularly humiliating them during the course of ordinary social interaction. When coupled with disfranchisement and the routine threat of violence, the Jim Crow regime enforced a brutal and devastating racial caste system that left African Americans as a hopeless and despised underclass. The problem with *Plessy*, then, is not that a system of "separate but equal" denied formal equality. Viewed from the standpoint of the equal protection doctrine we have so far discussed, the opinion is perfectly defensible. On its face, a segregation statute does not treat blacks worse than whites, thereby triggering heightened review, and even the fact that the statute might have had a disproportionate impact on African Americans (for example because it is more important for the economic well-being of African Americans to associate with members of the dominant culture than for whites to associate with members of a suppressed culture) is insufficient to change that conclusion. Moreover, the avoidance of racial violence or the desire of people not to commingle with other races might well provide a rational basis for the classification. One must go beyond the formal equality guaranteed by standard equal protection doctrine and resort to "background knowledge of educated men who live in the world," as Professor Charles Black put it,[17] to understand what is wrong with *Plessy*.

But this understanding introduces a problem of its own. A disavowal of *Plessy* premised on its actual *effect* in the social setting in which it was decided draws into question more than just "separate but equal." As we have seen, modern equal protection doctrine also ignores the actual effect of classifications and focuses instead on whether the classifications are facially neutral and not infected by discriminatory intent. Some of the statutes the modern Court has upheld might also be vulnerable if one thought seriously about the actual impact of these laws when they intersect with their social setting. For example, reconsider the actual effect of the test for police applicants that the Supreme Court validated in Washington v. Davis.

For this reason, there is an unavoidable tension between Court's treatment of facially neutral race-specific statutes and the rest of equal protection jurisprudence—a tension explored in the next section.

The Struggle against Jim Crow

In order to understand the events immediately following *Plessy*, one must grasp some other facts about the contemporary social setting. *Plessy* was decided against the backdrop of pervasive racism that was assumed as a given in both north and south. By the late nineteenth century, many north-

17. Charles Black, *The Lawfulness of the Segregation Decisions*, 69 Yale L. J. 421, 424–26 (1960).

erners had lost interest in a serious effort to enforce the promise of the Reconstruction Amendments. Preoccupied with problems produced by industrialization and urbanization and blinded by the virtually unshakable assumption of black inferiority, whites throughout the country were simply unconcerned about the plight of African Americans.

Plessy also arose at a moment when the Supreme Court was poised to embark upon its encounter with the doctrine of substantive due process. One year after *Plessy*, the Court decided Allgeyer v. Louisiana,[18] which held for the first time that the "liberty" protected by the due process clause included not only procedural rights, but unenumerated substantive rights, including economic freedoms. Eight years later, it decided Lochner v. New York,[19] where it invalidated a state statute providing for maximum hours for bakery workers. During the so-called "*Lochner* era," which extended from roughly 1905 to 1937, the Court frequently struck down redistributive economic and regulatory legislation. These decisions emphasized the importance of individual choice in the economic sphere and equated liberty with the absence of government intervention.

Given prevailing racial views in late nineteenth century America, it is hardly surprising that *Plessy* was greeted with little or no outrage. Moreover, early efforts to enforce the "equal" half of the "separate but equal" formulation amounted to a

18. 165 U.S. 578 (1897).
19. 198 U.S. 45 (1905).

cruel joke. For example, three years after *Plessy*, the Court was faced with a suit by African American taxpayers and parents who challenged their tax assessment on the ground that the school district was operating a white high school, but no comparable black school. This seems like an obvious denial of equality, yet Justice Harlan, the dissenter in *Plessy,* wrote for a unanimous Court in rejecting the challenge.[20]

Perhaps more surprising is the fact that elements of the then-dominant *Lochner* approach raised questions about some aspects of the Jim Crow system. A court that believed in individual, private choice as the essence of liberty was unlikely to be sympathetic to an argument against segregation that focused on its systemic effects on an entire class of persons. Still, the statute upheld in *Plessy*, like the statute invalidated in *Lochner*, involved government regulation of the market and interfered with the right of individuals to make market choices. When opponents of segregation were able to focus the Court's attention on government interference with individual market transactions, they were able to make some limited headway.

Two cases illustrate this point. In McCabe v. Atchison, Topeka & Santa Fe Railway,[21] a case decided in 1914, the Court struck down an Oklahoma statute that required railroads to provide separate but equal coach facilities, but permitted sleeping cars, dining cars, and chair cars only for

20. Cumming v. Board of Educ., 175 U.S. 528 (1899).
21. 235 U.S. 151 (1914).

whites. The state justified its failure to require these facilities for African Americans on the ground that there was minimal aggregate African American demand for them. The Supreme Court was unpersuaded. It pointed out that this position "makes the constitutional right depend on the number of persons who may be discriminated against, whereas the essence of the constitutional right is that it is a personal one."[22]

Three years later, in Buchanan v. Warley,[23] the Court invalidated a statute prohibiting whites from occupying a residence in a block where the majority of houses were occupied by African Americans and vice versa. On this occasion, the Court relied expressly on substantive due process grounds. In the Court's view, the ordinance was invalid because it constituted unwarranted government interference with the property rights of individuals.

Although these cases had some impact on the margins of the Jim Crow system, they did not change the underlying fact of systemic suppression of African Americans. Indeed, precisely because the cases focused on the rights of individuals, rather than on the status of social groups, their failure was guaranteed. More significantly, failure was certain because of the setting in which the cases were decided. In the early twentieth century, African Americans remained politically, socially, and economically isolated. Even if the Court had wanted to

22. *Id.* at 161.
23. 245 U.S. 60 (1917).

do so, it is doubtful it could have had much impact on the pervasive racism that gripped the country.

By mid-century, these social facts had begun to change. Massive immigration of African Americans from the south to northern cities gave them political power that they had never before enjoyed. The struggle against Hitler's racist policies in Europe made racism less acceptable in the United States, and African American veterans, returning from World War II, were unwilling to accept passively the treatment their parents had received. The integration of baseball in 1947, and Jackie Robinson's dignified, courageous, and well-publicized struggle for a place in America's "national pastime" symbolized the evils of racism and the heroism of those attempting to overcome it.

Against this shifting backdrop, the National Association for the Advancement of Colored People waged a legal campaign against segregated facilities. Under the leadership of future Supreme Court Justice Thurgood Marshall, the NAACP engaged in legal skirmishing in scores of communities. Often, these struggles had to overcome the threat of violence and economic sanctions, but they nonetheless not only produced some legal victories, but also served an important organizing and educational function. At first demanding that the "equal" half of the "separate but equal" formulation be given teeth, the NAACP gradually moved toward a direct confrontation with segregation.

In a series of decisions handed down during this period, the Supreme Court began to limit the scope of *Plessy*. As early as 1938, the Court held that Missouri had violated the equal protection clause when it provided a law school for white students, but sent prospective African American law students to out-of-state facilities.[24] In 1944, the Court held that exclusion of black voters from primary elections was unconstitutional,[25] and in 1948, the Court struck down enforcement of ostensibly "private" restrictive covenants on real property that prohibited sale to, or occupancy by, African Americans.[26]

By 1950, the Court was ready, for the first time, to order a state to admit black students to a white institution. In Sweatt v. Painter,[27] the African American plaintiff was denied admission to the University of Texas law school, but permitted to attend a parallel black institution, hastily organized only after litigation had begun. In a unanimous decision, the Supreme Court held that the African American institution was not "equal." Significantly, the Court emphasized a lack of equality that extended beyond objective factors like the size of the library or the number of faculty members. The Court thought that it was even more important that the schools were unequal in "qualities which were incapable of objective measurement, but which make for great-

24. Missouri ex rel. Gaines v. Canada, 305 U.S. 337 (1938).

25. Smith v. Allwright, 321 U.S. 649 (1944).

26. Shelley v. Kraemer, 334 U.S. 1 (1948).

27. 339 U.S. 629 (1950).

ness in a law school"[28] like the reputation of its faculty and influence of its alumni. Beyond this, the Court wrote,

> The law school, the proving ground for legal learning and practice, cannot be effective in isolation from the individuals and institutions with which the law interacts.... The law school to which Texas is willing to admit petitioner excludes from its student body members of the racial groups which number 85% of the population of the State and include most of the lawyers, witnesses, jurors, judges and other officials with whom petitioner will inevitably be dealing when he becomes a member of the Texas Bar. With such a substantial and significant segment of society excluded, we cannot conclude that the education offered petitioner is substantially equal to that which he would receive if admitted to the University of Texas law school.[29]

In a companion case decided on the same day, McLaurin v. Oklahoma State Regents,[30] the Court went even further. Under the threat of litigation, Oklahoma had actually admitted McLaurin, an African American, to a state graduate school. However, he was made to sit in a special seat in the classroom, could not eat with other students, and was given a special table in the library. The Court held that this treatment violated the equal protection clause because it inhibited "his ability to study, to

28. *Id.* at 633.
29. *Id.* at 634.
30. 339 U.S. 637 (1950).

engage in discussions and exchange views with other students, and, in general, to learn his profession."[31]

Sweatt and *McLaurin* effectively outlawed segregation in graduate institutions, but, as a formal matter at least, they left the "separate but equal" standard intact. The Court's frontal assault on that standard did not come until four years later, when it decided Brown v. Board of Education.[32]

Brown

Brown I concerned a challenge brought by black school children to laws that mandated segregated education in public elementary and high schools. As the Court formulated the issue, the case presented the question whether segregated public schools were constitutionally impermissible even when they were "equal." It is important to see that the issue need not have been presented in so stark a fashion. Given its earlier holdings in *Sweatt* and *McLauren*, the Court could easily have held that all the African American facilities before it were unequal to the parallel white institutions. Instead, in a famous opinion by Chief Justice Earl Warren, the Court held that "in the field of public education the doctrine of 'separate but equal' has no place. Separate educational facilities are inherently unequal."[33]

This holding obviously disavows *Plessy*, at least in the educational context. (Shortly after *Brown I*, the

31. *Id.* at 641
32. 347 U.S. 483 (1954).
33. *Id.* at 495.

Court, without explanation, extended its holding to other public facilities[34]). Less obviously, it is also inconsistent with a *Lochner*-like approach to the problem of segregation and racial justice. In this sense, *Brown* is in tension not only with *Plessy*, but also with cases like *McCabe* and *Buchanan*, which had used the rhetoric of individual choice to reduce *Plessy*'s scope.

These earlier cases had conceptualized segregation as government interference with private choice. They involved individuals who wished to engage in market transactions—buying a home or a railroad ticket—but who were prevented from doing so by government coercion. In contrast, *Brown* involved a *public* institution. Instead of requiring restrictions on government interference with a private sphere, *Brown* emphasized the affirmative obligations of government. As the Court put it:

> Today, education is perhaps the most important function of state and local governments. Compulsory school attendance laws and the great expenditures for education both demonstrate our recognition of the importance of education to our democratic society. It is required in the performance of our most basic public responsibilities, even service in the armed forces. It is the very foundation of good citizenship. Today, it is a principal instrument in awakening the child to

34. *See* Gayle v. Browder, 352 U.S. 903 (1956) (buses); Holmes v. City of Atlanta, 350 U.S. 879 (1955) (municipal golf courses); Baltimore v. Dawson, 350 U.S. 877 (1955) (public beaches).

cultural values, in preparing him for later professional training, and in helping him to adjust normally to his environment. In these days, it is doubtful that any child may reasonably be expected to succeed in life if he is denied the opportunity of an education. Such an opportunity, where the state has undertaken to provide it, is a right which must be made available to all on equal terms.[35]

Similarly, the model of individual choice does not fit very well within the framework established in *Brown*. Individuals might decide for themselves what kind of rail accommodations to purchase or what home to live in, but, as the Court noted, school attendance is compulsory, and public schools must be either segregated or integrated.

Relying on (probably flawed) social science data, the *Brown* court concluded that racial segregation "generates a feeling of inferiority as to [the] status [of African American children] in the community that may affect their hearts and minds in a way unlikely ever to be undone."[36] It is clear, though, that the *Brown* court did not mean to insist that *every* African American child performed better in an integrated environment. If one focuses on individual

35. Brown v. Board of Education, 347 U.S. 483, 493 (1954).

36. *Id.* at 494.

The Court cited, *inter alia*, Kenneth B. Clark, Effect of Prejudice and Discrimination on Personality Development (1950). *See* 347 U.S., at 495 n. 11. For criticism of the social science data, see Mark Yudof, *School Desegregation: Legal Realism, Reasoned Elaboration, and Social Science Research in the Supreme Court*, 42 J. of Law & Contemp. Prob. 57, 70 (1978).

African Americans, then segregation might be permissible (indeed, mandatory) in places where it could be shown, as an empirical matter, that black children perform better in a segregated than an integrated environment. But surely the Court did not mean to allow a particular school district to avoid desegregation by showing that, whatever was true in general, individual African Americans were not harmed by segregation in that district.

It is only by focusing on the status of African Americans as a group that we can understand the Court's conclusion that "[s]eparate educational facilities are inherently unequal." Taken literally, this statement is obviously false. As a purely conceptual matter, it is certainly not beyond the realm of possibility that there might be a particular segregated African American facility that is equal to or better than a particular segregated white facility. Indeed, to deny this possibility is to flirt with the very racist assumptions that the *Brown* court meant to disown.

The statement makes sense only if one thinks about the *system* of segregation and about the *effect* of that system on the social, economic, and political status of African Americans as a class. As already noted, this understanding of *Brown* is in considerable tension with the rest of equal protection doctrine, which is mostly blind to the social effects of government action and preoccupied with facial neutrality and with unfair categorizations of particular individuals. It is also in tension with *Washington*'s implicit assumption that the Court's role is limited to the remedying of isolated, nonsystemic instances of racial discrimination.

This tension became increasingly apparent as the Court moved from the announcement of *Plessy*'s demise to implementation of Brown's requirements.

Enforcing *Brown*

Although the rhetoric of the initial *Brown* decision was quite sweeping, the Court chose to remain silent about how the decision was to be implemented. Instead, it set the case for reargument on the issue of remedy. A year later, in *Brown II*,[37] the Court stepped back from an immediate confrontation over desegregation. Pointing to the "varied local school problems"[38] that would have to be solved before desegregation could occur, the Court invoked the "practical flexibility in shaping [equitable] remedies."[39] The upshot was that school boards were required to "make a prompt and reasonable start toward full compliance"[40] with *Brown I*, but were to proceed "with all deliberate speed."[41] With this pronouncement, the Court effectively washed its hands of the matter, remanding the cases to the lower federal courts to fashion whatever remedies they chose.

Brown II has been widely criticized as unnecessarily emboldening the Court's opponents and as

37. Brown v. Board of Educ., 349 U.S. 294 (1955).

38. *Id.* at 299.

39. *Id.* at 300.

40. *Id.*

41. *Id.* at 301.

inconsistent with the Court's earlier recognition that segregation violated the constitutional rights of African American school children. There is surely something to these criticisms. As we shall see, *Brown II* presaged a humiliating, decade-long demonstration of judicial impotence, during which the Court did virtually nothing in the teeth of widespread and unambiguous defiance of its mandate.

Paradoxically, however, there is also a sense in which *Brown II* reenforced the radicalism of *Brown I*. This is true in two respects, First, *Brown II* made clear that *Brown I* was something more than the simple, nondiscretionary application of the Constitution to a new set of facts. The Court, in effect, acknowledged that it was engaged in the high politics of social transformation rather than technical exegesis of a legal text. As a matter of politics, the Justices no doubt understood that they were in an exposed and vulnerable position. President Eisenhower had conspicuously refused to endorse *Brown I*, and Congress was completely dominated by southern segregationists who, virtually without exception, were prepared to defy it. Had the Court insisted on immediate enforcement, it is entirely possible that nothing would have happened. The Justices elected instead to bide their time and wait for the other branches to provide necessary support.

Relatedly, *Brown II* served to emphasize the systemic thrust of *Brown I*. If one conceptualizes *Brown I* as declaring the rights of individual, African American school children denied an integrated education, it is hard to justify the Court's refusal to enforce these rights for the individuals claiming them, many of whom had become adults by the time any actual desegregation occurred. As argued above, however, this interpretation reflects a misunderstanding of what *Brown I* was all about. If, instead, *Brown I* is conceptualized as a political intervention designed to dismantle a *system* and promote broadbased social change, the sacrifice of individual interests in order to facilitate a broader strategy with a better chance of success might be more defensible.

Perhaps a sounder criticism of *Brown II* is that the strategy itself was misconceived. It is at least possible that if the Court had been firmer, the transformation it favored would have occurred more quickly. In the event, for a decade following *Brown II*, there was virtually no desegregation in the deep south. Local communities responded with a variety of subterfuges, outright defiance, school closures, and, on occasion, violence.

It is not true that nothing of significance occurred during this period, however. Whether because of *Brown* or for other reasons, the civil rights movement began to pick up steam. Under the leadership of activists like Martin Luther King, African Americans began to engage in direct action throughout the south, including sit-ins, freedom rides, boycotts, marches, and demonstrations. In many communities, the authorities responded by instigating or tolerating sickening acts of violence directed against African Americans who were peaceably asserting their constitutional rights. The result was an upsurge of northern sympathy for the plight of southern blacks, which, in turn, helped to galvanize congressional and presidential support for desegregation by the mid 1960's.

In this more friendly political environment, the Court returned to the fray. When it did so, its decisions reemphasized the systemic and public character of the right it was defending. For example, in Green v. County School Board,[42] the Court invalidated a "freedom of choice" plan under which students were given the individual choice to attend either the formally all black or the formally all white school. As a matter of practical effect, the plan produced virtually no integration. Had the Court adopted a *Lochner*-like approach, it might have been satisfied with the fact that school assignments were now made in a color-blind fashion. It would have emphasized the freedom of choice granted to individual students and treated the practical effect of this "choice" is irrelevant. But practical effect was all that mattered to the Warren Court. The question was not whether the school district had provided freedom of choice, the Court insisted, but whether the plan "promises realistically to work, and promises realistically to work *now.*"[43]

Without quite so holding, the *Green* Court implied that it was requiring more than the simple dismantling of the formal legal obstacles to integration. Instead, school districts had an obligation to produce *actual* integration. As the Court put it,

42.   391 U.S. 430 (1968).

43.   *Id.* at 438.

the ultimate test was whether the plan "promise[s] realistically to convert promptly to a system without a 'white' school and a 'Negro' school, but just schools."[44]

Although the Court did not say so, the logic of *Green* also suggested that merely instituting "neighborhood" schools with geographical districting would not satisfy *Brown*. After all, if freedom of choice that failed to produce actual integration was unconstitutional, then it would seem to follow that a system where students were *compelled* to attend one-race schools in their neighborhood would also be invalid.

The Court took a big step toward converting this logical inference into a holding in Swann v. Charlotte–Mecklenburg Board of Education.[45] After years of defiance and delay, the Charlotte–Mecklenburg school district converted to a system of formally desegregated neighborhood schools. Nonetheless, because of geographical segregation, over half the black students were still attending schools that were at least ninety-nine percent black. In response to these statistics, the district court ordered the gerrymandering of school district lines and the bussing of students between schools so as to achieve greater racial balance. In an unanimous opinion written by Chief Justice Warren Burger, the Supreme Court affirmed this decision.

44. *Id.* at 432.
45. 402 U.S. 1 (1971).

The Court's *Swann* opinion has something of a schizophrenic quality, probably produced by the effort to reconcile the Court's result-oriented desegregation jurisprudence with broader equal protection doctrine focusing on formal equality. On the one hand, Chief Justice Burger emphasized that the underlying right protected by *Brown* was rooted in formal color-blindness. African American students had a right to a facially neutral school assignment process, not a right to attend schools that were in fact integrated. Yet on the other hand, as a matter of remedy, the Court squarely accepted a test based upon effects. Thus, once a court found that schools had at one point been deliberately segregated, district judges were permitted to adopt remedial measures that went far beyond dismantling de jure segregation. Instead, they could order the district to adopt measures that would produce actual, de facto integration. This understanding had the effect of disowning as a matter of remedy the individualist theory relied upon to establish the right. Far from requiring the color-blindness that the first Justice Harlan had praised in the previous century, *Swann* permitted district courts to assign students to various schools based upon their race so as to produce appropriate ratios of blacks to whites.

Swann marked the effective end of the *Brown* era. By the time the case was decided, southern resistance to *Brown* was in retreat almost everywhere and, within a short time, the south became the most integrated section of the country. At the same time, however, *Swann*'s focus on actual results made the line between southern de jure and northern de facto segregation difficult to defend. The result was pressure on northern school districts to produce integrated schools—pressure that contributed to the sharp diminution of northern, white support for desegregation. Moreover, as a doctrinal matter, the emergence of Washington v. Davis made the Court's treatment of school desegregation seem increasingly anomalous.

The upshot is that in recent years, the Court has returned to an understanding of *Brown* that is more consistent with Washington v. Davis and its approach to facially neutral statutes with discriminatory impact. Post-*Swann* decisions have sharply limited the remedial discretion of the lower courts, holding for example that interdistrict remedies, designed to deal with white flight to suburban, segregated schools, are impermissible[46] and that district judges may not readjust school district lines so as to maintain integration over time or insist on racial balance in the absence of a prior constitutional violation.[47] Moreover, the Court has now provided a blueprint for school districts wishing to rid themselves of court supervision so as to terminate result-oriented desegregation plans.[48]

In short, by the early twenty-first century, the *Brown* experiment was effectively over. Today,

46. *See* Milliken v. Bradley, 418 U.S. 717 (1974); Missouri v. Jenkins, 515 U.S. 70 (1995).

47. *See* Pasadena Bd. of Educ. v. Spangler, 427 U.S. 424 (1976).

48. *See* Board of Educ. v. Dowell, 498 U.S. 237 (1991); Freeman v. Pitts, 503 U.S. 467 (1992).

judges no longer order implementation of integration plans, many schools remain racially segregated, and almost no one believes that the Supreme Court or constitutional law will make a major difference in promoting significant racial change. *Brown* is of continuing significance mostly as a triumphal narrative that, ironically, serves as rhetorical support for the racial status quo and, only occasionally, as a dim reminder of a constitutional world that might have been.

Modern Examples of Strict Scrutiny for Race–Specific but Facially Neutral Statutes

Yet the equal protection doctrine established in *Brown*—the requirement of strict scrutiny for race specific but facially neutral statutes—lives on despite the collapse of the general theoretical approach that supported it. The doctrine has been normalized and reconciled with the rest of equal protection jurisprudence by focusing on the formal requirement of color-blindness and ignoring the concern about systemic effects that made sense of cases like *Brown*. Because it has been severed from its theoretical roots, the doctrine has produced some odd results when applied in a modern context. Two separate lines of contemporary cases illustrate the point.

By far, the more important of the two concerns the problem of electoral districting. Recall that in Gomillion v. Lightfoot,[49] the Court held that district lines that had the purpose and effect of depriv-

49.   364 U.S. 339 (1960).

ing African Americans of full representation were subject to strict scrutiny. Suppose, though, that a jurisdiction draws lines with the conscious purpose of reflecting, rather than understating, African American representation? For example, in a state where African Americans constituted a substantial minority of the population but were geographically dispersed, legislative district lines drawn on a nonracial basis might lead to underrepresentation of African Americans if there were racial bloc voting. Because African Americans would be in a minority in every district, they might gain no seats even though they represented a substantial percentage of the total population.

Suppose that a jurisdiction decided to remedy this problem by taking race into account when it drew legislative district lines. These lines might be deliberately gerrymandered so that if African Americans represent, say, thirty percent of the population, they would end up with thirty percent of the seats. A plan like this is similar to *Gomillion* in that the drawing of the district lines is influenced by race. Yet it is facially neutral because, unlike the *Gomillion* statute, the plan does not dilute the voting strength of any racial group in the sense that voting strength is not made disproportionate to that group's percentage of the total population. Should districting of this sort be strictly scrutinized?

The Supreme Court's answer to this question has been an ambiguous "yes." In Shaw v. Reno,[50] plaintiffs challenged the constitutionality of a "dramati-

50. 509 U.S. 630 (1993).

cally irregular[ly] shaped congressional district with a majority of African American residents. There was no claim that white voting strength was diluted by the creation of this district. On the contrary, the district had been drawn so as to accurately reflect the racial composition of the state as a whole. Rather, plaintiffs' complaint was that the districting involved a " 'deliberate segregation of voters' that interfered with their right to a 'color-blind' electoral process.' "

In a 5–4 opinion written by Justice Sandra Day O'Connor, the Court held that these allegations stated a valid cause of action:

> [W]e believe that reapportionment is one area in which appearances do matter. A reapportionment plan that includes in one district individuals who belong to the same race, but who are otherwise widely separated by geographical and political boundaries, and who may have little in common with one another but the color of their skin, bears an uncomfortable resemblance to political apartheid. It reinforces the perception that members of the same racial group—regardless of their age, education, economic status, or community in which they live—think alike, share the same political interests, and will prefer the same candidates at the polls. We have rejected such perceptions elsewhere as impermissible racial stereotypes. By perpetuating such notions, a racial gerrymander may exacerbate the very pat-

terns of racial bloc voting the majority-minority districting is sometimes said to counteract.[51]

Yet, despite these concerns, the Court stopped short of a holding that all use of race in districting decisions is subject to strict scrutiny. As it later explained in Johnson v. Miller, the test is whether race is

the predominant factor motivating the legislature's decision to place a significant number of voters within or without a particular district. To make this showing, a plaintiff must prove that the legislature subordinated traditional race-neutral districting principles, including but not limited to compactness, contiguity, respect for political subdivisions or communities defined by actual shared interests, to racial considerations.[52]

Moreover, the Court has indicated that even when strict scrutiny is applied, remedying the effects of past voting discrimination,[53] and, perhaps, compliance with the Voting Rights Act (which, to a limited extent requires the drawing of district lines so as to reflect minority voting strength)[54] may count as compelling government interests.

It is not hard to see why the Court is concerned about race-based districting. There is, after all, some force to the argument for formal equality.

51. *Id.* at 647–48.

52. *Id.* at 916.

53. *See* Shaw v. Hunt, 517 U.S. 899, 908 (1996).

54. *See* Bush v. Vera, 517 U.S. 952, 990 (1996) (O'Connor, J., concurring).

Imagine, for example, that a jurisdiction decided to remedy the underrepresentation of African Americans by creating "race elections," whereby separate, jurisdiction-wide elections are held for each racial group and the seats are then proportionately divided according to each group's percentage of the total population. Many people would find a plan of this sort, which reduces voters to nothing more than their race, very troubling. The race based districting that has troubled the Court can be seen as a watered-down version of such a plan.

Shaw and its progeny nonetheless illustrate the problems created by the effort to assimilate the *Brown* line of cases into standard equal protection doctrine. These problems may explain the Court's unwillingness to embrace the full implications of its logic by prohibiting all use of race in legislative districting.

One problem results from treating the *Brown* cases as if they guaranteed individual rights rather than protecting against group subordination. This orientation confronts the *Shaw* court with the difficulty of determining which individuals are harmed by racial districting. In United States v. Hays,[55] the Court held that plaintiffs living within a district subject to racial gerrymandering had standing to contest the districting, but that plaintiffs outside the district lacked standing. But how is an individual white voter harmed by being in a district deliberately drawn so as to contain an African American majority? Harm occurs only if we assume that

55.   515 U.S. 737 (1995).

whites and blacks have different interests and will vote for different candidates. But acknowledging this sort of harm seems to endorse the very race-conscious stereotypes that the Court wishes to discredit.

Of course, the *Shaw* court might have treated *Brown* as standing for a ban on group subordination, but, on this understanding, it requires some work to make out the case against racial districting. It is not immediately obvious that proportional, racial representation, designed to give African Americans a "fair share" of political power, carries the same message of racial inferiority conveyed by the Jim Crow policies invalidated in *Brown*. There are more subtle theories that suggest risks of racial subordination lurking in racial districting. It is possible, for example, that concentrating minority voters in certain districts will dilute their strength elsewhere, thereby leading to more racially polarized representation that will leave minorities as the ultimate losers. Racial districting might also promote the assumption that all minority voters share the same interests and political commitments—a view that might be taken as reenforcing a culture of subordination. The Court has hinted at these possibilities, but its preoccupation with the formalist version of *Brown* has prevented it from developing them fully.

The same preoccupation with formalism has tended to blind the Court to the systemic effects of the *Shaw* rule. As the *Shaw* Court itself acknowledged, grouping people with "actual shared interests" is a common, traditional feature of legislative districting. Often these interests are a product of culture or ethnicity. Thus, the systemic effect of the Court's decision is to deny to African Americans the recognition of group solidarity permitted, and indeed, encouraged for other groups. As Justice Ruth Bader Ginsburg wrote in a dissenting opinion in Miller v. Johnson.

> If Chinese–Americans and Russian–Americans may seek and secure group recognition in the delineation of voting districts, then African–Americans should not be dissimilarly treated. Otherwise, in the name of equal protection, we would shut out "the very minority group whose history in the United States gave birth to the Equal Protection Clause."[56]

The second line of cases involving race specific but neutral classifications is of much less practical significance, but demonstrates even more forcefully the anomalous position these cases hold in contemporary equal protection jurisprudence. This line concerns supposed efforts to change the political process so as to discourage measures benefitting racial minorities.

The leading case is Washington v. Seattle School District,[57] decided in 1982. The Seattle School Board voluntarily adopted a plan that went beyond the requirements of *Brown* to reduce racial isolation in its schools. Opponents of the plan thereupon

56.   515 U.S. at 947 (Ginsburg, J., dissenting).

57.   458 U.S. 457 (1982).

secured passage through referendum of a statewide initiative that prohibited school boards from requiring students to attend schools that were not nearest or next nearest to their place of residence. However, the initiative included exceptions that permitted such assignments for a variety of nonracial reasons.

In an opinion by Justice Harry Blackmun, a 5–4 majority of the Court held that the initiative violated the equal protection clause. The Court thought that the case was governed by "a simple but central principle."[58]

> [T]he political majority may generally restructure the political process to place obstacles in the path of everyone seeking to secure the benefits of government action. But a different analysis is required when the State allocates governmental power non-neutrally, by explicitly using the *racial* nature of a decision to determine the decision-making process. State action of this kind ... "places *special* burdens on racial minorities within in the governmental process."[59]

In the Court's view, the initiative created a special burden because nonmandatory integration efforts, unlike many other government actions, now had to be undertaken on the state, rather than the local, level.

The principle enunciated in *Seattle School District* may, indeed, be "central," as the Court claims, but it is certainly not "simple." At least superficial-

58. *Id.* at 469.

59. *Id.* at 470.

ly, the legislative classification invalidated in the case appears to be both non-race-specific and facially neutral. True, the classification relates in some way to race, but, as the Court explicitly acknowledged, members of all races favor and oppose measures to counteract racial isolation in public schools and members of all races benefit from racial integration. According to standard doctrine, then, the classification should be subject to low level review.

The Court nonetheless treated the classification as race-specific because "our cases suggest that desegregation of the public schools ... at bottom inures primarily to the benefit of the minority, and is designed for that purpose."[60] But even if it is true that desegregation primarily benefits minorities, this is a statement about the *effect* of such a program, and *Washington v. Davis* makes clear that effect alone is insufficient to trigger heightened review. Justice Blackmun also says that desegregation is "designed for [the] purpose" of creating this effect, but this is not the sort of purpose that triggers heightened scrutiny under the *Feeney* test. There was no proof that the *Seattle School District* initiative was adopted "because of" rather than "in spite of" its adverse effect on African Americans, as *Feeney* would seem to require. Even if supporters of the initiative knew that integration benefited blacks more than whites, it is unlikely that they voted for it out of a sadistic desire to reduce the welfare of blacks.

60. *Id.* at 472.

Like *Shaw*, *Seattle School District* illustrates the uneasy status of the *Brown* doctrine in a post-Washington v. Davis world. Much of the Court's opinion is focused on the requirement of process neutrality. The Court discerns an equal protection violation in the state's insistence on a more rigorous process for measures beneficial to racial minorities than for other measures. The impulse to reduce the issue to a problem about process and neutrality no doubt derives from the desire to reconcile the result with the Washington v. Davis approach. The problem, of course, is that it is not at all uncommon for jurisdictions to erect special barriers to statutes that may benefit racial minorities. Consider, for example, a provision in a state constitution that requires a super majority before the state can issue bonds to finance public works. Perhaps African Americans benefit more from such public works than other racial groups. Does this mean that the state constitutional provision violates equal protection? To paraphrase *Washington v. Davis*, such a holding "would be far reaching and would raise serious questions about, and perhaps invalidate a whole range of tax, welfare, public service, regulatory, and licensing statutes that may be more burdensome to the poor and to the average black than to the more affluent white."[61]

In part because of this tension with *Washington v. Davis*, the precedential value of *Seattle School District* is dubious. A 5–4 decision in the first place, the decision has not been relied upon by the Court

61. Washington v. Davis, 426 U.S. 229, 248 (1976).

in the twenty years since it was first rendered. Moreover, the Court conspicuously passed up an opportunity to reaffirm *Seattle School District* in Romer v. Evans.[62] The lower court in *Romer* had cited *Seattle School District* as the basis for invalidating a state constitutional amendment that prevented local jurisdictions from enacting statutes that outlawed discrimination against gay men and lesbians. Although it affirmed the decision below, the Supreme Court pointedly disavowed the lower court's reasoning and found a way to strike down the amendment without reference to *Seattle School District*.

But although *Seattle School District* has hardly been generative, neither has it been expressly overruled. The case therefore symbolizes *Brown*'s tenuous but tenacious hold on our legal imagination a half century after the decision was first announced.

62.   517 U.S. 620 (1996).

CHAPTER SEVEN

RACE–SPECIFIC CLASSIFICATIONS THAT BENEFIT RACIAL MINORITIES

The last variety of racial classification that the Court has addressed is race specific (in the sense that the government policy facially distinguishes between racial groups), but at least superficially is favorable to a racial minority (in the sense that it grants to members of a minority group some benefit or preference not accorded to others). Classifications of this type are commonly referred to as involving "affirmative action," although, as we shall see, the issue is so controversial that even the appropriate label is in dispute.

After a long period of confusion, the Supreme Court in Adarand Constructors, Inc. v. Pena[1] announced three principles that, it claims, now govern in this area: skepticism; consistency; and congruence. By "skepticism," the Court means that affirmative action measures, like race-specific measures disadvantaging racial minorities, are subject to strict scrutiny. "Consistency" refers to the principle that "the standard of review under the Equal Protection Clause is not dependent on the race of those burdened or benefitted by the particular classifica-

1. 515 U.S. 200 (1995).

tion."[2] Finally, "congruence" means that analysis of the equal protection component of the fifth amendment's due process clause, which applies to the federal government, is no different from analysis under the fourteenth amendment's equal protection clause, which applies to the states. Taken together, the Court has said,

> these three propositions lead to the conclusion that any person, of whatever race, has the right to demand that any governmental actor subject to the Constitution justify any racial classification subjecting that person to unequal treatment under the strictest judicial scrutiny.[3]

This command seems clear enough, but in fact, the Court has yet to resolve some of the most important issues surrounding affirmative action. In order to understand what those issues are and why they are difficult, it is first necessary to see how the affirmative action problem relates to the other sorts of racial classifications discussed above.

Washington v. Davis, Racial Integration, and Affirmative Action

As we saw in the last chapter, Brown v. Board of Education[4] inaugurated a brief period during which the Court attempted to use the equal protection clause to bring about a fundamental social change in race relations. The meaning of *Brown* was and is

2. *Id.* at 222 (quoting Richmond v. J.A. Croson Co., 488 U.S. 469, 493–94 (1989)).

3. 515 U.S. at 224.

4. 347 U.S. 483 (1954).

controversial, but it seems beyond question that the Court was concerned not just with the "hearts and minds" of the particular children before it, but with the status of black Americans generally.

It followed naturally from this concern that mere acquiescence in outcomes produced by exercises of private power might be insufficient to satisfy the government's constitutional obligation. Thus, it is no coincidence that the *Brown* Court focused on the affirmative obligation of government to prepare children for "the performance of our most basic public responsibilities."[5]

In this respect, the Court recaptured the original impetus behind the equal protection clause, which was to ensure that government provided the same protection of the laws for African Americans threatened with private acts of power that it provided for white Americans. The *Brown*-era Court recognized, at least implicitly, that almost a century after "bad men" threatened newly freed slaves because the laws "were insufficient or were not enforced,"[6] the social status of African Americans was still the product of a complex interaction between "private" prejudice and "public" decisions that gave effect to that prejudice. Whereas *Plessy* located "social prejudices" in the private sphere and rejected a government obligation to "eradicate racial instincts," the modern court has written that "[P]rivate biases

5. *Id.* at 493.

6. The Slaughter–House Cases, 83 U.S. (16 Wall.) 36, 70 (1872).

may be outside the reach of the law, but the law cannot, directly or indirectly give them effect."[7]

During the *Brown* era, the Court recognized this intersection of private and public power in a number of different ways. For example, the Court held that the Constitution was violated when public officials enforced private racially restrictive covenants,[8] when a state-owned garage leased space to a restaurant that engaged in racial discrimination,[9] when public aid was provided to racially discriminatory private schools,[10] and when a private park that had earlier been administered by public officials refused to admit African Americans.[11] Perhaps most significantly, the Court made clear that state recognition of private choice would not shield governments from their affirmative obligation to dismantle previously segregated schools.[12]

Moreover, even when the Court refused to acknowledge a constitutional *obligation* to dismantle private preserves of racial prejudice, it held that there were no constitutional *obstacles* to affirmative government measures designed to accomplish this end. The Court came close to holding that the invocation of the criminal law by private merchants who refused to serve African Americans was

7. Palmore v. Sidoti, 466 U.S. 429, 433 (1984).

8. Shelley v. Kraemer, 334 U.S. 1 (1948).

9. Burton v. Wilmington Parking Auth., 365 U.S. 715 (1961).

10. Norwood v. Harrison, 413 U.S. 455 (1973).

11. Evans v. Newton, 382 U.S. 296 (1966).

12. *See, e.g.,* Green v. County School Bd., 391 U.S. 430 (1968).

unconstitutional, but it never quite reached this conclusion.[13] Instead, it managed to reverse all the convictions of African Americans challenging these policies without deciding the ultimate constitutional issue, and it was saved from having to face the question by passage in 1964 of a civil rights act that broadly barred discrimination in public accommodations. But although the Court never squarely held that the Constitution prohibited private merchants from engaging in racial discrimination, it was unanimous in upholding the power of Congress to reach this conduct.[14] Similarly, the Court had relatively little difficulty upholding statutes that barred racial discrimination in private schools and employment[15] or in the private housing market.[16]

The determination to change the actual status of African Americans and the realization that their inferior status was enforced by a mixture of public and private power led naturally to race-conscious remedies. If school desegregation amounted to no more than invalidating the laws that established it, the mandate of *Brown* could easily be accomplished by race-neutral measures. In the beginning, the justices who decided *Brown* may have thought that no more was required. As time went on, however,

13. *See. e.g.,* Peterson v. Greenville, 373 U.S. 244 (1963).

14. *See* Heart of Atlanta Motel v. United States, 379 U.S. 241 (1964); Katzenbach v. McClung, 379 U.S. 294 (1964).

15. *See* Runyon v. McCrary, 427 U.S. 160 (1976).

16. *See* Jones v. Alfred H. Mayer Co., 392 U.S. 409 (1968).

perhaps radicalized by southern intransigence, the justices began to insist upon actual results.

This insistence, in turn, necessarily involved race-consciousness. Thus, as discussed above, in Green v. County School Board,[17] the Court rejected a "freedom of choice" plan because the plan did not produce actual integration. Of course, the only way to measure such integration is by keeping track of the number of black and white school children attending a particular school and by adjusting policies so as to produce the "right number." This point, only implicit in *Green*, became explicit in *Swann*,[18] where the Court expressly endorsed race-conscious remedies. As Chief Justice Warren Burger wrote, although a court could not require that "every school in every community must always reflect the racial composition of the school system as a whole," it was permissible to use "racial ratio[s] [as] a starting point in shaping a remedy."[19] And, as if to drive the point home, in a companion case, the Court held unconstitutional a North Carolina statute that prohibited taking race into account in school assignments.[20]

To be sure, the Court continued to insist that race-consciousness was appropriate only as a remedy, and that the substantive right entailed no more

17. 391 U.S. 430 (1968).

18. Swann v. Charlotte–Mecklenburg Bd. of Educ., 402 U.S. 1 (1971).

19. *Id.* at 23.

20. North Carolina State Bd. of Educ. v. Swann, 402 U.S. 43 (1971).

than race neutrality. Still, southerners could be forgiven for failing to perceive a hard distinction between right and remedy when the same neighborhood school policies that were common in the north were found to be unconstitutional in the south. Moreover, even if race-consciousness was not constitutionally mandatory as a matter of substantive right, the *Swann* Court was strikingly matter-of-fact in its assumption that assignment of students according to race was at least constitutionally permissible. As Chief Justice Burger observed:

School authorities are traditionally charged with broad power to formulate and implement educational policy and might well conclude, for example, that in order to prepare students to live in a pluralistic society each school should have a prescribed ration of Negro and white students reflecting the proportion for the district as a whole. To do this as an educational policy is within the broad discretionary powers of school authorities.[21]

With the collapse of the *Brown* experiment in the 1970's, all of this changed. A crucial turning point, discussed in Chapter Five, was Washington v. Davis.[22] As we have already seen, *Washington* held that race-neutral statutes were not subject to strict scrutiny simply because of their disproportionate impact on racial minorities. We are now in a better position to understand another way of stating this holding: *Washington* meant that, in general, affir-

21. Swann v. Charlotte–Mecklenburg Bd. of Educ., 402 U.S. 1, 16 (1971).

22. 426 U.S. 229 (1976).

mative action was not constitutionally required. On this view, so long as the government adhered to race neutrality, it was not constitutionally obligated to counteract supposedly private forces that produced racial disadvantage. Instead, the decision whether to address issues of racial impact was discretionary, with the Constitution neither mandating nor prohibiting race-conscious remediation (at least so long as the failure to remedy was not influenced by an impermissible discriminatory purpose). Thus, *Washington* standing alone left the District of Columbia free to adjust test scores in a race-conscious fashion, but it was not obligated to do so.

Around the same time that *Washington* was decided, the Court decided a number of other cases that also seemed to step back from the conclusion that the political branches were obligated to regulate private activity that produced racial disadvantage. For example, whereas the Court had earlier found that state encouragement of private discrimination through the leasing of space to a discriminatory restaurant was unconstitutional,[23] the Court now found that state licensing of a supposedly private club was insufficient state action to trigger the equal protection clause.[24] Findings of no "state action," like the *Washington* doctrine, left the political branches free either to adopt or refrain from adopting public measures that curbed private, racial power.

23. Burton v. Wilmington Parking Auth., 365 U.S. 715 (1961).

24. Moose Lodge No. 107 v. Irvis, 407 U.S. 163 (1972).

There is a sense in which this resolution of the problem reflects a more general effort to come to terms with the discrediting of Lochner v. New York.[25] As discussed in Chapter Six, *Lochner* had announced the existence of unenumerated rights that bounded a private sphere of freedom outside the realm of government regulation. A common and important criticism of *Lochner* was that it involved impermissible judicial activism. Accordingly, a post-*Lochner* understanding grew up that regulation of social and economic affairs was discretionary—an understanding that manifested itself among other places in the low level equal protection scrutiny afforded so-called "ordinary social and economic legislation." *Washington* can be seen as remitting race problems to the same discretionary sphere occupied by other areas of government regulation.

It turned out, however, that the *Washington* compromise was short-lived. In more recent years, the Court has moved to the other end of the spectrum. Whereas cases like *Swann* suggested that government intervention was mandatory, and *Washington* suggested that it was discretionary, the Court has now said that it may be impermissible.

This shift can be seen over a range of cases. For example, whereas the Warren Court flirted with the idea that the government might be constitutionally obligated to outlaw private discriminatory acts,[26] the modern Court has held that under some circumstances such efforts are an unconstitutional in-

25. 198 U.S. 45 (1905).

26. *See* note 13, *supra*.

fringement on individual rights.[27] Whereas the Warren Court upheld the power of federal *courts* to mandate state remedies for private discrimination,[28] the modern Court has held that even the federal *legislature* sometimes lacks the power to impose such remedies.[29]

The Modern Law of Affirmative Action

The doctrinal area where this turnabout has been most dramatic concerns the law of affirmative action. In recent years, the Court has rejected the result-oriented, color-consciousness of the Warren Court era and attempted to recapture the individualist, color-blind rhetoric of the nineteenth century. Thus, whereas the Warren Court had made some forms of affirmative action mandatory, and located the decision within the judicial sphere, and Washington v. Davis had made the decision discretionary and located it within the political sphere, more recent cases have made its prohibition mandatory and located the decision once again within the judicial sphere. There is a sense, then, in which modern affirmative action doctrine reflects a full-throated return to a *Lochner*-like approach.

It would be a mistake, however, to suppose that this shift has been easy or complete. Here, as elsewhere, the view that constitutional rights sometimes impose affirmative obligations on government, or at least permit affirmative government

27. *See* Boy Scouts of America v. Dale, 530 U.S. 640 (2000).

28. *See* notes 8–10, *supra*.

29. *See, e.g.,* United States v. Morrison, 529 U.S. 598 (2000).

responses, has vestigial strength and continues to complicate the doctrine.

For years, this ambivalence was reflected in the inability of the Court to agree on either a standard of review for affirmative action cases or a set of permissible ends that might be advanced by affirmative action. For over a decade, the Court decided a large number of cases concerning racial preferences in admission to public universities,[30] government contracting,[31] and employment,[32] upholding some and striking down others without ever producing an opinion signed by a majority of the justices.

The best known of these early cases was University of California v. Bakke,[33] which concerned a program at the University of California at Davis medical school pursuant to which 16 of the school's 100 seats were reserved each year for members of minority groups found by a special committee to have suffered from economic or educational deprivations. Four justices voted to evaluate this program under "intermediate" review, somewhere between strict scrutiny and rational basis analysis. These justices would have upheld the program as a means of remedying prior discrimination. Four other justices failed to reach the constitutional question be-

30. *See, e.g.,* University of California v. Bakke, 438 U.S. 265 (1978).

31. *See, e.g.,* Fullilove v. Klutznick, 448 U.S. 448 (1980).

32. *See, e.g.,* Wygant v. Jackson Bd. of Educ., 476 U.S. 267 (1986).

33. 438 U.S. 265 (1978).

cause, in their view, the program violated Title VI of the 1964 Civil Rights Act.

The deciding vote was cast by Justice Lewis Powell. In an influential opinion, he set out his belief that strict scrutiny was appropriate and that the Davis program failed this test. However, he also thought that some uses of race in order to achieve educational diversity would satisfy such scrutiny. For Powell, it was unconstitutional to reserve a certain number of seats for minority candidates, but it was constitutionally permissible to put in place a more flexible plan pursuant to which every applicant could compete for every seat, but admissions directors considered "all pertinent elements of diversity in light of the particular qualifications of each applicant."[34]

Bakke was decided only two years after Washington v. Davis, and the Powell opinion, as well as the Court's inability to reach a majority judgment, perfectly captures the justices' ambivalence as the Court migrated from its earlier approach. Powell's opinion is especially notable for its uneasy attempt to marry individualism (every applicant must be afforded an individual chance to compete for every seat) with group consciousness (universities can recognize that African Americans, as a group, offer a perspective that would be missing without them).

It turned out, however, that the *Bakke* compromise was unstable, and by the late 1980's, it had at least partially collapsed. For the first time, a majori-

34. *Id.* at 317.

ty was able to agree on a single approach to affirmative action—an approach that sharply limited the discretionary authority of the political branches to adopt race-specific forms of remediation and diversification. The Court explained this approach in two cases involving statutes that required race-based preferences for the awarding of government contracts. City of Richmond v. J.A. Croson Co.[35] involved a challenge to a "set-aside"program adopted by the City of Richmond. Proponents of the program submitted a study showing that although the general population of Richmond was 50% black, only .67% of the city's prime construction contracts had been awarded to minority businesses over the previous five years. Moreover, the relevant contractors' associations had virtually no minority businesses within their membership. In order to remedy this situation, the City ordered prime contractors on city projects to subcontract at least 30% of their business to minority business enterprises. Although it was possible to obtain a waiver from this requirement, waivers were granted only when "every feasible attempt [had] been made to comply, and it [was] demonstrated that sufficient, relevant, qualified Minority Business Enterprises ... are unavailable or unwilling to participate in the contract."[36] "Minority Business Enterprises" were defined as organizations controlled by "Blacks, Spanish-speak[ers],

35. 488 U.S. 469 (1989).

36. *Id.* at 478.

Orientals, Indians, Eskimos, or Aleuts."[37]

Adarand Constructors, Inc. v. Pena[38] involved the federal government's practice of giving general contractors on government projects a financial incentive to hire subcontractors controlled by "socially and economically disadvantaged individuals," and a race-based presumption in identifying such individuals.

Justice Sandra Day O'Connor wrote the controlling opinion in both cases. In *Croson*, she announced the Court's judgment that the program was unconstitutional. In *Adarand*, she made clear that the *Croson* requirements for such programs applied to the federal government as well as the states and remanded the case for a determination as to whether those requirements had been met.

Both opinions make clear that affirmative action measures, like race-specific statutes harming racial minorities, should be subject to the highest tier of review. Justice O'Connor advanced two major arguments in support of this position. First, in her view, the fourteenth amendment protected "personal" rather than "group" rights. Because every person had a right to be treated "with equal dignity and respect," a rigid rule depriving a person of a benefit because of race was constitutionally suspect.

Second, O'Connor argued that searching scrutiny was necessary to discern whether a given classification was in fact "benign" or "remedial."

37. *Id.*
38. 515 U.S. 200 (1995).

[T]he purpose of strict scrutiny is to "smoke out" illegitimate uses of race by assuring that the legislative body is pursuing a goal important enough to warrant use of a highly suspect tool. The test also ensures that the means chosen "fit" this compelling goal so closely that there is little or no possibility that the motive for the classification was illegitimate racial prejudice or stereotype.

Classifications based on race carry a danger of stigmatic harm. Unless they are strictly reserved for remedial settings, they may in fact promote notions of racial inferiority and lead to a politics of racial hostility.[39]

Justice O'Connor made clear, however, that rigid scrutiny should not be equated with automatic invalidity. She emphasized that

strict scrutiny is [not] "strict in theory, but fatal in fact." ... The unhappy persistence of both the practice and lingering effects of racial discrimination against minority groups in this country is an unfortunate reality, and government is not disqualified from acting in response to it. [40]

The end of remedying prior specific acts of discrimination by the government itself might be sufficiently "compelling," in her view, to justify a narrowly tailored racial preference. Similarly, "if [a govern-

39. City of Richmond v. J.A. Croson Co., 488 U.S. 469, 483 (1989).

40. Adarand Constructors, Inc. v. Pena, 515 U.S. 200, 236 (1995).

ment entity] could show that it had essentially become a 'passive participant' in a system of racial exclusion practiced by elements of the local construction industry," it could take "affirmative steps to dismantle such a system." [41]

There were nonetheless two reasons why Richmond's showing in *Croson* failed to meet this test. First, the City had failed to show that it was remedying specific acts of prior or present discrimination. To be sure, there was no doubt that there had been general, society-wide discrimination against African Americans. But this showing alone was insufficient.

> It is sheer speculation how many minority firms there would be in Richmond absent past societal discrimination.... Defining these sorts of injuries as "identified discrimination" would give local governments license to create a patchwork of racial preferences based on statistical generalizations about any particular field of endeavor.[42]

The Court was similarly skeptical about evidence before the Richmond City Council purporting to demonstrate more specific patterns of discrimination. The mere declaration by the City Council that its plan was remedial was "entitled to little or no weight."[43] Similarly, "highly conclusory" statements by the plan's proponents that there was discrimination in the construction industry was "of

41. City of Richmond v. J.A. Croson Co., 488 U.S. 469, 492 (1989).

42. *Id.* at 499.

43. *Id.* at 500.

little probative value."[44] Nor could the City Council rely upon statistical disparities between the number of contracts awarded to minority firms and the percentage of the population belonging to minority groups. This disparity was irrelevant, in the Court's view, because "the city does not even know how many [minority business enterprises] in the relevant market are qualified to undertake prime or subcontracting work in public construction projects."[45]

The second problem with the Richmond plan was that it was insufficiently "narrowly tailored." There had been no showing that the city had attempted race-neutral means to remedy the problem. Moreover, "the 30% quota cannot be said to be narrowly tailored to any goal, except perhaps outright racial balancing."[46] According to the Court

[T]he city's only interest in maintaining a quota system rather than investigating the need for remedial action in particular cases would seem to be simple administrative convenience. But the interest in avoiding the bureaucratic effort necessary to tailor remedial relief to those who truly have suffered the effects of prior discrimination cannot justify a rigid line drawn on the basis of a suspect classification.[47]

Justice O'Connor was careful not to rule out all affirmative action programs, however. Government

44. Id.
45. Id. at 501.
46. Id. at 507.
47. Id. at 508.

entities remained free, she insisted, to "rectify the effects of identified discrimination within [their] jurisdiction[s]."[48] If there were evidence of systematic exclusion of minorities, the government could take action to end it. Moreover an inference of discriminatory exclusion might arise from "a significant statistical disparity between the number of qualified minority contractors willing and able to perform a particular service and the number of such contractors actually engaged by the locality."[49] In an "extreme case," the government might resort to "some form of narrowly tailored racial preference."[50] What the Court would not permit was a system of "rigid racial preferences" based upon "past societal discrimination alone." To allow such a system

> would open the door to competing claims for "remedial relief" for every disadvantaged group. The dream of a Nation of equal citizens in a society where race is irrelevant to personal opportunity and achievement would be lost in a mosaic of shifting preferences based on inherently unmeasurable claims of past wrongs.[51]

Two Unanswered Questions

After *Croson* and *Adarand*, it is obvious that the Court is skeptical of race-specific statutes said to benefit racial minorities and is ready to invalidate

48. *Id.*

49. *Id.*

50. *Id.*

51. *Id.* at 505.

at least some of them. Still, the Court has left ambiguous just how "strict" its "strict scrutiny" will be. Despite the Court's insistence on the "consistency" prong of its test, it seems clear that it is applying something less rigorous than the review that it purports to apply to other race-specific classifications. A majority of the Court has gone to some pains to distance itself from the position, forcefully articulated by Justices Scalia and Thomas, that race-based remediation is never justified except when necessary to place a particular person back in the position she would have been in but for a specific, identifiable act of discrimination.[52]

The remaining unanswered questions fall into two categories. First, what ends are sufficiently "compelling" to justify race-specific measures? We know that some forms of remediation are sufficient, so long as they concern well-documented and specific acts of discrimination, and that efforts to remedy general societal discrimination will not do. We do not yet know how well-documented and how specific the discrimination must be.

Moreover, there is a curious contradiction between the Court's approach to this problem in *Croson* and what it has said in the Washington v. Davis context. Recall that in cases like *Arlington Heights*[53]

52. *See* Adarand Constructors Inc. v. Pena, 515 U.S. 200, 240 (1995) (Thomas, J., concurring in part and concurring in the judgment); City of Richmond v. J.A. Croson Co., 488 U.S. 469, 520 (1989) (Scalia, J., concurring in the judgment).

53. Village of Arlington Heights v. Metropolitan Housing Dev. Corp., 429 U.S. 252 (1977).

and *McCleskey*,[54] the Court has been very skeptical about attempts to prove a discriminatory purpose based upon statistical disparities. *Arlington Heights* holds that cases where such an attempt will be successful "are rare," and *McCleskey* suggests that even where a general statistical pattern of discrimination has been made out, there must be a further proof that the particular party has been victimized by it. Yet *Croson* states that "[w]here there is a significant statistical disparity between the number of qualified minority contractors willing and able to perform a particular service and the number of such contractors actually engaged by the locality ... an inference of discriminatory exclusion could arise."[55] This difference in approach might be explained by the Court's view (if, indeed it *is* the Court's view) that the remedying of discrimination that does not rise to the level of a constitutional violation is a sufficiently compelling governmental interest to justify racial preferences. The justices have not yet explicitly addressed this issue, however, and its approach to nonconstitutional discrimination therefore remains murky.

Nor has the Court yet determined whether goals other than remediation might justify race-specific measures. The most significant possibility, here, is an interest in diversity. Recall that in *Bakke*, Justice Powell found this interest sufficiently important to justify a flexible race-based approach to medical school admissions. In Metro Broadcasting,

54. McCleskey v. Kemp, 481 U.S. 279 (1987).
55. 488 U.S. at 508.

Inc. v. Federal Communications Commission,[56] a case decided in the period between *Croson* and *Adarand*, the Court upheld two Federal Communications Commission policies that favored minority firms applying for broadcast licenses on the ground that greater minority representation would enhance the diversification of programming. The *Metro Broadcasting* court distinguished *Croson* on the ground that the *Metro Broadcasting* policies had been approved by Congress. *Adarand* overruled *Metro Broadcasting* to the extent that the case had established a less stringent standard of review for federal race-specific programs. However, *Adarand* did not speak specifically to *Metro Broadcasting's* reliance on a diversity rationale. Whether the Court will ultimately endorse this goal is crucial to the future of affirmative action programs in state universities, which are typically justified as advancing educational diversity.

A second set of unanswered questions relates to the "narrow tailoring" prong of the Court's analysis. After *Croson* and *Adarand*, there can be no doubt that the Court is extremely hostile to rigid quotas, especially where the numbers are not directly tied to identified acts of discrimination. It remains to be seen whether more flexible and nuanced preferences will survive.

The status of race-neutral substitutes as an aspect of narrow tailoring is also in some doubt. In *Croson*, the Court chastised the city for not exhausting race-neutral measures that might increase

56. 497 U.S. 547 (1990).

the number of minority contractors. Yet there is some controversy concerning whether even race-neutral measures are constitutionally permissible.

The issue turns on whether the usual rules governing race-neutral classifications with a disproportionate racial impact apply. Recall that when these classifications harm racial minorities, they are strictly scrutinized if they have a discriminatory purpose. Does the same standard apply when they help racial minorities?

Consider two hypothetical cases. First, imagine that after Richmond's racial preference program is invalidated, it enacts a new program granting a special preference for contractors who live in certain neighborhoods. The city knows that contractors living in these neighborhoods are overwhelmingly African American and enacts the program for this reason. Surely, the Court would not allow *Croson*'s requirements to be eviscerated by a subterfuge of this sort.

But now consider a hypothetical variant on the facts of Washington v. Davis. Suppose that a city has been administering a test for police recruits that would barely survive low level scrutiny, but that has little or no value in predicting who will become a good policeman. If the city notices that the test is also excluding large numbers of minorities and abolishes it for this reason, is that decision subject to strict scrutiny? It seems odd that a jurisdiction would be prevented from eliminating an outmoded or useless examination just because the examination also had a disproportionate racial impact.

The Court has not yet faced the task of distinguishing between these two cases, if they are, indeed, distinguishable. What it says about the matter has real significance as, for example, public universities struggle to maintain minority enrollment through race-neutral measures.

A Normative Appraisal

Is the Court's approach to race-specific measures benefitting racial minorities sensible? Is it consistent with the rest of equal protection jurisprudence?

The Court's approach is in some tension with standard methods of constitutional analysis. The language of the equal protection clause contains no hint that the framers meant to subject statutes benefitting racial minorities to special scrutiny and, as we have seen, the framers were primarily motivated by the desire to *shield* Reconstruction measures from judicial invalidation. Some of these measures bear at least a family resemblance to modern affirmative action statutes.

Of course, as we have also seen, *Brown* and its progeny are similarly in tension with the history of the equal protection clause, and it is far from certain that the framers meant to subject all race-specific classifications disadvantaging minorities to strict scrutiny. (Recall, for example, the framers' distinction between "social," "civil," and "political" rights.) But these outcomes are at least reconcilable with widely shared metaconstitutional views about judicial restraint and democracy. As explained in Chapter Four, the modern court has sometimes justified its suspicion of statutes disadvantaging racial minorities on the ground that these groups are not fairly represented in the political process. Invalidating statutes that are passed only because of a defect in the political process might, therefore, actually reinforce democracy and not constitute an "activist" effort by the Court to impose its own values on society.

In contrast, it is hard to make a similar argument when a democratic majority passes legislation that disadvantages itself. Professor David Strauss has proposed a thought experiment that neatly demonstrates the problem:[57] As we will see in Chapter Nine, the Court does not presently treat homosexuals as a "suspect class." It follows that laws providing affirmative action intended to remedy prior discrimination against homosexuals are now subject to only "rational basis" review. Suppose that a future court were persuaded that prejudice against homosexuals prevents them from securing fair access to the political process and that they therefore form a suspect class after all. Under the *Adarand* Court's "consistency" requirement, this change would mean that measures attempting to remedy prior discrimination against them would now be subject to strict scrutiny. But surely it is perverse to think that it should be harder to pass statutes remedying discrimination just because the group

57. *See* David A. Strauss, *Affirmative Action and the Public Interest*, 1995 Sup. Ct. Rev. 1, 12.

benefitting from these measures lacks fair access to the political process.

Despite these difficulties, there remains something to be said for the Court's position. As we have seen, the affirmative action decisions can be understood as a defense of racial outcomes produced in the private sphere. What strict scrutiny amounts to is judicial suspicion of public efforts to intervene in private markets so as to upset the racial status quo. Even conceding all the difficulties with outcomes produced by the private sphere, there are surely reasons for this suspicion. Over the history of American race relations, government intervention has often made things worse rather than better. It is worth recalling, for example, that the segregation statutes validated by *Plessy* amounted to a political effort to counteract private, market pressures that were producing integrated facilities. There is evidence, as well, that government regulatory programs through the New Deal period tended to benefit white workers at the expense of racial minorities. Some people maintain that minimum wage legislation continues to have this effect today.

A defender of affirmative action might sensibly respond by arguing that political interventions designed to make things better for racial minorities should not be discredited just because there have been other measures designed to make things worse for them. But at this point, Justice O'Connor's skepticism about our ability to recognize what makes things better or worse takes hold. Although affirmative action has unquestionably helped some members of minority groups, it also entails substantial risks. It may reinforce racial prejudice by subtly suggesting that racial minorities are unable to compete without special preferences. When African Americans succeed, whites may (consciously or unconsciously) attribute their success to affirmative action, thereby discounting evidence that counters racial stereotypes. And, more globally, race-conscious government policies might lead to a general increase in racial politics which, over the long run, might frustrate the aspirations of members of racial minorities. In short, we may need strict scrutiny of race-specific classifications in order to separate authentic affirmative action measures from measures that actually make things worse for racial minorities.

Of course, this defense of the Court's position assumes that "affirmative action" itself is an analytically coherent category. There is reason to think that it is not. The Court's theory is premised on the view that race-specific categories are in fact "affirmative" rather than simply "neutral" and that they therefore involve government intervention in a private sphere. There are three difficulties with this view.

First, there is voluminous social science evidence indicating that supposedly race-blind decisions are often influenced by unconscious racism.[58] When an employer selects someone for a job or a university

---

58. For a summary of the evidence, see Linda Krieger, *Civil Rights Perestroika: Intergroup Relations after Affirmative Action*, 86 Cal. L. Rev. 1251 (1998).

admissions officer selects students for an entering class, these individuals may honestly believe that they are acting without regard to race. Despite this belief, race is a salient characteristic, virtually impossible to ignore in our culture, that carries with it stereotypes that are all the more powerful because they are frequently unconscious. What we think of as "affirmative" action, then, may not be affirmative at all, but rather what is required to compensate for subtle bias and to return us to a level playing field.

The second problem is that in some circumstances, the very failure to adopt affirmative action amounts to a kind of race discrimination. Imagine, for example, a public university that has adopted a program giving preference to applicants who have had to overcome substantial obstacles in order to excel. The program gives preferences to individuals with physical handicaps, individuals for whom English is not a first language, and individuals who are economically disadvantaged. Because this program does not involve a race-specific classification, it is almost certainly virtually immune from constitutional challenge. Now imagine that an African American applicant wishes to apply for admission under this program. The applicant claims that just as other students have had to overcome severe disadvantages in order to achieve, she has overcome generations of pervasive governmental and societal racism. *Croson* means that this claim, unlike the claim of other students with comparable disabilities, must be rejected. But a rejection of the claims of

African Americans in a context where claims of other disadvantaged groups are recognized might be said to constitute racial discrimination rather than neutrality.

Finally, the Court's position on affirmative action assumes that the standards of "merit" utilized to allocate benefits are neutral and objective. But this claim is open to dispute. What counts as merit turns on what one is trying to maximize, and if communities are divided by race on this question, then these standards will inevitably be tilted in one direction or another.

Of course, it does not follow from the fact that they are tilted one way that they *ought to be* tilted the other. At most, the attack on merit means only that we must give up on a certain kind of argument, premised on racial neutrality. It remains open to an opponent of affirmative action to claim that the majority standard of merit is the "right" standard.

Nor does it follow from the arguments set out above that affirmative action is in the long-range interests of either racial minorities or majorities. In large measure, issues about the efficacy and morality of affirmative action turn on empirical predictions about the actual effects of these programs. Unfortunately, these predictions must be made with radically incomplete information and no real ability to run controlled experiments.

One might, of course, take the view that the fundamental intractability of these questions argues for leaving them to the political sphere. An advocate of this view would have to explain why democracy is the right response to intractability. Moreover, notice that respect for political judgments in this context would amount to judicial deference to measures that (at least arguably) harm racial minorities. Judicial deference would therefore not only reverse the Court's current affirmative action jurisprudence, but also raise fundamental questions about the supposedly bedrock assumption that laws facially disadvantaging racial minorities should be strictly scrutinized.

Perhaps, then, the Court's strict scrutiny amounts to no more than a warning that we should be cautious about the long-term effects of affirmative action. The best case for current doctrine is that it is sufficiently vague and open textured to force policy makers to give such programs a "hard look" without predetermining the outcome of this examination. The risk for the future is that the doctrine will eventually calcify (has already calcified?) into more or less automatic opposition to race-based remediation as a matter of deep constitutional principle that is impervious to empirical or normative examination.

CHAPTER EIGHT

GENDER DISCRIMINATION

Unsurprisingly, the Supreme Court's modern treatment of gender discrimination is modeled after the law of race discrimination. Race discrimination is the paradigm case for and the historical lynchpin of equal protection clause analysis. Accordingly, consciously or unconsciously, the Court has often begun its analysis of other kinds of discrimination by asking whether they can be analogized to race.

For this reason, much of what follows in this chapter will seem familiar to readers of the previous chapters. Here, too, we have heightened scrutiny for classifications that treat people differently along putatively suspect lines, reduced scrutiny for laws with a "merely" disproportionate impact, and controversies about motivation, affirmative action, and the merits of formal equality.

But instead of producing the comfort that comes from the recognition of a well-traversed landscape, the similarity between the law of race and of gender sometimes produces a vague sense of unease. After all, gender discrimination has its own history, its own etiology, its own constitutional language,[1] and

1. Although the equal protection clause does not mention gender, the nineteenth amendment does. It provides: "The right

its own cures. Oddly, this sense of unease is shared by the Court's critics who think that it has gone too far in striking down laws that putatively harm women and its critics who think that it has not gone far enough. Critics who think that the Court has gone too far complain that gender, unlike race, is sometimes a "real difference" that justifies different treatment of women and men. Paradoxically, some critics who think that it has not gone far enough agree. They, too, insist that formal equality is insufficient to protect women from the unthinking application of male standards to them.

Some readers of the material that follows will no doubt conclude that these criticisms are overblown and that the Court's treatment of gender appropriately and sensitively applies the equality norm to men and women. Readers who disagree and share the unease described above might draw two different conclusions from it. Perhaps the Court should erect a special set of rules, specifically tailored to the problem of gender, that are self-consciously different from race doctrine. Alternatively, perhaps the difficulties uncovered by the Court's encounter with gender discrimination should lead it to revise not only gender doctrine, but race doctrine as well.

of citizens of the United States to vote shall not be denied or abridged by the United States or by any State on account of sex." For an argument that the Court should make more use of the nineteenth amendment in developing gender discrimination law, see Riva Siegel, *She the People: The Nineteenth Amendment, Sex Equality, Federalism, and the Family*, 115 Harv. L. Rev. 949 (2002).

Heightened Scrutiny for Gender–Specific Classifications

Despite the general language of the equal protection clause, it has been clear from the beginning that it had special application to racial discrimination. In contrast, for over a century, the conventional wisdom was that it spoke not at all to the issue of gender discrimination. Indeed, the same fourteenth amendment that contained the equal protection clause also introduced gender discrimination into the Constitution for the first time. The second section of the amendment required the reduction of representation in the House of Representatives for states that "denied [the right to vote] to any male inhabitant of such State, being twenty-one years of age and citizens of the United States." The provision was adopted despite the strong opposition of contemporary feminists.

Early interpretations of the fourteenth amendment reflected the view that gender discrimination was outside its scope. Perhaps the most notorious example is Bradwell v. Illinois,[2] a companion to the Slaughter–House Cases.[3] In the Slaughter–House Cases, the Court's majority held that Louisiana did not violate the fourteenth amendment when it prevented competing slaughterhouses from infringing on a statutory monopoly in the City of New Orleans. Justice Joseph Bradley dissented, arguing that "a law which prohibits a large class of citizens from adopting a lawful employment ... deprive[s]

2. 83 U.S. (16 Wall.) 130 (1872).

3. 83 U.S. (16 Wall.) 36 (1872).

them of liberty as well as property without due process of law."[4] In *Bradwell*, the Court confronted a constitutional challenge to an Illinois statute that prohibited women from practicing law. The Court's majority, in an opinion by Justice Samuel Miller, had little difficulty concluding that the right to practice law, like the right to operate a slaughterhouse, was not protected by the Constitution. Justice Bradley concurred, but, having just disagreed with the majority about the constitutional status of employment, he obviously had some explaining to do. Here is what he said:

> The natural and proper timidity and delicacy which belongs to the female sex evidently unfits it for many of the occupations of civil life. The constitution of the family organization, which is founded in the divine ordinance, as well as in the nature of things, indicates the domestic sphere as that which properly belongs to the domain and functions of womanhood. The harmony, not to say identity, of interests and views which belong or should belong to the family institution is repugnant to the idea of a woman adopting a distinct and independent career from that of her husband. . . .

> It is true that many women are unmarried and not affected by any of the duties, complications, and incapacities arising out of the married state but these are exceptions to the general rule. The paramount destiny and mission of woman are to fulfill the noble and benign offices of wife and

4. *Id.* at 122 (Bradley, J., dissenting).

mother. This is the law of the Creator. And the rules of civil society must be adapted to the general constitution of things, and cannot be based upon exceptional cases.[5]

The Court continued to rely on the "natural" roles of men and women within "separate spheres" to shape constitutional doctrine and frustrate claims of gender discrimination well into the twentieth century, and, indeed, some would argue that the reliance has continued into the twenty-first century. In 1875, the Court rejected a fourteenth amendment challenge to prohibitions on women's right to vote.[6] In 1908, it upheld a statute prohibiting the employment of women in factories for more than ten hours per day,[7] even though five years earlier, it had invalidated a similar statute that applied to men.[8] In 1948, the Court rejected a challenge to a statute prohibiting women from working as bartenders unless they were the wife or daughter of a male owner.[9] And in 1961, the Court upheld the exclusion of women from juries except when they indicated a desire to serve.[10]

Finally, beginning in the 1970's, in the midst of widespread questioning of traditional gender roles in society at large, the Court began to express more skepticism about gender classifications. In Reed v.

5.   *Id.* at 141 (Bradley, J., concurring).

6.   Minor v. Happersett, 88 U.S. (21 Wall.) 162 (1874).

7.   Muller v. Oregon, 208 U.S. 412 (1908).

8.   Lochner v. New York, 198 U.S. 45 (1905).

9.   Goesaert v. Cleary, 335 U.S. 464 (1948).

10.   Hoyt v. Florida, 368 U.S. 57 (1961).

Reed,[11] for the first time in its history, the Court invalidated a gender-specific statute under the equal protection clause. The statute in question established a preference for men over women when a court was charged with choosing an administrator for the estate of individuals who died without a will. Without much explanation, the Court, in an opinion by Chief Justice Warren Burger, found that the distinction was "irrational" and invalidated it under the equal protection clause.

Although the Court purported to utilize no more than low level scrutiny in *Reed*, it seemed obvious to many observers that the justices had, without saying so, heightened the level of review. Matters came to a head two years later, in Frontiero v. Richardson,[12] where the Court engaged in a full-scale debate about the appropriate level of scrutiny. At issue was a federal statute that allowed men enrolled in the uniform services automatically to claim a spouse as a dependent and thereby receive a larger allowance for quarters and medical benefits. In contrast, women received these benefits only if they demonstrated that their spouses were in fact dependent upon them for more than half of their support.

Eight justices agreed that the statute was unconstitutional, but only four of the eight joined Justice William Brennan's opinion maintaining that the statute should be subject to strict scrutiny. Brennan argued that the United States had suffered

11. 404 U.S. 71 (1971).
12. 411 U.S. 677 (1973).

from a "long and unfortunate history of sex discrimination,"[13] and that throughout much of the nineteenth century, "the position of women in our society was, in many respects, comparable to that of blacks under the pre-Civil War slave codes."[14] He pointed out that historically women, like slaves, could not serve on juries, bring suits, vote, or (in the case of married women) hold or convey property or serve as legal guardians of their own children. Although the disabilities imposed on women had abated somewhat since the nineteenth century, women still faced "pervasive, although at times more subtle, discrimination in our education institutions, in the job market and, perhaps most conspicuously, in the political arena."[15] Moreover, gender, like race, was an immutable, unchosen characteristic and that often bore no relationship to the ability to "perform or contribute to society."[16]

Justice Brennan's *Frontiero* opinion failed to convince a majority of the Court to adopt the most rigid standard of review for gender classifications, but three years later, he got at least part of what he wanted. In Craig v. Boren,[17] the Court invalidated an Oklahoma statute that prohibited the sale of "nonintoxicating" 3.2% beer to males under the age of 21 and to females under the age of 18. Again,

13. *Id.* at 684 (Brennan, J., announcing the judgment of the Court).

14. *Id.* at 685.

15. *Id.*

16. *Id.* at 686.

17. 429 U.S. 190 (1976).

Justice Brennan wrote the lead opinion, but on this occasion, he spoke for a majority of the Court.

Instead of insisting on the highest tier of review, as he had in *Frontiero*, or resorting to the low-level scrutiny that the Court had historically employed for gender classifications, Justice Brennan announced a "middle tier" of review. In order to satisfy mid-level scrutiny, gender classifications need not serve a "compelling" purpose (as with strict scrutiny), but neither was it sufficient for them to serve a merely "legitimate" purpose (as with low-level scrutiny). Instead, gender classifications had to "serve important governmental objectives."[18] Moreover, a merely rational relationship between these objectives and the classification would not save the statute, although it was not required that the classification be "necessary" to achieve the goal. Instead, gender classifications "must be substantially related to the achievement of those objectives."[19]

In the years since *Craig*, the Court has not been exactly unwavering in its use of this standard. For example, Justice William Rehnquist, who dissented in *Craig*, seemed to water down the standard in his majority opinion in Michael M. v. Sonoma County Superior Court, when he wrote that "this Court has consistently upheld statutes where the gender classification is not invidious, but rather realistically reflects the fact that the sexes are not similarly situated in certain circumstances."[20] Conversely,

18. *Id.* at 197.
19. *Id.*
20. 450 U.S. 464, 469 (1981).

Justice Ruth Bader Ginsburg, perhaps the Court's most vigorous opponent of gender discrimination, seemed to strengthen the standard when she wrote for the Court's majority in United States v. Virginia that "the reviewing court must determine whether the proffered justification is 'exceedingly persuasive.' The burden of justification is demanding and it rests entirely on the State."[21] In general, however, the Court seems to have settled on the *Craig* test. It has justified this enhanced scrutiny as necessary to uncover statutes that involve "archaic and overbroad generalizations" about gender or that are based upon "old notions."[22] In contrast, statutes that reflect supposedly real differences between the genders survive enhanced review.

Of course, there is disagreement as to which generalizations are "archaic" and which are "real." Here, as elsewhere, it may be a mistake to focus too carefully on the Court's verbal formulation rather than on how it has actually applied the test. Unfortunately, the applications are not altogether consistent and resist easy summary. On the one hand, it is apparent that the Court is willing to tolerate gender-specific statutes more readily than statutes that are race-specific. For example, the Court has upheld statutes that punish only men for statutory rape,[23] that require men but not women to register

21. 518 U.S. 515, 533 (1996).

22. Craig v. Boren, 429 U.S. 190, 198 (1976).

23. *See* Michael M. v. Sonoma County Superior Court, 450 U.S. 464 (1981).

for the military draft[24] and establish different time periods within which men and women receive military promotions,[25] and that distinguish between the children of unwed men and women for purposes of eligibility for U.S. citizenship.[26] On the other hand, it has invalidated statutes permitting only men to enroll in a state-run military academy,[27] restricting jury service for women,[28] permitting married men but not married women to alienate property without the consent of the other spouse,[29] and imposing certain gender-based generalizations on the awarding of social security and other government benefits.[30]

Should There Be Heightened Scrutiny for Gender–Specific Classifications?

Are there good reasons for heightened scrutiny of gender classifications? As discussed above, neither the text nor the history of the fourteenth amendment suggests that the framers meant to problematize gender discrimination. Moreover, women, unlike African Americans, are not a minority. And far from being "insular," they have regular and intimate contact with men.

24. *See* Rostker v. Goldberg, 453 U.S. 57 (1981).

25. *See* Schlesinger v. Ballard, 419 U.S. 498 (1975).

26. *See* Nguyen v. Immigration and Naturalization Service, 533 U.S. 53 (2001).

27. *See* United States v. Virginia, 518 U.S. 515 (1996).

28. *See* Taylor v. Louisiana, 419 U.S. 522 (1975).

29. *See* Kirchberg v. Feenstra, 450 U.S. 455 (1981).

30. *See, e.g.*, Califano v. Goldfarb, 430 U.S. 199 (1977).

On the other hand, women remain substantially underrepresented in the political process. They are still often paid less than men for doing the same work, and when they do different work (including work in the home), the work is sometimes undervalued just because they do it. They are subject to physical and psychological harassment and violence on the job, at home, and at places of employment. Many more women than men are poor. The concerns and problems of women are sometimes trivialized or ignored.

Still, even if one assumes that these facts establish the unequal status of women, it remains unclear that the right way to solve the problem is by heightened scrutiny for gender classifications. Ironically, *Craig*, the very case establishing heightened review, demonstrates some of the difficulties. As noted above, *Craig* concerned an Oklahoma statute that allowed women, but not men, between the ages of 18 and 21 to drink 3.2% beer. The stated purpose of the law was to protect highway safety. Justice Brennan's opinion for the Court conceded that highway safety is an "important" end, but attempted to argue that the classification was not "substantially" related to that end.

There are two difficulties with the Court's analysis. First, assuming *arguendo* that women are in need of enhanced constitutional protection, the Court fails to explain why this statute, which at least superficially discriminates against *men*, should be subject to enhanced scrutiny.

Second, the Court's argument for why the statute fails to survive this scrutiny is remarkably weak. Justice Brennan himself cited a study showing that 2.2% of young men but only .18% of young women are arrested for driving while drunk. He claimed that this correlation "must be considered an unduly tenuous 'fit,'"[31] but given the fact that more than ten times the number of young men are arrested for the offense than young women, it is hard to see the basis for this conclusion. Of course, 2.2% represents a tiny fraction of the young male population, but it might also represent a very large number of people, who could cause considerable havoc on the roadways.

Justice Brennan came closer to uncovering a problem with the statute when he pointed out that the statistics themselves may be an artifact of gender discrimination. This is true in two respects. First,

> The very social stereotypes that find reflection in age-differential laws ... are likely substantially to distort the accuracy of these comparative statistics. Hence, "reckless" young men who drink and drive are transformed into arrest statistics, whereas their female counterparts are chivalrously escorted home.[32]

The second point is more subtle, but also more important. Standard equal protection analysis involves a comparison between a legal mechanism

31. Craig v. Boren, 429 U.S. 190, 201 (1976).

32. *Id.* at 203 n.14.

(here, prohibitions on the sale of 3.2% beer) and a state of the world (here, the percentages of men and women who drive while drunk). Typically the state of the world is treated as fixed, and the legal mechanism is treated as a variable. The point of equal protection review is to adjust the legal mechanism so that it "fits" the state of the world. But what if the state of the world is, itself, a product of gender subjugation, to which the legal mechanism contributes? After all, it is neither "natural" nor inevitable that men drive while drunk more frequently than women. This fact is part of a culturally determined web of behaviors and suppositions that define gender roles—a web of which the statute under review also forms a part.

For example, it may still be true that when men and women get in a car together, men end up driving more often than women. Drinking too much alcohol is, somehow, a sign of masculinity, whereas women who drink too much are not behaving in a "ladylike" fashion. The Oklahoma statute takes account of these social facts, but perhaps it also contributes to and validates them.

There is a risk, then, that laws like the one struck down in *Craig* will become partially self-validating. The laws serve to reinforce stereotypes about how men and women behave—stereotypes that, when acted out, provide an empirical basis for the laws. It is just this problem that Justice Brennan hinted at when he argued in *Craig* that "proving broad sociological propositions by statistics is a dubious business, and one that inevitably is in tension with the normative philosophy of the Equal Protection Clause."[33]

If one thinks of the problem from this perspective, then it becomes less clear that the *Craig* statute in fact discriminates against men rather than women. True, superficially, the statute allows women to do something forbidden to men—viz., to drink 3.2% beer before reaching the age of 21. But women pay heavily for this dubious privilege. This particular statute forms a small part of much larger a network of legal and extralegal norms, expectations, customs, and requirements that, taken as a whole, produce less satisfactory lives for women than for men.

An argument along these lines is probably the best defense of the result in *Craig,* but it also produces problems of its own. If the argument is correct, then the only way to break out of the vicious circle of self-validating laws and norms is to try to imagine how the world would be if there were not the cultural conditioning that confines people to the gender roles they currently occupy. Put differently, one must try to determine which differences between men and women are "real" and desirable, and which are simply an artifact of oppressive cultural conditioning. Justice Brennan was surely right when he hinted that one cannot do this simply by looking at how people behave in our current, sexist world. But the coherence of this approach depends upon the existence of some "natural," way that men and women would behave in the absence of

33. *Id.* at 204.

social conditioning and upon some theory that privileges the natural over the constructed. It might give us pause that Justice Bradley's *Bradwell* concurrence was also premised on the existence of some "natural" state of affairs sometimes at variance with what he called "exceptional cases." Arguably, much of the struggle for gender equality has involved the effort to escape the sort of essentialist thinking that Justice Brennan, together with Justice Bradley, implicitly accepts.

The example of Justice Bradley raises a related caution. Even if it is coherent to imagine a utopian world where the genders would interact in the absence of social conditioning, it is unclear that we would want judges to do the imagining. There is reason for skepticism that judges will be able to disentangle themselves from the very social norms that they purport to be criticizing.

These difficulties are compounded by the analogical reasoning at the heart of equal protection analysis. Recall from Chapter One that equality arguments always involve an assertion that one thing is *like* another and, therefore, should be treated alike. Likeness and difference are not facts about the world, however. Instead, they are attributes we impose on the world. There will therefore be some analogies that make sense to us and some that do not, and it is likely that the force of a given analogy will depend in part on exercise of the very social power that the Court is attempting to transcend.

Formal versus Interventionist Equality

These difficulties, in turn, raise doubts about the value of the requirement of formal equality, around which the Court has organized gender discrimination law. Formal equality values facial neutrality in government policy. It begins with the presumption that women are "like" men and that they therefore ought to be treated alike. (It is this presumption that leads to heightened scrutiny of statutes that treat them differently.) But since this assumption is not necessarily rooted in empirical reality (because of the circularity problem described above), it must be rooted in some imaginative reconstruction of that reality. Once we are in the realm of imagination, is it so clear that men and women are, or ought to be, alike? If men and women are in "fact" different, or if they ought to be different, then treating them as if they were alike might actually discriminate against women. Worse, yet, treating women as if they were like men risks holding women to standards set for the benefit of men, a stance that builds inequality into the very starting point of the analysis.

United States v. Virginia[34] provides a good example of both the attractions and the pitfalls of the formal equality paradigm. At issue was the admissions policy of the Virginia Military Institute (VMI)—a state supported military academy that refused to admit women. VMI had a huge endowment and many alumni in positions of power and prestige. It used the "adversative" method of in-

34. 518 U.S. 515 (1996).

struction, which involved intense harassment, abusive treatment, a near total absence of privacy, and pervasive indoctrination into a set of values.

Plaintiffs brought a suit to integrate VMI, but the trial court found that if women were admitted, some aspects of the VMI culture would have to change. Applying the *Craig* test, the court found that these changes would jeopardize an "important" governmental interest in educational diversity. The Court of Appeals reversed this decision, and remanded the case to the trial court for selection of a remedy. In response to the appellate ruling, Virginia proposed a "separate but equal" program for women. Under this plan, a Virginia Women's Institute for Leadership would be established. Its purpose would be to prepare women for leadership roles, but the model of instruction would be very different from, and supposedly more suited to, women than VMI's.

The Court of Appeals was satisfied with this remedy, but the Supreme Court was not. In an opinion by Justice Ginsburg, the Court reversed the judgment below. Ginsburg's opinion made a powerful argument for the formal position. It may be true, she conceded, that few women will have the interest or ability to succeed at VMI, but there is no reason why the women who can and want to succeed there should be captives of their gender. Some men and some women are alike in their ability to perform at VMI, and these men and women are entitled to be treated alike. It followed that VMI could abandon its discriminatory admissions policy without sacrificing the core of its educational approach.

This argument captures an important strength of the formal position. The rhetoric of formal equality provides a tool that allows individuals to overcome barriers that might otherwise appear insurmountable. There is no reason why a young girl, like a young boy, cannot aspire to being a student at VMI. Formal equality can be transformative and liberating by opening up possibilities that were previously unimagined.

This argument is strengthened by a second insight: The history of gender discrimination teaches that when the government purports to "compensate" for women's putative differences by providing separate rules for them, it often ends up treating them worse. The point is illustrated by the facts of *Virginia* itself. Virginia claimed that it was creating a separate institution that would benefit women, but in fact, the institution it promised had only a fraction of the resources available to VMI. Just as the separate black law school in Sweatt v. Painter[35] could not possibly compete with the University of Texas, so too, the separate Virginia Women's Leadership Institute was not close to equal to its all-male counterpart.

But despite these strengths, there are also reasons to be skeptical about the argument for formalism. There are two related problems. First, whatever may be the case in some imaginary world, in our world there are significant differences between men

35. 339 U.S. 629 (1950).

and women, when considered as groups. For these reasons, although formal equality may be transformative for individual women, it may not be worth much to women as a whole. Thus, while it is surely true that there are a few women who will thrive in the VMI environment, it is also true that the percentage of women for whom this education is appropriate is much smaller than the percentage of men.

Second, we are confronted again with the problem that equal protection analysis is usually about means rather than ends. Thus, the *Virginia* Court takes as a given the "adversative" method of instruction and confines its discussion to whether the admission of women is compatible with this end. The Court overlooks the problem that the end itself might be gender-biased. Critics of the Court's position might argue that if women indeed apply to VMI, they will be judged according to a standard devised by and for men. This arrangement virtually guarantees failure for many women—failure that can now be blamed on them, rather than on the discrimination supposedly cured by their admission on an "equal" basis.

These problems with the Court's approach are brought into sharp relief by Chief Justice Rehnquist's concurring opinion in *Virginia*.[36] Rehnquist, like the majority, thought that the proposed Virginia Women's Institute for Leadership was inadequate to satisfy the state's constitutional obligations. But for Rehnquist, the solution to this

36. United States v. Virginia, 518 U.S. 515, 558 (1996) (Rehnquist, C. J., concurring in the judgment).

problem was not the desegregation of VMI, but more resources devoted to the Leadership Institute.

The Ginsburg and Rehnquist approaches might be compared along two dimensions. First, whereas the Ginsburg approach focuses on liberty for individual women, the Rehnquist approach focuses on group equality. (In this sense, the dispute might be analogized to the difference between Justice Harlan's position in his *Plessy* dissent and Justice Warren's in his *Brown* majority opinion.) What matters for Ginsburg is that individual women who have the ability to succeed at VMI will be prevented from doing so by the "artificial" barrier of gender. This individual liberty is doubtless important, but it comes at a price. In exchange for individualized judgments, Ginsburg must give up the possibility of a solution that might better empower women as a group. In contrast, Rehnquist's remedy would probably provide more of value to women generally, but it does so at the expense of individual freedom for women who want to escape from confining gender stereotypes.

The second dimension is closely related to the first. Whereas the Ginsburg approach takes current distributions of resources between men and women as a given, the Rehnquist approach would force government intervention to change these distributions. (Here again there are echos of Justices Harlan and Warren.) Recall from Chapter One that equality rhetoric can sometimes be utilized to change negative rights (the right to be left alone in a private sphere) into positive rights (the right to government intervention in the private sphere). Although constitutional rights are generally conceptualized as negative, equality rights are special because the government will often respond to a finding of inequality by ratcheting up benefits given to the less favored group, rather than ratcheting down benefits provided to the more favored group.

The Rehnquist remedy provides an example. Had his approach been followed, the government would have been encouraged to respond to the finding of inequality by what would have amounted to a massive "affirmative action" program for women. True, as a theoretical matter, Virginia might have solved its legal difficulty by closing VMI, but, as a practical matter, this outcome was extremely unlikely. Instead, the state would have been forced into an affirmative intervention into the lives of women so as to provide them with resources they previously lacked.

These dilemmas should be familiar because of their previous appearance in the discussion of racial discrimination. They have special bite in the gender area, however, because of another important feature of gender discrimination. Historically, gender discrimination has been condoned in part because of protections surrounding the private sphere. Relationships between men and women—especially in the setting of the family—were considered too intimate and personal to be regulated by law. Standard forms of constitutional argument equate the private sphere with liberty, but critics of the gender status quo have argued that the supposed freedom enjoyed in the private sphere has shielded a pervasive pattern of violence and subjugation suffered by women.

To the extent that this criticism is accurate, it argues for a conception of equality that triggers affirmative government intervention into private preserves of power. Formal equality will often not be up to this task. Judging men and women alike by a standard that favors men does nothing to force government redistributions. In contrast, an approach that insists that women must be treated differently because they are different has some potential to unravel status quo private distributions of wealth and power between the genders.

Yet here, as always, it is a mistake to think that there are easy solutions. Although the private sphere has sometimes shielded patriarchy, it can also be a haven for women. Consider, for example, the abortion right. The holding of Roe v. Wade,[37] establishing a constitutional right to abortion, is firmly grounded in the rhetoric of privacy and nonintervention. As we saw with regard to race, there is no guarantee that a more activist government will be more favorable to disadvantaged groups than private arrangements. In at least some contexts, women may do better fending off employers and family members than fending off government.

Examples

The dilemmas outlined above have been played out in a series of cases concerning supposed "archaic generalizations" and "real differences."

37. 410 U.S. 113 (1973).

Consider, for example, the fact that some women, but no men are capable of becoming pregnant. Is this a "real" difference that ought to make a difference? A formal approach insists on treating men and women alike in the face of this difference. An interventionist approach argues for different treatment that takes account of the difference.

The contrast between the approaches is illustrated by Geduldig v. Aiello.[38] California's disability insurance program excluded pregnancy-related disabilities. The Court held that this exclusion did not constitute gender discrimination because the exclusion distinguished between pregnant and nonpregnant persons, rather than between men and women. This decision has been widely criticized—even ridiculed—yet, from the perspective of rigorous formalism, it is correct. Of course, no men become pregnant, but it is an "archaic and overbroad generalization" to assume that all women are, will become, or even are capable of becoming, pregnant.

Congress responded to *Geduldig* by enacting a statute that was interventionist in character. It provided, in essence, that employers could not discriminate against pregnant persons.[39] The effect of the statute was to force employers to provide new resources to pregnant individuals. But the problem of formalism reemerged under this statute. Suppose that an employer provides benefits to pregnant women but fails to provide similar benefits to expectant fathers? The statute could easily have been

38. 417 U.S. 484 (1974).

39. 42 U.S.C. § 2000(e)(k).

read as establishing a formal requirement that mandated facially "equal" treatment between pregnant and nonpregnant persons, despite the fact that perspective fathers and mothers are obviously differently situated. Instead, the Court interpreted the statute as distinguishing between the two situations by permitting benefits for pregnant persons, while outlawing burdens on such persons.[40]

In the constitutional arena, the Court has frequently treated the possibility of pregnancy as a "real difference" that justifies different treatment. For example, in Michael M. v. Sonoma County Superior Court,[41] a majority of the justices voted to uphold a California statute defining statutory rape as "an act of sexual intercourse accomplished with a female not the wife of the perpetrator, where the female is under the age of 18 years."[42] This definition meant that if, for example, a fifteen-year-old male had consensual sex with a seventeen-year-old female, the male, but not the female, would be guilty of a criminal offense.

Writing for the Court, Justice Rehnquist relied upon the potential for pregnancy as a grounds for upholding the statute. According to Rehnquist, "the risk of pregnancy itself constitutes a substantial deterrence to young females. No similar natural sanctions deter males. A criminal sanction imposed

40. *See* California Federal Savings & Loan Assn. v. Guerra, 479 U.S. 272 (1987).

41. 450 U.S. 464 (1981).

42. *Id.* at 466.

solely on males thus serves to roughly 'equalize' the deterrents on the sexes."[43]

There are at least two puzzling aspects of this reasoning. First, it fails to justify the gender classification as applied to cases where there is no risk of pregnancy because, for example, the female is too young.[44] More seriously, the argument seems askew because the statute only takes hold with regard to females who are not deterred by the risk of pregnancy. A female who is deterred would not consent to sex, and, if sexual intercourse occurred, she would be raped. The statutory rape law applies only when the female agrees to sex. Thus, the fact that there is some other group of females who are deterred by the risk of pregnancy but to whom the statute does not apply, hardly justifies the statute's gender classification.

These problems with the Court's reasoning suggest some of the virtues of a formal approach. Formalism rests in part on the view that we sometimes unthinkingly accept gender classifications without careful analysis of whether they are really necessary. Moreover, gender classifications that are supposedly justified by "natural" differences, like

43. *Id.* at 473.

44. The Court responds to this difficulty as follows:

[Q]uite apart from the fact that the statute could well be justified on the grounds that very young females are particularly susceptible to physical injury from sexual intercourse, it is ludicrous to suggest that the Constitution requires the California Legislature to limit the scope or its rape statute to older teenagers and exclude young girls.

Id. at 475.

the possibility of pregnancy, are sometimes a cover for less respectable assumptions about the roles of men and women. Here, given the weakness of the pregnancy argument, there is at least the possibility that the law rests instead on (perhaps unconscious) differential valuations of male and female virginity, on the assumption that men, but not women, can be trusted to make wise decisions about sex, or on the view that young women who have sex are acting immorally, while young men who have sex are merely "sowing wild oats."

Yet despite these problems, there is also something to be said for the majority's position. For example, the critique of the majority's deterrence theory is persuasive only if rape law presently captures all cases of nonconsensual intercourse. That assumption, in turn, rests on the view that "consent" and "nonconsent" are binary concepts that, together, exhaust the mental states people might have regarding sex. In fact, there is much evidence that rape law does not adequately protect nonconsenting females, and, as a matter of common sense, we know that there are degrees of consent and coercion. Suppose it is true that young men use subtle and not so subtle pressure to talk young women into sex more often than young women talk young men into sex. Of course, this difference might be the product of sexist conditioning and might not exist in an imaginary world where men and women were not hampered by restrictive gender roles. Still, if the difference exists in our world, there may be a basis for gender-based statutory rape laws.

Similarly, it is another fact about our world—as opposed to facts that might exist in a "just" imaginary world—that women bear more of the costs of pregnancy than men. This is not merely a matter of the physical burdens of pregnancy, although these burdens should not be underestimated. More than a generation after the sexual revolution of the 1970's, it remains true that women do much more of the child rearing than men, and that many more single women than single men end up raising children in poverty. One might argue that the law in *Michael M.*, like the law in *Craig,* is part of a web of social signals that entrenches this state of affairs. Still, an insistence on gender-neutral statutes in the face of these differences that in fact exist may hurt rather than help women.

Statutes that differentiate between birth mothers and birth fathers pose a similar dilemma. Consider, for example, Nguyen v. Immigration and Naturalization Service.[45] At issue was a federal statute providing that nonmarital children born outside the United States to a citizen mother, but noncitizen father, were automatically United States citizens if the mother had been present in the United States for one year. In contrast, nonmarital children born to a citizen father and noncitizen mother were United States citizens only if the child obtained formal proof of paternity before age 18. The Court, in an opinion by Justice Anthony Kennedy, upheld the statute as applied to a nonmarital child despite

45.   533 U.S. 53 (2001).

DNA evidence conclusively demonstrating that his father was American.

Justice Kennedy once again relied upon "natural" differences between men and women to support his argument:

> In the case of the mother, the [biological] relationship is verifiable from the birth itself. . . .

> In the case of the father, the uncontestable fact is that he need not be present at the birth. If he is present, furthermore, that circumstance is not incontrovertible proof of fatherhood. . . .

> Congress could have required both mothers and fathers to prove parenthood within 30 days or, for that matter, 18 years of the child's birth. Given that the mother is always present at birth, but that the father need not be, the facially neutral rule would sometimes require fathers to take additional affirmative steps which would not be required of mothers. . . . Just as neutral terms can mark discrimination that is unlawful, gender specific terms can mark a permissible distinction. . . . Here, the use of gender specific terms takes into account a biological difference between the parents. The differential treatment is inherent in a sensible statutory scheme, given the unique relationship of the mother to the event of birth.[46]

In light of the fact that Nguyen's biological relationship to his American father had been established beyond question, this result may seem undu-

46. *Id.* at 62–63.

ly harsh. There is also a risk that here, as in *Michael M.*, the majority has fallen victim to a gender stereotype. There are, to be sure, instances where women will have an easier time establishing parenthood than men, but there will also be cases where a man can conclusively demonstrate fatherhood, but (perhaps because of lost or disputed records), a woman will have more difficulty. Given these weaknesses in the Court's argument, it seems possible that the statute may instead be motivated by the stereotype that women are more likely than men to have an intimate relationship with their children. Indeed, Justice Kennedy himself acknowledged as much and defends the statute on this basis as well.[47]

The problem, of course, is that there is some truth to this stereotype, and, to the extent that it is true, it is unjust to treat men and women in the same way when in fact they are different. The statute, in effect, gives fathers an incentive to establish the kind of relationship with their children that many mothers will establish without the incentive. Thus, depending on one's disposition, the classification can be seen as entrenching, compensating for, or even undermining traditional gender roles.

Affirmative Action

There are similar problems at the heart of the affirmative action debate in the gender context. One "real" difference between men and women is that

47. *See Id.* at 64.

women have suffered from discrimination that men have escaped. Yet here, as in the race context, responding to this difference risks making things worse rather than better.

Consider, for example, Califano v. Goldfarb.[48] Under the social security law, widows were automatically entitled to survivor benefits, but widowers received the benefits only if they could show that they were dependent on their wives for more than half of their earnings. The Court, in a judgment announced by Justice Brennan, invalidated the statute. Viewed from one perspective, the statute might be considered laudatory compensation for past discrimination against women. The statute responded to a "real" difference between men and women— that job discrimination made many more wives dependent upon their husbands than husbands dependent on their wives.

Instead, the Court saw the statute as involving an unthinking and unnecessary overgeneralization. True, more women than men are dependents, but this stereotype is not universally accurate. Moreover, the effect of the statute was to make comparable work by men and women of different value. Men who worked earned a survivor benefit for their nondependent wives, whereas women who did the same work did not earn a similar benefit for their nondependent husbands. The upshot is a subsidy for male employment not provided for female em-

48. 430 U.S. 199 (1977).

ployment, thereby entrenching the very discrimination that the statute allegedly compensated for.

The fragility of these conclusions is illustrated by comparing *Goldfarb* to Califono v. Webster,[49] a case decided less than three weeks later. On this occasion, the Court unanimously upheld a provision in the same act that granted retired female workers a higher monthly old-age pension than comparable male workers. The Court thought that the statute was a permissible affirmative action measure that compensated women workers for the discriminatorily low wages they received while employed. This defense of the statute is not altogether implausible, yet here, as in *Goldfarb*, there is the risk of entrenchment as well as the possibility of compensation. The statute effectively subsidized women who choose to work part time by granting them the same benefits as men who earn higher salaries by working full time. One can view this subsidy as either taking account of the fact that, in the real world, more women spend time working at home than men, or as obstructing our pursuit of a new world where men and women share work at home and away from home in equal fashion.

In both *Goldfarb* and *Webster* the Court, without much discussion, applied the intermediate scrutiny mandated by *Craig*. However, both cases were decided before *Croson*,[50] which, as we have seen, man-

49. 430 U.S. 313 (1977).

50. City of Richmond v. J.A. Croson Co., 488 U.S. 469 (1989).

dated the highest level of scrutiny for race-based affirmative action. The intersection between *Croson* and gender-based affirmative action creates a serious dilemma for the Court, to which it has yet to respond.

One possibility is that the Court will adhere to *Goldfarb* and *Webster*, thereby mandating only intermediate scrutiny for gender-based affirmative action, even though strict scrutiny is required for race-based affirmative action. But given the history of the equal protection clause, it would be ironic to have a legal regime that made it harder to remedy racial discrimination than gender discrimination. On the other hand, the Court might import the *Croson* standard into the gender area, thereby making both race and gender affirmative action measures subject to strict scrutiny. But this approach also produces an outcome that is difficult to defend. Unless *Craig* is overruled, this regime would make it harder to pass laws designed to help women than laws designed to help men (which would still be subject to only intermediate scrutiny).

It is hard to predict how the Court will resolve this dilemma, but it is at least possible that its effort to do so will refocus its attention on the problem with which this chapter begins. Race and gender are the two greatest challenges to our aspirations for an equal society. There is therefore a natural tendency to attempt to reconcile our approaches to the two problems. But although analogies between the two can be useful, they can also be misleading. The Court's task is to develop a law of race and gender that at once applies lessons we have learned in one arena to the other and is responsive to the complexity and distinctiveness of each.

CHAPTER NINE

THE BOUNDARIES OF EQUALITY

How far should the domain of equality extend? The logic and history of equal protection push against boundaries. Analogical reasoning, at the core of equal protection analysis, directs our attention to similarities, and historically, excluded groups have used this reasoning to focus attention on their claims.

Yet boundaries cannot be completely elastic. Three forces push back against expansion. First, at least in its ethical form, equality arguments are about the moral irrelevance of "superficial" difference. But to include everyone within the boundaries of an all-encompassing moral community is to define that community so broadly as to make it meaningless. Hence, arguments for inclusion are always made against the backdrop of some sort of exclusion, which must be maintained lest we destroy the value of inclusion. After all, if everyone in every situation is alike, then we have lost track of the distinction between alike and different.

Second, for reasons set out in Chapter One, equality claims tend to be public-regarding. They often involve an extension of government power into a private sphere. Moreover, they are frequently infused with public-regarding values. Unlike due process claims, which often privilege the right of individual, idiosyncratic choice, equality claims are usually about treating groups in similar fashion. Equality rhetoric therefore sounds in universalism, rather than particularism. But human beings are not just public. They also value a private sphere where individual, particularist judgments are immune from universalist criticism. Protection of this private sphere entails some limits on the domain of equality rhetoric.

Finally, there are a set of practical constraints. Equality judgments are always socially situated. As we have seen repeatedly, likeness and difference are not facts about the world, but social constructs that we impose on physical reality. At any particular moment, some analogies will make sense and others will not. It follows that when courts decide equal protection cases, they are inevitably reflecting, as well as changing, existing social norms.

As a doctrinal matter, many of the boundary skirmishes in our equality wars have been fought over whether particular groups are entitled to heightened review when government policies disadvantage them. This chapter examines the claims of a number of these groups.

Gay Men and Lesbians

The Supreme Court's first encounter with gay rights came in the context of a due process challenge to a state sodomy statute. In Bowers v.

Hardwick,[1] a narrowly divided Court held that the statute, at least when applied to sex between homosexuals, did not invade the kind of fundamental liberty interest protected by the due process clause.

A decade after *Bowers*, the Court upheld an equal protection claim pressed by gay men and lesbians in Romer v. Evans.[2] At issue was a provision of the Colorado Constitution, which provided

Neither the State of Colorado, through any of its branches or departments, nor any of its agencies, political subdivisions, municipalities or school districts, shall enact, adopt or enforce any statute, regulation, ordinance or policy whereby homosexual, lesbian or bisexual orientation, conduct, practices or relationships shall constitute or otherwise be the basis of or entitle any person or class of persons to have or claim any minority status, quota preferences, protected status or claim of discrimination.[3]

The provision, adopted through Colorado's initiative and referendum process, had the effect of repealing local ordinances prohibiting discrimination on the basis of sexual orientation in matters like housing, employment, and public accommodations. Viewed from a due process perspective, it would seem that *Bowers* immunized the amendment from constitutional challenge, at least to the extent that it applied to homosexual "conduct." After all, if the

1. 478 U.S. 186 (1986).
2. 517 U.S. 620 (1996).
3. *Id.* at 624.

Constitution permits criminal punishment of gay sex, then surely it does not mandate antidiscrimination protection for those who engage in it.

Nonetheless, in an opinion written by Justice Anthony Kennedy, the Court held that the amendment violated the equal protection clause. Justice Kennedy's opinion did not even mention *Bowers*. Nor did the Court hold that gay men and lesbians constituted a suspect class triggering heightened scrutiny. Instead, the Court held that the amendment "fails, indeed, defies even [rational basis] inquiry."[4] This was because the amendment's "sheer breadth is so discontinuous with the reasons offered for it that [it] seems inexplicable by anything but animus toward the class that it affects.... "[5]

A striking feature of *Romer* is that the Court's resort to the equal protection clause made the decision public-regarding. If *Bowers* had been decided differently, the protected right would have been a right *against* government interference. Individual gays and lesbians would have enjoyed immunity when they engaged in sexual acts in the private sphere. In contrast, the equal protection analysis in *Romer* had the effect of creating a right *to* government intervention. The *Romer* Court began with a baseline of government protection against discriminatory acts targeted at other groups. As Justice Kennedy put the point:

4. *Id.* at 621.

5. *Id.* at 632.

[M]ost States have chosen to counter discrimination by enacting detailed statutory schemes....

In following this approach, Colorado's state and local governments have not limited anti-discrimination laws to groups that have so far been given the protection of heightened equal protection scrutiny under our cases. Rather, they set forth an extensive catalogue of traits which cannot be the basis for discrimination, including age, military status, marital status, pregnancy, parenthood, custody of a minor child, political affiliation, physical or mental disability of an individual or of his or her associates and, in recent times, sexual orientation....

We find nothing special in the protections Amendment 2 withholds. These are protections taken for granted by most people either because they already have them or do not need them; these are protections against exclusion from an almost limitless number of transaction and endeavors that constitute ordinary civic life in a free society.[6]

Thus, on the Court's view, the effect of the disputed amendment was to divide residents of Colorado into two classes: the majority of people who either are protected against discrimination or do not need protection, and gay people, who are unprotected. The Court declared that this classification denied gay people equal protection of the laws, in

6. *Id.* at 628–30.

the most literal sense of that term. Theoretically, Colorado could have responded to this holding by establishing a state-wide ban on antidiscrimination measures protecting other groups. As a practical matter, the effect of the holding was to revive government regulation of private transactions disadvantaging gay people.

This holding is quite dramatic. In important ways, it runs against the main direction of most of American constitutional law, which is dedicated to negative rights—i.e., the carving out of a private sphere free of government regulation. Nonetheless, the Court's cryptic opinion raises more questions than it answers. The difficulties are made clear by Justice Antonin Scalia's biting dissent.[7] Justice Scalia pointed out that the disputed amendment is, in fact, perfectly rational if one starts from the premise that homosexuality is a moral evil. If this were true, then there would be a rational basis for the distinction between the treatment of gay people and the treatment of other groups who benefit from antidiscrimination protection.

Suppose, for example, that Colorado adopted a state-wide amendment providing that spouse abusers were not entitled to this protection. Surely this provision would withstand equal protection scrutiny: The statute is rationally related to the discouragement of spouse abuse. Put differently, there is a sensible and obvious distinction between spouse abusers and, say, the mentally or physically dis-

7. *Id.* at 635.

abled, because spouse abusers have done something wrong.

If homosexuality is like spouse abuse, then the Court is mistaken and the Colorado amendment should have been upheld. Is it like spouse abuse? Justice Scalia reasons that because the Constitution does not speak to homosexuality, therefore, the matter should be left to the political sphere. But this is surely a non sequitur. The Constitution *does* speak to homosexuality if homosexuality is like, say, physical or mental disability, for if gay men and lesbians are "like" the disabled, then it would violate the equal protection clause to treat them differently. It follows that in order to resolve the claim before it, the Court had no choice but to make a moral judgment about the nature of homosexuality.

The necessity for this moral judgment may make us uncomfortable, but it should come as no surprise. All equal protection claims involve extraconstitutional moral judgments about likeness and difference. Suppose, for example, that Colorado provided that men, but not women, were entitled to antidiscrimination protection. The equal protection clause says nothing in so many words about the moral equality of men and women, but surely Justice Scalia would not claim that the statute is therefore valid. A Court that struck down this statute would be making a moral judgment about the likeness of men and women—a judgment that is inevitable so long as the Court retains the power to enforce the equal protection clause.

But although Justice Scalia's attack on the majority opinion is less powerful than he supposes, it nonetheless uncovers significant weaknesses in the Court's approach. Writing for the majority, Justice Kennedy attempted to narrow the force of the decision by emphasizing the extraordinary breadth of the Colorado amendment. As the spouse abuse example makes clear, however, this breadth would be of no concern unless gay people were relevantly similar to other groups protected by antidiscrimination law. They are relevantly similar only if it is impermissible to categorize homosexuality as a moral evil, since, if it is a moral evil, then this status makes it different from other traits protected by antidiscrimination law. But if as a constitutional matter, homosexuality is morally neutral, then much more than the Colorado amendment is at risk.

To be sure, some putatively discriminatory treatment of homosexuals might be justified on premises unrelated to the morality of the practice. Perhaps there are rational reasons for excluding gay people from military service that rest on problems of "order and discipline" rather than moral condemnation. Even here, though, the widespread disapproval of gay sex, as well as inaccurate or overbroad negative stereotypes about gay people, might make one suspicious that this is the real reason for the exclusion. Moreover, at bottom, problems of order and discipline stem mostly from private disapproval of the conduct, and, in other contexts, the Court has made plain that the government may no more submit to private prejudice than it may act from prejudicial motives of its own.[8]

Moreover, in other situations, it is hard to imagine a rationale for antihomosexual government policies that does not entail moral disapproval. Consider the problem of gay marriage. In Loving v. Virginia,[9] the Court held that prohibitions against interracial marriage are unconstitutional. This holding rested on the moral equality of members of different races. If homosexuals and heterosexuals also enjoy moral equality, then the rational basis for the ban on gay marriages would seem to collapse.

Nonetheless, it is quite doubtful that the Justices joining the *Romer* majority opinion meant to draw into question the ban on gay marriage. If the ban remains relatively impervious to constitutional challenge, this is not because of anything about the logic of equal protection analysis, but because of the reality of social power. As a social fact, the analogy between blacks and whites makes sense to us in a way that it did not to many in the nineteenth century. The analogy between gays and straights makes more sense to more people today than it did, even relatively recently. Still, enough people remain sufficiently shocked by the prospect of gay marriage to make its constitutional protection, for the time being at least, outside the realm of "sensible" legal outcomes.

8. *See, e.g.,* Palmore v. Sidoti, 466 U.S. 429 (1984).
9. 388 U.S. 1 (1967).

There is a natural tendency to see equal protection analysis as pushing us toward a more inclusive moral community, and there is little doubt that, at the margins at least, it can have this effect. Thus, *Romer* provided an occasion for the Court to think empathically about the plight of gay Americans and to stretch the blanket of government protection to include them as well. Yet we should not lose sight of the other side of equal protection analysis. Equal protection is about likeness, but it is also inevitably about difference. Indeed, as emphasized above, difference is necessary to make likeness meaningful.

Thus, it is not as if most advocates of gay rights favor protecting all forms of sexual expression. There are few people, indeed, who think that adults who have sex with children, or parents who marry their own adult offspring, should be protected by antidiscrimination laws. Many gay rights advocates are angered by efforts to group them with less reputable sexual nonconformists. Their anger is understandable because their moral status depends upon their being different from the "other" who remain outside the moral community.

Social facts are not static, so there is no way to predict whether the analogical claims of other sexual nonconformists—claims that seem bizarre or worse to us today—will make perfect sense tomorrow. We can be certain, though, that these claims, too, will be made against the backdrop of some other set of claims that will seem absurd to "sensible" people.

Noncitizens

The argument about gay men and lesbians concerns the boundaries of our moral community. In contrast, dispute about how noncitizens should be treated raises questions about the scope of our political community.

There is a vantage point from which discriminatory treatment of noncitizens seems immoral and irrational. When we look at the world from a universalist perspective, we can see that all people of all nations are fundamentally the same and entitled to equal regard. Why should we care less about someone who, through an accident of birth, came into the world in Tijuana rather than in San Diego?

None of us is a pure universalist, however. Although we retain the capacity to be moved by claims of universal brotherhood and sisterhood, most of us are also patriots with special devotion to our own country and its people. Few Americans think that the United States government should provide exactly the same amount of assistance for flood victims in Bangladesh as for flood victims in North Dakota.

Suppose, however, that some of the flood victims in North Dakota are citizens of Bangladesh? When a noncitizen is within the physical boundaries of this country, it is much harder to shield ourselves from the fundamental similarity between her and the rest of us. Yet such a person has no constitutional right to be here, and no right to equal treatment if she were not here. Why then should the mere fact of geography change the result?

Part of the answer, no doubt, lies in the fourteenth amendment's text. The equal protection clause protects "any person within [a state's] jurisdiction." A Bangladeshi residing in North Dakota may not be an American citizen, but she is nonetheless within North Dakota's jurisdiction. All that this establishes, however, is that such a person is within the domain of the clause. If there is a sound basis for distinguishing between noncitizens and citizens, the clause has nonetheless not been violated. And there might be a sound basis if political membership provides a just ground for differential regard.

As this discussion illustrates, our universalist and particularist urges are fundamentally inconsistent. This tension, in turn, means that it is easy to destabilize our intuitions and that the constitutional status of noncitizens is bound to be confused.

As a doctrinal matter, the Court announced in 1971 that noncitizens were a "discrete and insular minority" and that, consequently, classifications based on alienage were subject to heightened judicial scrutiny.[10] The decision came in the context of a state statute that denied noncitizens various forms of welfare assistance. Applying strict scrutiny to the statutes, the Court, in an opinion by Justice Harry Blackmun, concluded that the "state's desire to preserve limited welfare benefits for its own citizens is inadequate to justify ... making noncitizens inel-

10. *See* Graham v. Richardson, 403 U.S. 365 (1971).

igible for public assistance."[11] In subsequent cases, the Court invalidated laws that broadly banned all noncitizens from state civil service positions,[12] from higher education financial assistance,[13] from becoming lawyers,[14] and from becoming notaries public.[15] And, although it purported to use only rational basis review, the Court went so far as to strike down a state prohibition on public school attendance by noncitizens who were here illegally.[16]

The argument for strict scrutiny of statutes that discriminate against noncitizens is relatively straightforward. To the extent that heightened scrutiny is designed to compensate for the absence of political power, alienage classifications seem like an easy case, since noncitizens are almost always denied the franchise. Moreover, the country has a long and disreputable history of prejudice against noncitizens.

Yet even this brief summary of the case for heightened scrutiny reveals significant problems. After all, if disfranchisement really justifies heightened scrutiny, why isn't the disfranchisement itself unconstitutional? Our history of discrimination against noncitizens is an argument for heightened scrutiny only if such discrimination is inappropriate. But the very issue in dispute is whether or not

11. *Id.* at 374.
12. *See* Sugarman v. Dougall, 413 U.S. 634 (1973).
13. *See* Nyquist v. Mauclet, 432 U.S. 1 (1977).
14. *See* In re Griffiths, 413 U.S. 717 (1973).
15. *See* Bernal v. Fainter, 467 U.S. 216 (1984).
16. *See* Plyler v. Doe, 457 U.S. 202 (1982).

membership in our political community makes different treatment appropriate. Given this dispute, nothing would seem to follow from evidence of prior different treatment.

It is also worth emphasizing that noncitizens do not have a right to come to the United States in the first place. This fact is most dramatically apparent when noncitizens arrive illegally. An undocumented alien has no right to be in this country. If the undocumented alien were not in this country, he would have no right to attend an American public school. Why, then, do noncitizens who violate our immigration laws have rights that noncitizens who obey them do not have?

Even when noncitizens are legally here, the problem does not go away. The federal government often conditions the privilege of visitation or residence on restrictions that seem justified in light of the discretionary character of admission. The prohibition on seeking employment while in the United States is only the most obvious example. Surely, this differential treatment of noncitizens does not violate equal protection. Why, then, can't the government condition admission on not applying for welfare or for civil service jobs (after all, a category of employment)?

No doubt because of these difficulties, the Court's declaration that alienage classifications should be strictly scrutinized has involved less than meets the eye. The Court has developed two important limitations on this doctrine. First, states are permitted to utilize alienage classifications when they are defining the contours of their own political community. Hence, although a broad-based disqualification from all civil service positions is unconstitutional, the Court has upheld exclusion from positions involving the formulation or execution of public policy. On this theory, it has validated prohibitions on noncitizens serving as state police officers,[17] as public school teachers,[18] and as probation officers.[19]

Unfortunately, the distinction between government positions that do and do not involve public policy determinations is not precise. Perhaps the best summary of the Court's position is in its opinion in Cabell v. Chavez–Salido:

> The Court [has distinguished] between the economic and sovereign functions of government.... [A]lthough citizenship is not a relevant ground for the distribution of economic benefits, it is a relevant ground for determining membership in the political community.[20]

The *Cabell* Court went on to hold that this distinction could be drawn by utilizing a two-pronged test. "First, the specificity of the classification will be examined: a classification that is substantially overinclusive or underinclusive tends to undercut the governmental claim that the classification serves legitimate political ends."[21] Second, even

17. *See* Foley v. Connelie, 435 U.S. 291 (1978).

18. *See* Ambach v. Norwick, 441 U.S. 68 (1979).

19. *See* Cabell v. Chavez–Salido, 454 U.S. 432 (1982).

20. *Id.* at 438.

21. *Id.* at 440.

narrowly tailored statutes might be "economic" rather than "political" unless they were applied only to " 'persons holding state elective or important nonelective executive, legislative and judicial positions,' those officers who 'participate directly in the formulation, execution, or review of broad public policy' and hence 'perform functions that go to the heart of representative government.' "[22]

A second limitation on the heightened scrutiny afforded alienage classifications is based upon the difference between federal and state policy. The Court has been suspicious of state alienage restrictions in part because states have no proper role in making judgments about immigration policy. In contrast, the federal government has plenary power to control our borders. On a "greater includes the lesser" theory, the Court has upheld federal limitations on noncitizens who are granted visitation or residency rights. For example, in Mathews v. Diaz,[23] the Court upheld a federal statute limiting noncitizen participation in a medical insurance program. On the other hand, the Court invalidated even a federal policy when it was clear that the policy was not enacted as an adjunct to the immigration power. In Hampton v. Mow Sun Wong,[24] a case decided on the same day as *Mathews*, the Court considered a Civil Service Commission policy excluding noncitizens from most federal civil service jobs. In an

22. *Id.*
23. 426 U.S. 67 (1976).
24. 426 U.S. 88 (1976).

opinion written by Justice John Paul Stevens, the Court said the following:

> We may assume ... that if the Congress or the President had expressly imposed the citizenship requirement, it would be justified by the national interest in providing an incentive for aliens to become naturalized, or possibly even as providing the President with an expendable token for treaty negotiating purposes; but we are not willing to presume that the Chairman of the Civil Service Commission ... was deliberately fostering an interest so far removed from his normal responsibilities.[25]

The limitations the Court has imposed on strict scrutiny for alienage classifications leave the doctrine in a less than fully satisfactory state. Given the ability of states to exclude noncitizens from their political communities, the case for heightened review is paradoxical. Recall that a central element of that case is the very political exclusion that the Court has validated. If the denial of fundamental political rights is justified because of the "otherness" of noncitizens, then why is the state more constrained in the denial of discretionary subsidies like welfare?

The second limitation is equally puzzling. Recall the Court's endorsement of the "congruence" principle in the context of racial affirmative action. As the Court defined the principle, "equal protection analysis in the Fifth Amendment area [applicable

25. *Id.* at 104.

to the federal government] is the same as that under the Fourteenth Amendment [applicable to the states]."[26] Congruence might be reconciled with the Court's treatment of federal discrimination against noncitizens on the theory that the federal government has a legitimate (compelling?) interest in immigration and naturalization that the states lack. But even if this interest exists, it is hard to see how it justifies discrimination once noncitizens have immigrated. True, the government could entirely exclude noncitizens. But all equal protection arguments are vulnerable to "greater includes the lesser" type arguments. The government could also abolish public schools, but it hardly follows that it can operate segregated schools.

These weaknesses in the doctrine should not surprise us. They are the predictable consequence of a contradiction at the core of the equal protection clause. Our treatment of noncitizens brings to the fore the competing impulses toward the definition of an all-inclusive community and the need to limit the scope of equality. The Court's uneasy reconciliation of these impulses demonstrates what should, by now, be a familiar point: Equal protection analysis is much better at exposing tensions than resolving them.

Poor People

We have seen that although the Court has announced the "suspect" status of classifications based upon citizenship, it has nonetheless upheld

26. Adarand Constructors, Inc. v. Pena, 515 U.S. 200, 224 (1995).

many such classifications. There is something like the opposite pattern with regard to wealth classifications. The Court has strongly resisted the argument that classifications based upon wealth are suspect; yet it continues to exhibit considerable suspicion toward such classifications.

The problem of wealth classifications reintroduces the conflict between public- and private-regarding versions of constitutional law. As we shall see, claims of wealth discrimination usually involve the implicit assertion that there is a constitutional entitlement to government intervention—most often in the form of some sort of government subsidy. Because our constitutional tradition is dominated by a theory of negative rights, these claims are often unsuccessful. Yet the countertradition of positive liberty remains strong enough to occasionally make the case for subsidies seem persuasive.

At mid-twentieth century, the Warren Court flirted with the idea that wealth classifications were suspect. During this period, the Court invalidated the poll tax[27] and laws limiting the franchise to property holders.[28] It struck down durational residency requirements for receipt of welfare,[29] held that indigent criminal defendants were entitled to free trial transcripts on appeal[30] and to a free law-

27. *See* Harper v. Virginia State Board of Elections, 383 U.S. 663 (1966).

28. *See, e.g.,* Cipriano v. City of Houma, 395 U.S. 701 (1969).

29. *See* Shapiro v. Thompson, 394 U.S. 618 (1969).

30. *See* Griffin v. Illinois, 351 U.S. 12 (1956).

yer on a first appeal of right,[31] and held (on due process grounds) that the government could not prevent an indigent person from obtaining a divorce because of inability to pay court fees.[32] Some of the rhetoric in these cases was quite sweeping. For example, in Harper v. Virginia the Court wrote that "[l]ines drawn on the basis of wealth or property, like those of race, are traditionally disfavored."[33]

By the late 1970's, the Court seemed to move sharply away from this position. For example, in Maher v. Roe, in the course of denying the claim of indigent women to government subsidized abortions, the Court wrote the following:

An indigent woman desiring an abortion does not come within the limited category of disadvantaged classes so recognized by our cases. Nor does the fact that the impact of the regulation falls upon those who cannot pay lead to a different conclusion. In a sense, every denial of welfare to an indigent creates a wealth classification as compared to nonindigents who are able to pay for the desired goods or services. But this Court has never held that financial need alone identifies a suspect class for purposes of equal protection analysis.[34]

During the same period, the Court refused to extend the right of indigents to appellate lawyers

31. *See* Douglas v. California, 372 U.S. 353 (1963).
32. *See* Boddie v. Connecticut, 401 U.S. 371 (1971).
33. 383 U.S. 663, 668 (1966).
34. 432 U.S. 464, 470–71 (1977).

beyond the first appeal of right,[35] upheld the imposition of filing fees on indigents in ordinary civil litigation,[36] rejected an equal protection challenge to the unequal funding of school districts in poor areas,[37] and made clear that the Constitution did not guarantee the provision of "necessities" to the poor.[38]

Yet despite this retrenchment, the Court has not overruled any of its earlier decisions, and some have even been extended. For example, in more recent years, the Court has held that a state may not condition appeals from decrees terminating parental rights on the parent's ability to pay record preparation fees,[39] that a state must pay for psychiatric assistance for indigent criminal defendants when insanity is an issue,[40] and that the state must pay for a blood test for an indigent defendant in a paternity action.[41]

Should wealth be a suspect classification? There can be no doubt that poor people have less ability to defend themselves in the political process. The poor are often both discrete and insular, and poverty is at least sometimes an unchosen and immutable

35. *See, e.g.,* Ross v. Moffitt, 417 U.S. 600 (1974).

36. *See* United States v. Kras, 409 U.S. 434 (1973).

37. *See* San Antonio Independent School Dist. v. Rodriguez, 411 U.S. 1 (1973).

38. *See* Dandridge v. Williams, 397 U.S. 471 (1970); Lindsey v. Normet, 405 U.S. 56 (1972).

39. *See* M.L.B. v. S.L.J., 519 U.S. 102 (1996).

40. *See* Ake v. Oklahoma, 470 U.S. 68 (1985).

41. *See* Little v. Streater, 452 U.S. 1 (1981).

characteristic. Poor people are victimized by prejudice and by overbroad generalizations about them.
On the other hand, in a market economy, ability to
pay plays a central role in the allocation of goods
and services. The subsidization that suspect status
would mandate might erode incentives to work or
lead to inefficient allocations of goods and services.

To some degree, the argument about whether
wealth classifications are suspect is a distraction
from the real issue. To see the point, compare these
two cases. City A owns a municipal swimming pool,
but does not permit any residents of the city to
swim in it unless their family income exceeds
$20,000 per year. City B owns a similar pool and
charges $200 for a summer membership to cover
the cost of running the pool.

Surely, virtually all courts would hold that City
A's policy violates the equal protection clause, and
this would be true even if there were some rational
relationship between family income and, say, a pro-
pensity to commit crime or to litter. On the other
hand, few courts would invalidate City B's policy
even if the policy had the effect of preventing people
with less than a $20,000 annual income from using
the pool.

The difference between the constitutional status
of the two policies is not a difference between
rational basis review and heightened scrutiny. Instead, the difference is a consequence of the Washington v. Davis doctrine. Recall that after *Washington,* a policy that facially discriminates on a suspect

basis is subject to heightened scrutiny, but a facially neutral policy need survive only rational basis review even if it has an (unintended) discriminatory impact on a "discrete and insular minority." The difference between the policies of City A and City B is that City A's policy facially discriminates against the poor, whereas City B's policy produces only a discriminatory impact. Thus, the reason why the modern Court is hostile to most wealth discrimination claims is not because of the nonsuspect character of wealth discrimination, but because most such discrimination amounts to no more than the disproportionate impact created by the utilization of market pricing.

Occasionally, the Court has attempted to deny this fact. For example, in M.L.B. v. S.L.J.[42] the Court invalidated a requirement that litigants pay record preparation fees before appealing from decisions terminating parental rights. The state attempted to defend the fees on the theory that they, like the police application exam upheld in *Washington*, had no more than a disproportionate impact on the disadvantaged group. The Court dealt with this argument as follows:

> Sanctions of [this] genre ... are not merely *disproportionate* in impact. Rather, they are wholly contingent on one's ability to pay, and thus "visit different consequences on two categories of persons"; they apply to all indigents and do not reach anyone outside that class.[43]

42. 519 U.S. 102 (1996).

43. *Id.* at 126.

But this argument is unpersuasive. The inability to appeal decisions terminating parental rights does not "apply to all indigents." For example, it does not apply to indigents whose friends give them the money to pay the fees. Nor is it true that market pricing affects only indigents. It affects anyone who, for whatever reason, does not pay the fee. Moreover, even if the policy did affect only indigents, this fact would not lead to heightened scrutiny according to standard equal protection doctrine. Only women can become pregnant, yet the Court has held that discrimination against pregnant persons is not gender discrimination.

Rather than being reconcilable with Washington v. Davis, the Court's scattered decisions protecting the poor demonstrate a lingering unease with the decision. *Washington* starts with the baseline of distributions produced by the private sphere. When the government forces a downward departure from this baseline, its conduct may be suspect, but it has no constitutional obligation to raise people above the baseline through the provision of subsidies.

Thus, the *Washington* approach depends on a sharp distinction between public and private, or, to say the same thing in a different way, between penalties and failures to subsidize. But this distinction is fragile. There is a sense in which all market transactions occur within a context created by various government interventions. Without some sort of government interventions, in the form of contract and property law for example, markets could not function. Therefore, it is often difficult to distinguish between the functioning of a "private" market, and government distortions of that market.

Consider, for example, the problem faced by indigent criminal defendants who lack the funds to prosecute an appeal. When the Court held that the failure to provide counsel denied equal protection, Justice John Harlan dissented. He argued that

> [a]ll that [the state] has done is to fail to alleviate the consequences of differences in economic circumstances that exist wholly apart from any state action. . . .

> [T]he issue here is not the typical equal protection question of the reasonableness of a 'classification' on the basis of which the State has imposed legal disabilities, but rather the reasonableness of the State's failure to remove natural disabilities.[44]

There is a sense in which this logic is unassailable, but another sense in which it is question begging. Criminal prosecutions, after all, are hardly "natural disabilities." In what sense is the criminal prosecution that brings about the need for a lawyer "wholly apart from any state action?" Because it seemed to the majority that criminal prosecutions were, obviously, government intervention designed to make things worse, rather than a subsidy designed to make things better, the Court thought that a lawyer was constitutionally mandated.

44. Griffin v. Illinois, 351 U.S. 12, 34–36 (1956) (Harlan, J., dissenting).

The trouble with this argument, though, is that it has no clear stopping point. There is also a sense in which government "intervention"—the Federal Reserve Board's regulation of interest rates, for example, or the fiscal and trade policies pursued by Congress and the President—lead to unemployment and homelessness. Does it follow that the government has an affirmative constitutional obligation to remedy these conditions? The fragility of the public-private distinction puts at risk the central building blocks of contemporary constitutional law. For this reason, the Court must find a stopping point, whether it is clear or not. It therefore codes some kinds of government action as intervention, which trigger equal protection analysis, and some kinds as mere failures to subsidize, which are left to the political branches.

The Future of Suspect Classification Analysis

In recent years, the Court has strongly resisted calls to expand the category of "discrete and insular minorities" entitled to heightened judicial scrutiny of statutes that facially disadvantage them. For example, it has rejected arguments that the mentally retarded[45] or the aged[46] are such minorities. Moreover, the Court's "consistency" principle, which extends the same protection to majorities that is extended to minorities, brings into question

45. *See* City of Cleburne v. Cleburne Living Center, 473 U.S. 432 (1985).

46. *See* Massachusetts Board of Retirement v. Murgia, 427 U.S. 307 (1976).

the entire enterprise of providing special protection for disadvantaged groups.

One might suppose that these changes have limited the outward push of equal protection analysis and, indeed, to some extent, they have. The Court seems much less ready to question political decisions harming identifiable "disadvantaged" groups than it was in the last century.

Yet at the same time that the Court has halted the proliferation of groups entitled to special judicial protection, it has also blurred the once sharp distinction between strict scrutiny and rational basis review. At one time, strict scrutiny meant more or less automatic invalidation, while rational basis review meant more or less automatic deference to political decisions. Today, the Court has experimented with various forms of intermediate review—most prominently in the context of gender, but also, occasionally, with regard to classifications disadvantaging nonmarital children.[47] Moreover, the automatic consequences that once flowed from the categorization are now more ambiguous. For example, in the very decision holding that discrimination against the mentally retarded did not trigger strict scrutiny, the Court, purporting to use rational basis review, nonetheless invalidated the challenged practice.[48] Similarly, we have seen in this chapter that the Court sometimes strikes down wealth classifica-

47. *See, e.g.,* Levy v. Louisiana, 391 U.S. 68 (1968); Gomez v. Perez, 409 U.S. 535 (1973).

48. *See* City of Cleburne v. Cleburne Living Center, 473 U.S. 432 (1985).

tions even though it has refused to denominate these classifications as "suspect." Conversely, the Court often upholds alienage classifications even though these are, supposedly, suspect.

This blurring of boundaries, in turn, raises questions as to whether the Court's analytic structure is really doing the work intended for it. A relatively rigid structure is attractive because it seems to constrain discretion and prevent equal protection judgments from becoming no more than intuitive, ad hoc judgments about the fairness of legislative classifications. But the problem of equality is too vexing, and the solution too contradictory, to be captured by any formal test. As a result, the Court is now vulnerable to the charge that the formal structure masks a series of undefended, unprincipled, perhaps even random, interventions.

A related criticism is that the very effort to pick particular groups meriting special judicial attention seems to imply that when these groups are not involved, the political system more or less automatically satisfies the demands of equality. Put differently, the Court's approach suggests that, aside from exceptional cases dealt with by heightened scrutiny, we need not much worry about the inequalities in our society. If one thinks that the equal protection clause, and the riddle of equality that lies behind it, best serve their purposes when they unsettle the outcome of ordinary politics, then one is bound to be dissatisfied with this approach.

These problems, in turn, raise questions about whether the effort to locate and define particular groups vulnerable to unequal treatment makes sense. An alternative might focus on *what* is denied, rather than *who* is victimized by the denial. The Court has experimented with this approach, as well, and that experiment is the subject of the next chapter.

CHAPTER TEN

EQUAL PROTECTION AND FUNDAMENTAL RIGHTS

As we have seen, most equal protection doctrine is organized around the identification of groups entitled to special judicial protection against discrimination. But there is another way to approach the problem. Instead of asking which groups have been disadvantaged, we might inquire into the importance of what has been taken away from them. When the Court analyzes cases from this perspective, it heightens the level of scrutiny when a group—any group—is denied something that is of special significance. This approach is sometimes referred to as "substantive equal protection" because it focuses on the substantive right or benefit at issue, and sometimes called the "fundamental rights" strand of equal protection because it involves an effort to define the kinds of fundamental rights that should heighten scrutiny.

An Example, Two Problems, and a Proposed Solution

Skinner v. Oklahoma,[1] decided in 1942, provides an early example of this approach. The Oklahoma Habitual Criminal Sterilization Act defined a "ha-

1.   316 U.S. 535 (1942).

bitual criminal" as a person who had been convicted of three or more crimes "amounting to felonies involving moral turpitude." The statute specifically excluded from this category "offenses arising out of the violation of the prohibitory laws, revenue acts, embezzlement, or political offenses." If a judge determined that a person was a habitual criminal, the person was to be "rendered sexually sterile" if the operation could be performed without "detriment to his or her general health."[2]

In an opinion written by Justice William Douglas, the Court held that the statute violated the equal protection clause because it subjected some, but not all, convicted criminals to sterilization. For example,

A person who enters a chicken coop and steals chickens commits a felony and he may be sterilized if he is thrice convicted. If, however, he is a bailee of the property and fraudulently appropriates it, he is an embezzler. Hence, no matter how habitual his proclivities for embezzlement are and no matter how often his conviction, he may not be sterilized.[3]

Two points are noteworthy about the Court's approach. First, the Court did not hold that there was a substantive constitutional right to procreate. The Court had rejected such a claim in its earlier decision in Buck v. Bell,[4] and *Skinner* specifically

2. *Id.* at 537.

3. *Id.* at 539.

4. 274 U.S. 200 (1927).

declined to reach the question whether *Buck* should be overruled. Second, the Court did not hold that the statute discriminated against a suspect class. On the contrary, the classification of criminals into different groups and providing different punishment for those groups was subject to only the most minimal scrutiny.

> Thus, if we had here only a question as to a State's classification of crimes, such as embezzlement or larceny, no substantial federal question would be raised. For a State is not constrained in the exercise of its police power to ignore experience which marks a class of offenders or a family of offenses for special treatment. Nor is it prevented by the equal protection clause from confining "its restrictions to those classes of cases where the need is deemed to be clearest."[5]

Yet despite the fact that there was no substantive constitutional right at stake and that Oklahoma had not discriminated along suspect lines, the Court held that the statute was subject to strict scrutiny. The reason for the heightened scrutiny was that

> We are dealing here with legislation which involves one of the basic civil rights of man. Marriage and procreation are fundamental to the very existence and survival of the race. The power to sterilize, if exercised, may have subtle, far-reaching and devastating effects. In evil or reckless hands it can cause races or types which are inimical to the dominant group to wither and disap-

5. 316 U.S. at 540.

pear. There is no redemption for the individual whom the law touches.... We mention these matters not to reexamine the scope of the police power of the States. We advert to them merely in emphasis of our view that strict scrutiny of the classification which a State makes in a sterilization law is essential, lest unwittingly or otherwise invidious discriminations are made against groups or types of individuals in violation of the constitutional guaranty of just and equal laws.[6]

Justice Douglas's approach to *Skinner* is illuminated by some background historical facts, which are hinted at but nowhere explicitly delineated in the opinion itself. Throughout the late nineteenth and early twentieth century, eugenics—the practice of controlling human reproduction so as to improve the gene pool and eliminate "antisocial" behavior— was widely accepted in "progressive" circles. By 1942, this view was beginning to change. The example of Nazi Germany, which explicitly and brutally embraced eugenics as a method of achieving racial purity, caused many Americans to question their earlier endorsement of the practice. In this regard, it is worth noting how the suspect classification and fundamental rights strands of equal protection analysis reinforce each other in cases like *Skinner*. It is true that *Skinner* itself did not involve a suspect classification. But, as Justice Douglas expressly acknowledged, one reason for treating procreation as a fundamental right is the risk that eugenic policies might be utilized against racial or

6. *Id.* at 541.

other disfavored minorities, as they had been in Germany.

One might suppose that emerging opposition to eugenics would cause the Court to overrule *Buck* and announce a substantive constitutional right to procreate, but here a second background fact becomes important. *Skinner* was decided only a few years after the Court had disowned its earlier decision in Lochner v. New York[7] and rejected the idea that it could use the vague language of the due process clause to provide special substantive protection for nontextual rights.

Given this background, it is not surprising that the Court was highly suspicious of forced sterilization and that it expressed this suspicion in the language of equal protection, rather than substantive due process. Still, this choice created two problems that have continued to dog the fundamental rights strand of equal protection throughout its history.

The first problem is how the Court can legitimately determine which rights are sufficiently "fundamental" to trigger heightened scrutiny. After all, either a right is protected by some substantive constitutional provision (e.g., the right to free speech or the free exercise of religion) or it is not. If the right already receives substantive constitutional protection, then, it would seem, the equal protection clause has no work to do. An invasion of the right is unconstitutional because of the substantive

7.   198 U.S. 45 (1905).

protection even if (indeed, especially if) *everyone* is denied it. Alternatively, if the framers of the Constitution chose not to protect a particular right, then what legitimate basis does the Court have for providing such protection through heightened scrutiny?

This first problem naturally leads to a second: How is the fundamental rights strand of equal protection different from the discredited *Lochner* doctrine? Liberals like Justice Douglas criticized the *Lochner* Court for invading the legislative sphere by overturning political decisions without any firm support in constitutional text. Doesn't substantive equal protection amount to the same thing?

There is a cynical answer to both these questions: Liberals who attacked *Lochner* favored judicial restraint when their opponents controlled the Court, but opposed it as soon as they gained control. Under the figleaf of equal protection rhetoric, liberals were just as ready as their conservative opponents to single out their own favored rights for protection.

There is no doubt some truth to the cynical explanation. Throughout the Court's history, dissenting justices have regularly decried judicial activism, only to engage in it themselves when they gained majority status. It turns out, though, that there is another, less cynical, explanation that also has considerable analytic power. The explanation requires reconceptualizing the argument over *Lochner* as involving a dispute about the appropriate boundaries of the public and private spheres, rather than about the boundaries of judicial and legislative power. On this view, the *Lochner* Court was devoted to expanding a private sphere free from public regulation. It used the due process clause to protect private markets because it equated nongovernmental decisions with individual freedom. In contrast, substantive equal protection was about protection of a public sphere from private invasion. It used the equal protection clause to promote government intervention because it equated such intervention with control over oppressive private power.

Even if this conceptualization of the problem is correct, it hardly follows that *Lochner* was wrong and *Skinner* was right. *Lochner* might be right and *Skinner* wrong if one thinks that human freedom is, indeed, best protected in a private sphere. Alternatively, both *Lochner* and *Skinner* might be wrong if one thinks that courts simply have no business interfering with legislative judgments absent clear constitutional text. What does follow from this reconceptualization, however, is that advocates of substantive equal protection are not necessarily hypocrites. Their position is authentically different from that of *Lochner*'s defenders because it is public- rather than private-regarding.

Ironically, *Skinner* itself provides relatively weak support for this reconceptualization. The right at stake in *Skinner*—procreation—seems quintessentially private. There are, after all, many public-regarding reasons why a legislature might want to limit reproduction. Some people are not good parents, and their poor parenting skills produce large social costs. Others may be unable to afford additional children, who end up being supported at public expense. Perhaps overpopulation and pressure on resources argue for restrictions on reproductive freedom. If any of these worries are valid, limits on procreation might be consistent with the norm of rational equality. A right to procreate stands in opposition to these public-regarding arguments. It is more consistent with the goals of ethical equality in the sense that enforced limits on reproduction might be motivated by a rejection of the equal worth of every individual. What a right to procreate amounts to is a claim that individuals need not defend this fundamental freedom by reference to the public good but, instead, can claim it as an aspect of individual personhood, whether or not it contributes to collective well-being.

As we shall see, the public-regarding character of substantive equal protection became more apparent when the Court turned to other rights triggering heightened scrutiny. Even in *Skinner*, however, the Court's choice of equal protection, rather than due process methodology has consequences for the struggle between public and private. Recall Justice Robert Jackson's argument in Railway Express Agency v. New York,[8] discussed in Chapter Three, about the difference between equal protection and due process. As Jackson pointed out, the effect of a decision holding that a government program violates substantive due process is to completely disable the public sphere. The government is simply

8. 336 U.S. 106 (1949).

prevented from pursuing the program in question. In contrast, at least in theory, the consequence of an equal protection invalidation is to allow the government to pursue the program, so long as it disadvantages a broader class. Thus, *Skinner* ostensibly left the government free to adopt a eugenics policy, so long as it applied the policy "equally" to embezzlers as well as larcenists.

If one thinks of procreation as a private right, this consequence of equal protection invalidation seems odd. Why does it make things better, rather than worse, to deny more people the right? The consequence seems less odd if one understands that equal protection invalidation is designed to promote public debate rather than private autonomy. Justice Antonin Scalia explained the difference in a concurring opinion rejecting a substantive due process attack on a statute restricting the "right to die."

> Are there ... no reasonable and humane limits that ought not to be exceeded in requiring an individual to preserve his own life? There obviously are, but they are not set forth in the Due Process Clause. What assures us that those limits will not be exceeded is the same constitutional guarantee that is the source of most of our protection—what protects us, for example, from being assessed a tax of 100% of our income above the subsistence level, from being forbidden to drive cars, or from being required to send our children to school for 10 hours a day, none of which horribles is categorically prohibited by the Constitution. Our salvation is the Equal Protec-

tion Clause, which requires the democratic majority to accept for themselves and their loved ones what they impose on you and me.[9]

Put differently, whereas a due process invalidation protects private decisions, the equal protection clause forces a collective resolution. Instead of disabling government, equal protection provides a guarantee that government decisions are truly public. Equal protection analysis is democracy forcing in the sense that it prevents a dominant private group from seizing public institutions and using them for private purposes.

As already noted, *Skinner* itself provides relatively weak support for a public conception of the equal protection clause. Indeed, the Court has frequently cited *Skinner* in subsequent due process decisions emphasizing the private character of reproductive decisions. However, when the Court turned to the protection of other fundamental rights under the equal protection clause, the public character of its intervention became more apparent.

The Right to Vote

Perhaps the most far-reaching of the Court's decisions heightening judicial scrutiny because of the nature of the restricted right concern the franchise. The Constitution does not explicitly guarantee a right to vote in state elections or in elections for President. It does provide that Congressmen and Senators shall be selected by the "People," and that

9. Cruzan v. Director, Missouri Dept. of Public Health, 497 U.S. 261, 300 (1990) (Scalia, J., concurring).

those voting "shall have the Qualifications requisite for Electors of the most numerous branch of the State legislatures."[10] Moreover, amendments to the Constitution prohibit limitations on the right to vote based upon race,[11] gender,[12] age (for those older than 18),[13] or (in the case of federal elections) failure to pay a poll tax.[14] However, these provisions might be read as necessary only because there is no general right to vote. This interpretation is reinforced by the second section of the fourteenth amendment, which seems to presuppose that states may legally restrict the right to vote. The section provides that if a state chooses to enact such restrictions, its representation in the House of Representatives shall be proportionally reduced.

Despite these textual embarrassments, the Court declared the right to vote "fundamental" and, starting in the 1960's, began strictly scrutinizing statutes that apportioned the franchise unequally. For example, in Harper v. Virginia State Board of Elections,[15] the Court invalidated a Virginia statute conditioning the right to vote on payment of a $1.50 poll tax. (As noted above, a constitutional amendment, enacted two years before *Harper* banned the poll tax in federal elections. *Harper* extended the

10. *See* U.S. Const., Art I, § 2, cl. 1; U.S. Const. Amend. XVII, § 1.

11. *Id.* at Amend. XV.

12. *Id.* at Amend. XIX.

13. *Id.* at Amend. XXVI.

14. *Id.* at Amend. XXIV.

15. 383 U.S. 663 (1966).

ban to state elections.) Justice Douglas, the author of *Skinner*, again spoke for the Court. As in *Skinner,* he expressly declined to find that there was a substantive constitutional right to vote. Instead, he argued that "once the franchise is granted to the electorate, lines may not be drawn which are inconsistent with the Equal Protection Clause of the Fourteenth Amendment."[16]

The Court advanced two reasons why the poll tax was subject to heightened scrutiny. First, Justice Douglas asserted that "[l]ines drawn on the basis of wealth or property, like those of race are traditionally disfavored."[17] This branch of the opinion, which sounds in suspect class analysis, is problematic. As explained in Chapter Nine, the poll tax does not discriminate facially on the basis of wealth, but only on the basis of payment of the tax. Even if one were concerned that the tax has a disproportionate impact on poor people, this concern does not justify the Court's invalidation of the tax as applied to rich people. And if it were really true that fee payment requirements constituted suspect wealth classifications, such a holding could not be confined to the poll tax. For example, licensing fees for automobile registration and property taxes on residences would also be drawn into question.

The Court's holding is more defensible on the second argument Justice Douglas advanced. Citing *Skinner*, Douglas observed that "We have long been mindful that where fundamental rights and liber-

16. *Id.* at 665.
17. *Id.* at 668.

ties are asserted under the Equal Protection Clause, classifications which might invade or restrain them must be closely scrutinized and carefully confined" and that "the right to vote is too precious, too fundamental to be so burdened or conditioned."[18]

Why is the right to vote fundamental? *Harper* is quite cryptic on this point, but the Court provided a somewhat fuller explanation in Kramer v. Union Free School District[19] where it invalidated a statute limiting the franchise in school district elections to people who owned or leased taxable property within the district and parents of children enrolled in the district. According to Chief Justice Earl Warren, strict scrutiny of the statute was required because

> Statutes granting the franchise to residents on a selective basis always pose the danger of denying some citizens any effective voice in the governmental affairs which substantially affect their lives....
>
> The presumption of constitutionality and the approval given "rational" classifications in other types of enactments are based on an assumption that the institutions of state government are structured so as to represent fairly all the people. However, when the challenge to the statute is in effect a challenge of this basic assumption, the assumption can no longer serve as the basis for presuming constitutionality.[20]

18. *Id.* at 670.

19. 395 U.S. 621 (1969).

20. *Id.* at 626–27.

It is easy to see how these conclusions flow from the public-regarding character of equal protection analysis. Precisely because the Court believed that public institutions should resolve our disputes, it was necessary to insure that these institutions were truly public. Limitations on the right to vote were suspect because they left these institutions as the preserve of only some of the people, instead of a forum in which all of the people could deliberate over the public good.

There is also a more subtle sense in which both *Harper* and *Kramer* reflect public values. Recall that *Harper* invalidated Virginia's $1.50 poll tax, even as applied to rich people. Surely, a $1.50 charge for voting is a trivial concern to a millionaire. Why should this sort of minor impediment trigger heightened scrutiny? Perhaps the difficulty with the charge is that, on a symbolic level, it encourages us to think of voting in the same way that we think of market transactions.

Suppose, for example, that someone must decide whether to pay $1.50 for a tube of toothpaste. Almost everyone makes this decision in a private-regarding fashion. The only relevant question is whether the purchaser would prefer to have the toothpaste or the $1.50. If people thought about voting in the same way, virtually no one would vote. On the one hand, voting can be quite inconvenient. On the other, there is a trivial chance that a single vote will change the outcome. Voting makes sense only as a form of symbolic identification with a public community. Indeed, its public character is emphasized by the irrationality of the act from a private perspective. But if we charged money for voting, like we do for toothpaste, the act of voting might come to be seen as a private purchase, rather than an affirmation of public solidarity.

Similarly, from a private point of view, the restrictions struck down in *Kramer* seem entirely sensible. Some people have more at stake in an election than others. If I am a taxpayer or a parent, from a private point of view, it may matter a great deal who is elected to the school board. If you are neither, the election might matter to you no more than my choice of toothpaste. On this view, then, if you insist upon voting, you are engaged in officious intermeddling in something that is none of your business. It is even possible to construct an argument that providing you and me with the same vote denies my right to equal protection.

But this argument is premised on the assumption that when people vote, they are expressing (or should express) only private-regarding preferences. Of course, voters do express such preferences to some extent, but there is also some evidence that people sometimes shift their preference structures when they regard themselves as engaged in civic obligation. Some people vote for candidates who promise to raise their own taxes even though they never make voluntary contributions to the Internal Revenue Service when filling out their tax returns. Indeed, it might even be argued that the entire experiment in representative government is premised on the faith that voters will at least occasionally be able to transcend their private preferences so as to do what is best for the community.

In any event, *Kramer* seems to be premised on such an assumption. If voters are no more than private consumers of public policy, then it makes sense to restrict the franchise to the people doing the consuming. But if voting constitutes a public declaration of solidarity and identification with a community, then all members of the community should share the franchise equally.

It must be conceded that *Harper* and *Kramer* are open to different interpretations. The *Kramer* Court expressly reserved the question whether a state "in some circumstances might limit the exercise of the franchise to those 'primarily interested' or 'primarily affected.' "[21] In later cases, the Court has upheld franchise limitations for limited purpose government units. For example, in Salyer Land Co. v. Tulare Lake Basin Water Storage District,[22] the Court upheld a statute permitting only landowners to vote for representatives to districts that provided water for farmers in the district. And in Holt Civic Club v. City of Tuscaloosa,[23] the Court held that the extraterritorial application of a municipality's laws did not create a constitutional right to vote in the municipality's elections.

Yet these holdings are also consistent with a public-regarding reading of *Harper* and *Kramer*.

21. *Id.* at 632.

22. 410 U.S. 719 (1973).

23. 439 U.S. 60 (1978).

Saylor Land Company might be explained precisely on the ground that special purpose governmental units exercising no general governmental power do not constitute true public communities. *Holt* can be read as disavowing the view that the franchise depends upon the impact of governmental action on particular individuals. Even though it was conceded that the municipality's actions had such an impact, it was constitutional to withhold the franchise because the impacted individuals were not part of the political community.

Vote Dilution

Harper and *Kramer* involved the complete denial of the franchise to classes of individuals. But providing everyone with the formal right to vote does not guarantee political equality. There are more subtle ways of limiting electoral power. For years, the malapportionment of legislative districts was a primary source of voting inequality. To be sure, malapportioned districts left every individual with the formal right to vote. (In this sense, the "one-person/one vote" slogan often associated with the Court's reapportionment decisions is misleading.) But these votes reflected disproportionate electoral power because some districts had many more residents than others.

Until 1962, the Court treated issues surrounding legislative districting as a nonjusticiable political question.[24] In that year, however, it decided Baker v. Carr,[25] which overruled its earlier precedent and

24. *See* Colegrove v. Green, 328 U.S. 549 (1946).

25. 369 U.S. 186 (1962).

indicated that claims of malapportionment might give rise to judicially enforceable remedies. Two years later, in Reynolds v. Sims,[26] the Court considered claims that one or both branches of state legislatures in six states were so malapportioned as to deny equal protection. In a landmark decision authored by Chief Justice Warren, the Court held that

the Equal Protection Clause requires that the seats in both houses of a bicameral state legislature must be apportioned on a population basis. Simply stated, an individual's right to vote for state legislators is unconstitutionally impaired when its weight is in a substantial fashion diluted when compared with votes of citizens living in other parts of the State.[27]

The evident simplicity of this requirement obscured a host of difficulties. One problem was the extent of deviation that was constitutionally permissible. Obviously, a requirement of absolute equality in population is not practical. The *Reynolds* Court recognized this fact, but insisted on "an honest and good faith effort"[28] to construct districts of equal population. While some deviation in pursuit of a "rational state policy"[29] was permissible, the deviation could not be based upon history, economic, or other group interests, or the geographical size of the district. Indeed, the only consideration mentioned

26. 377 U.S. 533 (1964).

27. *Id.* at 568.

28. *Id.* at 577.

29. *Id.* at 579.

by the Court that would justify a deviation was the need to keep political subdivisions intact, and, even here, the Court made clear that if "population [were] submerged as the controlling consideration,"[30] a substantial deviation would be impermissible.

In later cases, the Court has used the concept of maximum percentage deviation to put flesh on these requirements. To derive this number, one starts with the ideal distribution that would produce districts of exactly equal population. One then measures the percentage by which the largest and smallest districts deviate from this goal and sums the two percentages. In the case of federal congressional districting, the Court has invalidated plans with maximum deviations of as little as 0.7%,[31] but it has been a good deal more lenient in cases involving districting for state legislatures. In the state context, the Court has recognized a category of "minor" deviations of under 10% that require no justification at all.[32] Moreover, it has upheld even larger deviations where a "rational" justification, such as keeping districts compact and contiguous or protecting the seats of incumbents, is offered.[33]

Reynolds and its progeny are sometimes criticized for paying obsessive attention to very small population differences. The criticism is not without force, especially when one remembers that the census

30. *Id.* at 581.

31. *See* Karcher v. Daggett, 462 U.S. 725 (1983).

32. *See* Brown v. Thomson, 462 U.S. 835 (1983).

33. *See, e.g.,* Mahan v. Howell, 410 U.S. 315 (1973).

data upon which the numbers are based is somewhat inaccurate to begin with and is only revised once per decade. The Court has also paid scant attention to whether the relevant numbers are total population, voting population, or population eligible to vote.

On the other hand, the Court's insistence upon a relatively clear, bright-line rule has allowed it to implement the *Reynolds'* requirement, while largely avoiding the "political thicket" that the *Reynolds* dissenters feared. In fact, *Reynolds* has been a success story, at least on the Court's own terms. Although the initial decision met with considerable opposition, today it is relatively uncontroversial, and districts are no longer of the wildly divergent population sizes that were common a half century ago.

The virtue of a formal rule is that it is easy to implement. The problem with a formal rule is that it is easy to evade. Thus, although the *Reynolds* Court succeeded in implementing the requirement of equal population districting, it is far less clear that the decision has produced real equality in political power. One difficulty is that voting is not the only, and not even the most important, method through which political power is exercised. Does anyone suppose that a law professor who lives in Washington, D.C. (and therefore cannot vote for a Senator or Representative) has less political power than a poor person living in an inner city slum? Political power is exercised not just at the ballot box, but also through campaign contributions, letters to the editor of newspapers, citizen mobilization efforts, and community engagement.

The deeper inequalities in these other spheres may be beyond judicial remedy, but even with regard to legislative districting, *Reynolds* left important loopholes in place. Perhaps the most significant of these is the dilemma posed by winner-take-all election systems. Suppose, for example, that a state consists of two political groups—the A's, who make up 60% of the population, and the B's, who make up 40%. If the A's and the B's are spread uniformly throughout the state, geographical districting with a winner-take-all system in each district will result in a legislature consisting entirely of A's. This outcome arguably leaves the B's with no political power at all despite their substantial representation among the electorate. On the other hand, if all (or virtually all) of the A's are concentrated in a few districts, the B's might end up with most of the seats, even though they have only a minority of the population.

The Court's efforts to deal with this problem have not been entirely successful. One way to think about the issue is through the lens of suspect classification analysis. Suppose that either the A's or the B's consist of a class that triggers heightened scrutiny. Then, as explained in Chapter Five, the question will be whether facially neutral districting intentionally understates the voting strength of this group (in which case it will be strictly scrutinized and almost certainly invalidated) or whether it is simply the unintended byproduct of some other objective (in which case it is subject to only low-level scrutiny and almost certainly will be affirmed).

For example, in Gomillion v. Lightfoot,[34] discussed in Chapter Five, the Court held that the redrawing of a city's municipal boundaries so as to exclude virtually all African American voters from the City had the purpose and effect of reducing their voting power and, accordingly, was unconstitutional.

Conversely, in City of Mobile v. Bolden,[35] the Court considered a challenge to Mobile's City Commission, which consisted of three commissioners, all of whom were elected at large. Since there was racial bloc-voting and Mobile had a substantial African American minority, if the commissioners had been elected by district, there almost certainly would have been some African American representation. In fact, the Commission had never had an African American member. Nonetheless, the Court rejected the challenge to at large voting because, in the (somewhat implausible) view of a plurality of the Justices, the plaintiffs had failed to show that the system "was 'conceived or operated as [a] purposeful device to further racial ... discrimination.' "[36]

Suppose, though, that a particular voting system does not discriminate along suspect lines? One might think that the fundamental character of the

34. 364 U.S. 339 (1960).

35. 446 U.S. 55 (1980).

36. *Id.* at 66.

right to vote would nonetheless trigger heightened scrutiny of vote dilution. After all, there was no showing of suspect class discrimination in *Kramer* or *Reynolds*.

The Court has flirted with the idea that the fundamentality of the right to vote might lead to heightened scrutiny, but it has not fully embraced it. It set out its basic approach in Davis v. Bandemer,[37] a case involving a challenge to Indiana's legislative apportionment scheme. The scheme, drafted entirely by Republican members of the legislature, was clearly designed to understate Democratic representation. Although Democrats ended up receiving 51.9% of the total vote for House seats, and 53.1% of the total Senate vote, Democratic candidates won in only forty-three of the 100 House races and in only thirteen of the twenty-five Senate races.

Justice Byron White, who announced the Court's judgment, conceded the obvious: that the voting scheme had the purpose of discriminating against Democratic voters. Indeed, he pointed out, so long as politicians are in charge of drawing district lines, they will almost always be drawn at least in some measure in order to achieve political purposes. He nonetheless rejected the equal protection challenge because the scheme did not produce an unconstitutional effect. This was so, in Justice White's opinion, because the Constitution does not require proportional representation of groups. Instead, he argued, the primary protection for losers in elections is their ability to exercise influence on

37. 478 U.S. 109 (1986).

the winners. At first, this idea may seem very strange, but an understanding of the nature of gerrymandering may make it more plausible.

An effort to dilute the strength of substantial minorities by spreading them among districts will usually result in each district having a large number of losing voters in it. But the more minorities are diluted in this fashion, the more numerous they will be within each district. The result will be that the district will be contested to some degree, and the incumbent will be unable to ignore altogether the desires of the losing voters. Alternatively, districts might be gerrymandered by "packing" rather than "diluting" minorities. This strategy involves putting most of the minorities in a few districts. Packing leaves the other districts "safe" for the majority, but it does so at the cost of also creating a certain number of "safe" seats for the minority.

For these reasons, the ability of the majority to engage in gerrymandering is self-limiting. However, it did not follow for Justice White that there were no constitutional limits on political gerrymandering. Although the Indiana legislature had not exceeded these limits, Justice White wrote that the limits would be exceeded

wheel the electoral system substantially disadvantages certain voters in their opportunity to influence the political process effectively. In this context, such a finding of unconstitutionality must be supported by evidence of continued frustration of the will of a majority of the voters or effective denial of a minority of voters of a fair chance to influence the political process.[38]

As a practical matter, despite the Court's denial, this standard amounts to an insistence on a kind of loose proportionality. Some political gerrymandering is permissible, but when "the electoral system is arranged in a manner that will consistently degrade a voter's or a group of voters' influence on the political process as a whole,"[39] a constitutional violation has been made out.

Suppose that a jurisdiction decides to go beyond the constitutional minimum by deliberately creating safe seats so as to proportionally reflect the voting strength of a minority? It is at this point that the intersection of the fundamental rights and suspect class strands of equal protection produces results that are difficult to defend. On the one hand, *Davis* suggests that, from a fundamental rights perspective, there is no problem with a jurisdiction voluntarily agreeing to a "political fairness" principle that insures equal representation for minority groups.[40] True, such a system denies minorities *within the gerrymandered district* a chance to elect a representative reflecting their views, but this is a price that must be paid for insuring equality of representation *throughout the state*. It would be ironic if the equality requirement prevented a jurisdiction from insuring this equal representation.

38. *Id.* at 133.

39. *Id.* at 110.

40. *Id.* at 124.

Suppose, though that the minority is not just an ordinary group, but one that triggers heightened scrutiny? At this point, suspect class analysis kicks in. As we saw in Chapter Six, the Court has held that districting deliberately designed to produce "fair" representation for racial minorities is constitutionally suspect, at least when the use of race leads to the disregard of ordinary districting principles. As should be readily apparent, the intersection of these two lines of authority leads to a paradoxical conclusion: Districting designed to protect the interests of groups best able to protect themselves in the political process is relatively immune from constitutional challenge, whereas districting protecting "discrete and insular minorities" from lack of representation is constitutionally suspect.

Matters are further complicated by the Court's famous (some would say infamous) decision in Bush v. Gore.[41] As almost everyone knows, the 2000 presidential election ended in a virtual tie, with the outcome hinging on the excruciatingly close results in Florida. After several weeks of frenzied recounting and litigation, the Florida Supreme Court ordered a state-wide manual recount of ballots for which no vote had registered during the machine count.

In two intensely controversial 5–4 per curiam decisions, the Supreme Court first stayed[42] and then reversed[43] this order. In the second decision, the

41. 531 U.S. 98 (2000).

42. *See* Bush v. Gore, 531 U.S. 1046 (2000).

43. *See* Bush v. Gore, 531 U.S. 98 (2000).

Court held that the recount violated the equal protection clause because "[t]he recount mechanisms ... do not satisfy the minimum requirement for non-arbitrary treatment of voters necessary to secure the fundamental right [to vote]."[44]

The Florida Court had ordered officials conducting the recount to be guided by the "intent of the voter." The Supreme Court thought that this standard was "unobjectionable as an abstract proposition and a starting principle," but that this yardstick was insufficient "in the absence of specific standards to ensure its equal application."[45] By not providing such standards, the Florida Court had allowed individual counties to use different tests to determine what was a legal vote. Indeed, in some places different tests were used in the same county. According to the Court, these features of the recount were "inconsistent with the minimum procedures necessary to protect the fundamental right of each voter in the special instance of a statewide recount under the authority of a single state judicial officer."[46]

The Court's decision in *Bush* was intensely controversial and gave rise to suspicions that it was politically motivated, especially because the 5–4 lineup seemed to track the Court's ideological fault line. The Court contributed to these suspicions by going out of its way to attempt to limit the force of the holding to the case before it. According to the

44. *Id.* at 105.
45. *Id.* at 105.
46. *Id.* at 109.

per curiam opinion, its analysis was "limited to the present circumstances, for the problem of equal protection in election processes generally presents many complexities."[47]

If *Bush* was indeed a political decision, then it is likely to contribute little to doctrinal development. If we are to take the Court's reasoning seriously, however, it could be quite important. Since there was no allegation of discrimination against a suspect class in *Bush*, the case seems to stand for the proposition that the fundamentality of the right to vote alone triggers heightened scrutiny. Such a holding is in serious tension with *City of Mobile*, where the Court declined to utilize heightened scrutiny in the absence of a showing that a class of voters was deliberately disadvantaged, and with *Bandemer*, which held that even deliberate disadvantagement was not unconstitutional unless there was continued frustration of the principle of fair representation. Moreover, if local variation in vote counting methods is subject to strict scrutiny, then it is unclear why it was the Florida recount, rather than the underlying election, that violated equal protection. Like most states, Florida has a decentralized system of election administration, with different counties using different equipment with different error rates and different standards for judging the validity of a ballot.

Perhaps local control is a sufficiently compelling interest to justify these deviations. The Court hinted as much when it observed that

47. *Id.*

> [t]he question before the Court is not whether local entities, in the exercise of their expertise, may develop different systems for implementing elections. Instead, we are presented with a situation where a state court with the power to assure uniformity has ordered a statewide recount with minimal procedural safeguards.[48]

But this distinction seems unconvincing. Surely a state court should be allowed to displace only so much of a statutory scheme as is necessary to provide a remedy. If local control is a sufficiently compelling interest to justify statewide statutes that permit discrimination between residents living in different parts of the state, then, it would seem, a state court is also justified when it leaves this local control intact during a recount.

We will have to await future decisions before knowing whether or not *Bush* presages important future doctrinal developments. Suppose we ask instead why the current doctrine is so complex to make room for added word. One possibility is that the complexity is produced by the Court's unease about the public-regarding character of the equal protection law of voting. As explained above, voting is a method by which people affiliate themselves with groups and engage in collective political action. For this reason, the Court's effort to enforce equality in this area has also focused on the power of groups. Reapportionment, for example, is about the

48. *Id.*

relative power of people living in suburbs, cities, and rural areas.

The focus on groups, in turn, pushes one toward a norm of proportional representation. On this view, groups should enjoy political power that is comparable to their electoral strength. But the Court has also resisted the pull toward proportionality precisely because proportional representation subsumes individuals into groups. A competing, individualistic norm insists that voters are not just African American, Italian, Democrats, or union members. A private-regarding view of voting treats each voter as an individual with a set of goals and preferences that is unique to the individual. Because so much of our constitutional heritage is tied up with this individualistic conception, the Court has tended to backtrack whenever its equal protection analysis seems on the verge of full-throated endorsement of the public conception.

Access to Judicial Process

Whereas voting is primarily a public-regarding method of resolving conflict, litigation is primarily private-regarding. Traditionally, courts, unlike legislatures, deal with individual claims asserted by individual litigants. Perhaps for this reason, the Supreme Court has been ambivalent about whether to base its decisions ensuring access to the judicial process on equal protection or due process jurisprudence.

In two early cases, Griffin v. Illinois[49] and Douglas v. California,[50] the Court relied primarily on the

49. 351 U.S. 12 (1956).
50. 372 U.S. 353 (1963).

equal protection clause to hold that indigent criminal defendants were entitled to counsel and a transcript on their first appeal. As discussed in Chapter Nine, these cases suggested that indigency might form a suspect class triggering heightened scrutiny. But the cases also suggested that access to courts was a fundamental right, at least when personal liberty was at stake. The Court has also held unconstitutional as applied to indigents a requirement for payment of court fees in order to secure a divorce[51] and the conditioning of appeals from trial court decrees terminating parental rights on the payment of a fee for record preparation.[52] On the other hand, the Court has upheld filing fees for bankruptcy proceedings[53] and has refused to order states to provide counsel for indigent defendants petitioning for discretionary review after a first appeal of right.[54]

Interestingly, whereas *Harper* had held that the poll tax was unconstitutional even as applied to the rich, *Griffin* and *Douglas* provided benefits only to the poor. Perhaps this distinction rests on the fact that litigation is more privately oriented than voting. Perhaps for this reason as well, the Court has vacillated between resort to the equal protection clause and the due process clause in analyzing access to judicial process. For example, when the Court invalidated filing fees in divorce actions, it

51. Boddie v. Connecticut, 401 U.S. 371 (1971).
52. M.L.B. v. S.L.J., 519 U.S. 102 (1996).
53. United States v. Kras, 409 U.S. 434 (1973).
54. Ross v. Moffitt, 417 U.S. 600 (1974).

relied upon due process, rather than equal protection analysis.[55]

There is an obvious problem with conceptualizing these claims as grounded in due process, however. Due process, unlike equal protection, involves absolute, rather than comparative, rights. Thus, insofar as the due process clause is concerned, a violation occurs even if everyone is denied access to judicial process. But why should such process matter if there is no underlying right to be vindicated by the process? Thus, a holding that the due process clause is violated by charging a filing fee in divorce actions comes close to holding that there is an underlying right to divorce.

In contrast, equal protection analysis permits the government to abolish the right, so long as it does so for everyone. Here, as elsewhere, resort to the equal protection clause tends to make the analysis more public-regarding. As we have already seen, the equal protection clause can be used as a lever to encourage government intervention. Thus, insofar as the equal protection clause is concerned, the government could, if it wished, abolish criminal appeals generally. However, if it allows them, it must intervene in private markets to subsidize services necessary for the appeals like counsel and record preparation.

Travel

The Court's treatment of cases involving the right to travel illustrates the action-forcing poten-

55. *See* Boddie v. Connecticut, 401 U.S. 371 (1971).

tial of substantive equal protection. In Shapiro v. Thompson,[56] a case decided during the Warren Court era, the Court struck down a one year residency requirement for state residents seeking welfare benefits. In an opinion written by Justice William Brennan, the Court held that the waiting period infringed on the constitutional right to travel and, therefore, triggered heightened scrutiny. It followed that the putative state interest in preventing the influx of poor people seeking higher welfare benefits was simply illegitimate. Because the right to travel between states was constitutionally protected, the state could not legitimately act so as to penalize this right.

There are two difficulties with the Court's analysis. First, unlike the opinions in *Skinner, Harper*, and *Griffin*, Justice Brennan's *Shapiro* opinion suggests that the right to travel enjoys substantive constitutional protection. But if this is true, we are confronted yet again with the puzzle of what work the equal protection clause is doing. If there is already a constitutional right to travel, then why didn't the state law violate this right, rather than the right to equal protection?

Presumably, the answer to this question is that the substantive right to travel is private-regarding. Put differently, there is a right to be free from government constraints when one travels, but not a right to a government subsidy to assist people who wish to travel. A poor person who cannot afford the bus fare from New York to New Jersey is not

56. 394 U.S. 618 (1969).

constitutionally entitled to have the government pay for it. Similarly, since there is no right to affirmative government subvention in the form of welfare, it might be thought that the substantive right to travel is not violated by withholding this subsidy to newly arrived residents.

In contrast, equal protection has the potential to apply to subsidies as well as to burdens. True, there is no substantive right to government subvention of travel, but the right to travel might nonetheless trigger heightened scrutiny of classifications impinging on the right. Thus, the government may, if it chooses, abolish welfare altogether, but if it chooses to maintain a welfare program, it may not do so in a fashion that penalizes those who have exercised the travel right.

This formulation brings the second problem into sharp relief. Did *Shapiro*'s waiting period really impinge on the right to travel? Zobel v. Williams[57] illustrates the difficulty with the Court's analysis. After oil was discovered in Alaska, the state decided to use some of the revenue to make cash grants to its citizens. However, the state distributed the resources in varying amounts depending on the length of residence within the state. Citing *Shapiro*, the *Zobel* Court held that this discrimination penalized the right to travel. This holding is puzzling because individuals who did not exercise the right fared no worse than individuals who did. Obviously, people who did not migrate to Alaska were not eligible to receive the distribution. People who re-

57. 457 U.S. 55 (1982).

cently migrated were also ineligible, but this meant only that they got what they would have received had they stayed where they were.

This problem came to a head in Saenz v. Roe.[58] Unlike the laws invalidated in *Shapiro*, a California statute provided welfare benefits to newly arrived residents. However, the statute also provided that the benefits could not exceed the amount that the resident would have received had he remained in the state from which he migrated. California argued that this statute was distinguishable from the *Shapiro* law on the ground that paying mobile citizens the same amount as citizens who stayed in one place in no way penalized the right of movement.

The *Saenz* Court responded to this challenge by shifting the analysis from the equal protection clause to the fourteenth amendment's privileges and immunities clause. As we saw in Chapter Two, this provision, which guarantees inhabitants of the states the privileges and immunities of United States citizenship, had been a virtual dead letter since the Court's decision in the Slaughter–House cases decided shortly after enactment of the fourteenth amendment. In *Saenz*, the Court gave new life to the clause by holding that one of the privileges of United States citizenship is the right to full citizenship in the state in which a person resides. Hence, discriminatory treatment of newly arrived citizens is unconstitutional not because it deters or penalizes the right to travel, but because it treats

58. 526 U.S. 489 (1999).

new residents as something less than full state citizens.

This reinterpretation of *Shapiro* helps make sense of some other pre-*Saenz* cases that are otherwise mysterious. Compare, for example, Dunn v. Blumstein[59] with Sosna v. Iowa.[60] In *Dunn*, the Court struck down a durational residency requirement for voting. In *Sosna,* it upheld a durational residency requirement for securing a divorce. We know from prior cases that differential access to both divorce and voting can trigger heightened scrutiny.[61] Why, then, should durational residency requirements limiting access to the two rights be treated differently?

From the perspective of a right to travel, *Dunn* and *Sosna* are even more mysterious. It seems intuitively unlikely that many people are actually deterred from traveling to a new state because durational residency requirements prevent them from voting. In contrast, one can easily imagine individuals moving to a new state so as to secure a divorce. Indeed, the state enacted the *Sosna* durational residency requirement precisely so as to prevent it from becoming a "divorce mill" for newly arrived residents. In this sense, then, both cases seem wrongly decided.

59. 405 U.S. 330 (1972).

60. 419 U.S. 393 (1975).

61. *Compare* Boddie v. Connecticut, 401 U.S. 371 (1971) (divorce) *with* Harper v. Virginia State Board of Elections, 383 U.S. 663 (1966) (voting).

Thinking about the cases in terms of the privileges and immunities of United States citizenship makes more sense of them. The problem in these cases is not that the right to travel has been penalized, but that new residents have not been treated as full citizens. There is no more obvious mark of citizenship than the right to vote. Importantly, this right is public-regarding. In contrast, the right to divorce fits less easily under the rubric of citizenship. To be sure, the right may be important, but, because it is private-regarding, it is harder to conceptualize it as a right of citizenship.

This distinction does not fully explain the Court's treatment of welfare in *Shapiro*, which also seems more private-regarding. But here a second distinction takes hold. The whole purpose of the law imposing durational residency requirements on divorce is to respect the judgment of neighboring states that have more stringent divorce laws. Precisely because the residents of these states cannot vote in the state with liberal divorce laws, the liberal state has a sound reason for closing its courts to outsiders who move there temporarily in order to subvert their own state's laws. In contrast, it is hard to imagine why voters of one state would object if residents of that state migrate elsewhere to receive higher welfare benefits or to vote in the elections of another state. Thus, the very principle of state political sovereignty that argues for striking down limitations on the right to vote argues for sustaining such limitations on the right to a divorce.

The End of Substantive Equal Protection?

Many of the Court's substantive equal protection decisions were a product of the Warren Court years. By the early 1970's the politics of the Court—and of the country—had significantly changed, and substantive equal protection became much less important. For example, despite earlier hints to the contrary, during this period, the Court firmly rejected the notion that goods necessary for subsistence, like a minimum income[62] or decent housing,[63] were fundamental rights triggering heightened equal protection review.

A turning point came in San Antonio Independent School District v. Rodriguez.[64] Plaintiffs challenged Texas' system for financing public education, which depended mostly upon local property taxes. This system resulted in substantial interdistrict disparities in the amounts of money districts had to spend on education. Districts that contained valuable property spent much more per pupil than districts lacking such property, even if the two districts taxed the property at the same rate. Plaintiffs claimed that this system violated the equal protection clause. They argued that scrutiny should be heightened in part because it impinged upon the fundamental right to education.

The Supreme Court, in a decision written by Justice Lewis Powell, rejected this claim. In a pas-

62. *See* Dandridge v. Williams, 397 U.S. 471 (1970).

63. *See* Lindsey v. Normet, 405 U.S. 56 (1972).

64. 411 U.S. 1 (1973).

sage that seemed in considerable tension with the Court's earlier precedent, Justice Powell rejected the notion that

> It is ... the province of this Court to create substantive constitutional rights in the name of guaranteeing equal protection of the laws.... [T]he key to discovering whether education is "fundamental" is not to be found in comparisons of the relative societal significance of education as opposed to subsistence or housing. Nor is it to be found by weighing whether education is as important as the right to travel. Rather, the answer lies in assessing whether there is a right to education explicitly or implicitly guaranteed by the Constitution.[65]

Of course, the Constitution does not "explicitly or implicitly guarantee[]" the right to procreate, the right to vote, or the right of indigent defendants to appeal their convictions. Justice Powell's struggle to distinguish prior precedent suggested that an important change was occurring. It is easy to misunderstand what that change amounts to, however. The passage quoted above suggested that *Rodriguez* was grounded in respect for constitutional text. From this passage alone, one might think that the dispute involved the appropriate boundary between the judicial and political branches. When the Constitution "explicitly or implicitly" guarantees a right, the Court should enforce that right. But when the text is silent, it is for the political branches to decide whether the right should be vindicated.

65. *Id.* at 33.

The difficulty with this interpretation of *Rodriguez* is that the case was decided during the very Term when the Court also announced its decision in Roe v. Wade.[66] *Roe*, which upheld the due process right of a woman to secure an abortion, is perhaps the most famous nontextual decision ever rendered. Justice Powell, who decried the invention of nontextual rights under the equal protection clause in *Rodriguez*, joined the majority in inventing such a right under the due process clause in *Roe*.

The real significance of *Rodriguez* concerns the division between public and private, rather than between court and legislature. What is really at stake becomes apparent when one compares Justice Powell's majority opinion with Justice Thurgood Marshall's dissent.[67] Justice Marshall argued that the Court ought to adopt a "sliding scale" approach to equal protection scrutiny, adjusting the level of scrutiny to fit the importance of the right impinged. How does one determine how important a particular right is? Justice Marshall thought that this determination could be made fairly objectively by measuring how closely the nontextual right was tied to the vindication of a textual right. Thus, even though the constitutional text does not speak to education, it is nonetheless fundamental because it is necessary for the effective exercise of the right to speak and vote.

66. 410 U.S. 113 (1973).

67. San Antonio Independent School Dist. v. Rodriguez, 411 U.S. 1, 70 (1973) (Marshall, J., dissenting).

Justice Powell responded to Justice Marshall's dissent with the following argument:

> The Court has long afforded zealous protection against unjustifiable governmental interference with the individual's rights to speak and to vote. Yet we have never presumed to possess either the ability or the authority to guarantee to the citizenry the most *effective* speech or the most *informed* electoral choice. That these may be desirable goals ... is not to be doubted.... But they are not values to be implemented by judicial intrusion into otherwise legitimate state activities.[68]

As this passage makes clear, the difference between Justices Marshall and Powell is about whether the Constitution is public- or private-regarding. For Justice Marshall, individual rights are useless unless the government facilitates their exercise. Education is fundamental because it is a positive government intervention that makes the exercise of other rights possible. For Justice Powell, the Constitution is designed to wall off a private sphere free from government interference. To be sure, adequate education is desirable, but, unlike the abortion right, it not constitutionally mandatory because it involves protection *by* government rather than protection *from* government.

Rodriguez was a victory for the private-regarding conception. But no victories or defeats are permanent in constitutional law. Thus, in subsequent

68. *Id.* at 36.

cases, where a large-scale restructuring of school financing was not at stake, as it was in *Rodriguez*, the Court has suggested that education might be a fundamental right after all.[69] In other areas, such as voting rights and the right of access to appellate process, the Court continues to decide cases based upon the fundamental rights strand of equal protection doctrine. And, as Bush v. Gore indicates, sometimes support for this strand comes from quarters where one would hardly expect to find it.

In this sense, evolving substantive equal protection might be taken as a metaphor for all of equal protection jurisprudence. The various tests and doctrines described in this book constitute the vocabulary that the Court uses when it decides equal protection cases, but it would be a mistake to suppose that these tests and doctrines have the capacity to permanently resolve the underlying disputes. The concept of equal protection is too open-ended, amorphous, and contradictory for any resolution to be permanent. The struggles between universalism and particularism, between the public and the private, between likeness and difference—the stuff of equal protection controversy—are ongoing and unending.

Equal protection doctrine cannot "solve" these problems because the problems are built into how each of us perceives the world that surrounds us.

69. *See* Papasan v. Allain, 478 U.S. 265 (1986); Plyler v. Doe, 457 U.S. 202 (1982). *But see* Kadrmas v. Dickinson Pub. Schools, 487 U.S. 450 (1988).

We are all capable of perceiving analogies that make the different seem alike, yet we all need to bound the analogies so as to create a community that is special for us. So long as each of us retains these conflicting capacities, there will be arguments about the meaning and scope of equal protection.

TABLE OF CASES

References are to Pages.

Adarand Constructors, Inc. v. Pena, 28, 32, 157, 170, 171, 175, 236
Ake v. Oklahoma, 239
Allgeyer v. Louisiana, 129
Ambach v. Norwick, 29, 233
Application of (see name of party)
Arlington Heights, Village of v. Metropolitan Housing Development Corp., 114, 175
Armstrong, United States v., 108

Baker v. Carr, 264
Baltimore v. Dawson, 136
Batson v. Kentucky, 106
Bernal v. Fainter, 29, 231
Board of Educ. v. Dowell, 145
Board of Educ. v. Grumet, 125
Boddie v. Connecticut, 238, 278, 279, 283
Bolling v. Sharpe, 32
Bowers v. Hardwick, 220
Boy Scouts of America v. Dale, 36, 166
Bradwell v. Illinois, 188
Brown v. Board of Educ., 139
Brown v. Board of Ed. of Topeka, Shawnee County, Kan., 34, 135, 137, 158
Brown v. Thomson, 266
Buchanan v. Warley, 131
Buck v. Bell, 249
Burton v. Wilmington Parking Authority, 160, 164
Bush v. Gore, 273, 273
Bush v. Vera, 149

291

Cabell v. Chavez–Salido, 29, 233
Califano v. Goldfarb, 195, 215
Califano v. Webster, 216
California Federal Sav. & Loan Ass'n v. Guerra, 209
Carolene Products Co., United States v., 86
Cipriano v. City of Houma, 237
City of (see name of city)
Cleburne, City of v. Cleburne Living Center, 30, 55, 244, 245
Colegrove v. Green, 264
Craig v. Boren, 29, 192, 194, 197
Cruzan v. Director, Missouri Dept. of Health, 257
Cumming v. Board of Ed., 130

Dandridge v. Williams, 46, 239, 285
Davis v. Bandemer, 270
Douglas v. California, 31, 238, 277
Dunn v. Blumstein, 283

Evans v. Newton, 160

F.C.C. v. Beach Communications, Inc., 62
Foley v. Connelie, 29, 233
Freeman v. Pitts, 145
Frontiero v. Richardson, 30, 191
F.S. Royster Guano Co. v. Commonwealth of Virginia, 46
Fullilove v. Klutznick, 167

Gayle v. Browder, 136
Geduldig v. Aiello, 208
Glona v. American Guarantee & Liability Ins. Co., 29
Goesaert v. Cleary, 190
Gomez v. Perez, 29, 245
Gomillion v. Lightfoot, 104, 146, 269
Graham v. Richardson, 29, 230
Green v. County School Bd., 35, 142, 160, 162
Griffin v. Illinois, 31, 237, 243, 277
Griffiths, In re, 29, 231

Hampton v. Mow Sun Wong, 234
Harper v. Virginia, 31, 237, 238, 258, 283
Hays, United States v., 150
Heart of Atlanta Motel v. United States, 161
Holmes v. City of Atlanta, 136

Holt Civic Club v. City of Tuscaloosa, 263
Hooper v. Bernalillo County Assessor, 31
Hoyt v. Florida, 190
Hunter v. Underwood, 61, 108

Jefferson v. Hackney, 61
Jones v. Alfred H. Mayer Co., 161

Kadrmas v. Dickinson Public Schools, 289
Karcher v. Daggett, 266
Katzenbach v. McClung, 161
Kirchberg v. Feenstra, 195
Korematsu v. United States, 80
Kramer v. Union Free School Dist., 31, 260
Kras, United States v., 239, 278

Lalli v. Lalli, 29
Levy v. Louisiana, 29, 245
Lindsey v. Normet, 239, 285
Little v. Streater, 239
Lochner v. New York, 129, 165, 190, 252
Loving v. Virginia, 120, 227

Mahan v. Howell, 266
Maher v. Roe, 238
Martinez–Fuerte, United States v., 83
Massachusetts Bd. of Retirement v. Murgia, 244
Mathews v. Diaz, 29, 234
Mathews v. Lucas, 29
Mayor of City of Philadelphia v. Educational Equality League, 85
McCabe v. Atchison, T. & S.F. R. Co., 130
McCleskey v. Kemp, 113, 176
McGowan v. Maryland, 46
McLaughlin v. Florida, 77
McLaurin v. Oklahoma State Regents, 134
Metro Broadcasting, Inc. v. F.C.C., 176
Michael M. v. Sonoma County, 193, 194, 209
Milliken v. Bradley, 145
Minnesota v. Clover Leaf Creamery Co., 62
Minor v. Happersett, 190
Missouri v. Jenkins, 145
Missouri ex rel. Gaines v. Canada, 133
M.L.B. v. S.L.J., 31, 239, 241, 278
Mobile, City of v. Bolden, 269

Moose Lodge No. 107 v. Irvis, 164
Morrison, United States v., 33, 166
Mt. Healthy City School Dist. Bd. of Educ. v. Doyle, 117, 119
Muller v. Oregon, 190

New Orleans, City of v. Dukes, 46
New York City Transit Authority v. Beazer, 39
Nguyen v. I.N.S., 195, 212
Nordlinger v. Hahn, 62
North Carolina State Bd. of Ed. v. Swann, 162
Norwood v. Harrison, 160
Nyquist v. Mauclet, 29, 231

Palmer v. Thompson, 117
Palmore v. Sidoti, 83, 160, 227
Papasan v. Allain, 289
Pasadena City Bd. of Ed. v. Spangler, 145
Personnel Adm'r v. Feeney, 110
Peterson v. Greenville, 161
Plessy v. Ferguson, 16, 33, 122
Plyler v. Doe, 231, 289
Poe v. Ullman, 16

Railway Exp. Agency v. New York, 70, 255
Reed v. Reed, 190
Reynolds v. Sims, 31, 265
Richmond, City of v. J.A. Croson Co., 29, 78, 158, 169, 171, 172, 175, 216
Roe v. Wade, 207, 287
Romer v. Evans, 16, 30, 57, 156, 221
Ross v. Moffitt, 239, 278
Rostker v. Goldberg, 195
Runyon v. McCrary, 161

Saenz v. Roe, 282
Salyer Land Co. v. Tulare Lake Basin Water Storage Dist., 263
San Antonio Independent School Dist. v. Rodriguez, 239, 285, 287
Schlesinger v. Ballard, 195
Schweiker v. Wilson, 64
Shapiro v. Thompson, 31, 237, 280
Shaw v. Hunt, 149
Shaw v. Reno, 147
Shelley v. Kraemer, 35, 133, 160

Skinner v. Oklahoma, 31, 248
Slaughter–House Cases, 23, 159, 188
Smith v. Allwright, 133
Sosna v. Iowa, 283
State of (see name of state)
Strauder v. West Virginia, 27, 94, 97
Sugarman v. Dougall, 29, 231
Sunday Lake Iron Co. v. Wakefield Tp., 45
Swain v. Alabama, 106
Swann v. Charlotte–Mecklenburg Bd. of Ed., 35, 143, 162, 163
Sweatt v. Painter, 133, 203

Taylor v. Louisiana, 195
Trimble v. Gordon, 64

United States v. _____ (see opposing party)
United States Dept. of Agriculture v. Moreno, 55
United States R.R. Retirement Bd. v. Fritz, 53, 66
University of California v. Bakke, 167

Village of (see name of village)
Virginia, United States v., 29, 194, 195, 201, 204

Washington v. Davis, 36, 96, 97, 118, 155, 163
Washington v. Seattle School Dist., 152
Weaver, United States v., 83
Weber v. Aetna Cas. & Sur. Co., 29
West Virginia State Board of Education v. Barnette, 50
Williamson v. Lee Optical, 27, 69
Willowbrook, Village of v. Olech, 44
Wygant v. Jackson Bd. of Educ., 167

Yick Wo v. Hopkins, 104

Zobel v. Williams, 31, 281

＊

TABLE OF CASES

INDEX

References are to Pages

ABORTIONS
Subsidized abortions, right to, boundaries of equality, 238

ACCESS TO JUDICIAL PROCESS
Fundamental rights and equal protection, 277–279

ADMINISTRATOR OF ESTATE
Gender discrimination, male preference, 191

ADOPTION OF CHILDREN
Race based classifications, actual status of, 84, 85

AFFIRMATIVE ACTION
Gender discrimination, 214–218
Race–Specific Classifications Benefiting Racial Minorities, this
index

ALCOHOLIC BEVERAGES
Gender discrimination, only women between 18 and 21 permitted to drink 3.2 per cent beer, 196–200

ALIENS
Noncitizens, this index

ARMED FORCES
Military Service, this index

ATTORNEYS
Criminal defendants, free attorneys, 237–239
Gender discrimination, law practice, 189, 190
Noncitizens prohibited from becoming, 231

BOUNDARIES OF EQUALITY
General discussion, 219, 220

BOUNDARIES OF EQUALITY—Cont'd
Abortions, right to subsidized, 238
Criminal Defendants, this index
Divorce, inability to pay court fees, 238
Future of suspect classification analysis, 244–247
Homosexuals, this index
Initiative prohibiting discrimination against homosexuals, 221–228
Necessities, provision to poor, 239
Noncitizens, this index
Parental rights, termination of, poor persons, 239, 241, 242
Poll tax, poor people, 237
Poor people, 236–244
Probation officers, 233
Property owners, franchise limited to, poor people, 237
Public assistance, durational residency requirements for, 237

CAPITAL PUNISHMENT
Nonrace-specific classifications which disadvantage racial minorities, 113, 114, 117

CHILD CUSTODY
Race based classifications, actual status of, 83, 84

CITIZENSHIP
Gender discrimination
    distinguishing between children of unwed men and women
        for purposes of citizenship, 195
    nonmarital children born outside United States to citizen
        mother but noncitizen father, 212–214
Noncitizens, this index

CIVIL SERVICE POSITIONS
Noncitizens, 231, 232, 234–236
Veteran preferences, nonrace-specific classifications which disadvantage racial minorities, 110–112

COMPELLING ENDS
Race-specific measures, justifying, 175–177

CONGRUENCE
Race-specific classifications benefiting racial minorities, 158

CONSISTENCY
Race-specific classifications benefiting racial minorities, 157

CONSTRUCTION CONTRACTS
Race-specific classifications benefiting racial minorities, affirmative action, modern law of, 169–174

CRIMINAL DEFENDANTS
Appeal, right of counsel, 237–239, 243
Death penalty, nonrace-specific classifications which disadvantage racial minorities, 113
Free attorneys, 237–239
Free transcripts on appeal, 237–239

DEATH PENALTY
Nonrace-specific classifications which disadvantage racial minorities, 113, 114, 117

DIVORCE
Boundaries of equality, inability to pay court fees, 238

DRAFT, MILITARY
Gender discrimination, only men required to register, 194, 195

DRUGS
Employment refused to users of methadone, low level scrutiny, 39–41

EDUCATION
Schools, this index

ELECTIONS
Initiative prohibiting discrimination against homosexuals, 221–228
Voting Rights, this index

EMPLOYMENT
Noncitizens, prohibition on seeking employment, 232

EQUALITY
Boundaries of Equality, this index
Ethical equality, 7–10
Importance of, 10–14
Nature of, 1–17
Political valence of, 14–17
Rational equality, 5–7
Sameness and difference, problem of, 3–5

ESTATE ADMINISTRATION
Gender discrimination, male preference, 191

ETHICAL EQUALITY
General discussion, 7–10

FACIALLY NEUTRAL CLASSIFICATIONS
Race–Specific Classifications Which Are Facially Neutral, this index

FOOD STAMP PROGRAM
Low level scrutiny, households containing nonrelatives as ineligible, 55

FORMAL VERSUS INTERVENTIONIST EQUALITY
Gender discrimination, 201–207

FUNDAMENTAL RIGHTS AND EQUAL PROTECTION
General discussion, 248
Access to judicial process, 277–279
End of substantive equal protection, 285–290
Poll tax, 258–261
Property tax, funding of public education, end of substantive equal protection, 285–289
Sterilization of habitual criminals, 248–257
Travel, 279–284
Voting Rights, this index

GENDER DISCRIMINATION
General discussion, 186, 187
Affirmative action, 214–218
Alcoholic beverages, only women between 18 and 21 permitted to drink 3.2 per cent beer, 196–200
Citizenship, this index
Estate administration, male preference, 191
Examples, 207–214
Formal versus interventionist equality, 201–207
Heightened scrutiny for gender specific classifications, 188–200
Law practice, prohibiting women from, 189, 190
Military academy, only men permitted to enroll in, 195, 201–207
Military Service, this index
Pregnancy, this index
Social security
    retired females granted higher old age pension than comparable males, 216, 217
    widows' benefits different from widowers' benefits, 215, 216
Statutory rape, only men prosecuted for, 194, 209–212

GRADUATE SCHOOL
Race-specific classifications which are facially neutral, special seat in class and dining room, 134

GROUP HOMES FOR RETARDED PERSONS
Low level scrutiny, 55, 56

HASIDIC JEWS
Special school district for, race-specific classifications which are facially neutral, 125

HEIGHTENED SCRUTINY
Gender-specific classifications, 188–200
Race-specific classifications, 76–79

HIGHER EDUCATION FINANCIAL ASSISTANCE
Noncitizens prohibited from receiving, 231

HOMOSEXUALS
Initiative prohibiting discrimination against homosexuals, 221–228
Low level scrutiny, antidiscrimination measures, 57–61
Sodomy statute, 220, 221

IMMIGRATION POLICY
Noncitizens, 234

INDIGENTS
Poor Persons, this index

INITIATIVE
Homosexuals, discrimination against, initiative prohibiting, 221–228

INTERVENTIONIST EQUALITY
Gender discrimination, formal versus interventionist equality, 201–207

INTOXICATING BEVERAGES
Gender discrimination, only women between 18 and 21 permitted to drink 3.2 per cent beer, 196–200

JAPANESE RELOCATION CAMPS
Actual status of race based classifications, 80–83

JIM CROW, STRUGGLE AGAINST
Race-specific classifications which are facially neutral, 128–135

JUDICIAL PROCESS
Access to, fundamental rights and equal protection, 277–279

JURORS
Peremptory challenges, nonrace-specific classifications which dis-
    advantage racial minorities, 106, 109
Racially charged case, race specific statutes disadvantaging racial
    minorities, 94

LAUNDRY
Nonrace-specific classifications which disadvantage racial minori-
    ties, consent of municipality, 104, 105

LAW PRACTICE
Gender discrimination, 189, 190

LAW SCHOOLS
Race-specific classifications which are facially neutral, law school
    for white students only, 133, 134

LOW AND MODERATE INCOME HOUSING
Nonrace-specific classifications which disadvantage racial minori-
    ties, refusal to rezone, 114–116

LOW LEVEL SCRUTINY
Actual purpose review, 61–66
Choosing standard of review, 46–52
Examining nexus, 66–73
Example, 39–41
Homosexuals, antidiscrimination measures, 57–61
Identifying classification, 41–45
Identifying legislative purpose, 52–66
Overinclusion and underinclusion, 67–73

MARRIAGE
Race specific statutes, intermarriage of white and colored per-
    sons, 120–122

MATERNITY
Pregnancy, this index

MEDICAL INSURANCE PROGRAM
Noncitizens' participation in, 234

MEDICAL SCHOOLS
Race-specific classifications benefiting racial minorities, affirma-
    tive action, modern law of, 167, 168

METHADONE
Employment refused to users of, low level scrutiny, 39–41

MILITARY ACADEMY
Gender discrimination, only men permitted to enroll, 195, 201–207

MILITARY SERVICE
Gender discrimination
    dependents, spouses as, 191–193
    draft, only men required to register for, 194, 195
    promotions, different time periods for men and women to receive, 195

MINIMAL JUDICIAL SCRUTINY
Race-specific statutes disadvantaging racial minorities, 86

MISCEGENATION
Race specific statutes, 120–122

MORAL TURPITUDE
Nonrace-specific classifications which disadvantage racial minorities, disqualification of voter for committing crime of moral turpitude, 109

MOTIVE
Nonrace-Specific Classifications Which Disadvantage Racial Minorities, this index

MUNICIPAL SWIMMING POOL
Closing rather than desegregating, nonrace-specific classifications which disadvantage racial minorities, 117, 118

NARROW TAILORING APPROACH
Race-specific classifications benefiting racial minorities, 177–179

NECESSITIES
Poor, provision to, boundaries of equality, 239

NEXUS
Low level scrutiny, examining nexus, 66–73

NONCITIZENS
    General discussion, 229–233
Attorneys, noncitizens prohibited from becoming, 231
Civil service positions, 231, 232, 234–236
Employment, prohibition on seeking, 232
Gender discrimination, nonmarital children born outside United States to citizen mother, but noncitizen father, 212–214

NONCITIZENS—Cont'd
Higher education financial assistance, noncitizens prohibited from receiving, 231
Immigration policy, 234
Medical insurance program, participation in, 234
Notaries public, noncitizens prohibited from becoming, 231
Police officers, 233
Public assistance benefits, 230–232
Public employment, 231, 233, 234
Residency rights, 234
Visitation rights, 234

NONRACE–SPECIFIC CLASSIFICATIONS WHICH DISADVANTAGE RACIAL MINORITIES
General discussion, 95, 96
Capital punishment, 113, 114, 117
Improperly motivated classifications, 103–110
Laundry operation requiring consent of municipality, 104, 105
Limitations on review for improper motive, 110–119
Low and moderate income housing, refusal to rezone for, 114–116
Moral turpitude, disqualification of voter for committing crime of, 109
Motive
    improperly motivated classifications, 103–110
    limitations on review for improper motive, 110–119
Municipal swimming pool, closing rather than desegregating, 117, 118
Peremptory challenges, 106, 109
Police officers, tests for positions as, 96–100
Rational basis review, 96–103
Reapportionment, 104
Teacher, refusal to rehire, 118
Veteran preferences, civil service positions, 110–112

NORMATIVE APPRAISAL
Race-specific classifications benefiting racial minorities, 179–185

NOTARIES PUBLIC
Noncitizens prohibited from becoming, 231

ORIGINS OF EQUAL PROTECTION
General discussion, 19–23

OVERINCLUSION AND UNDERINCLUSION
Low level scrutiny, 67–73

OVERVIEW OF EQUAL PROTECTION CLAUSE
General discussion, 18
Basic structure of equal protection review, 23–36
Origins of equal protection, 19–23
Summary, 36–38

PARENTAL RIGHTS, TERMINATION OF
Poor persons, boundaries of equality, 239, 241, 242

PEREMPTORY CHALLENGES
Nonrace-specific classifications which disadvantage racial minorities, 106, 109

POLICE OFFICERS
Noncitizens, 233
Tests for positions as, nonrace-specific classifications which disadvantage racial minorities, 96–100

POLITICAL VALENCE
Equality, 14–17

POLL TAX
Fundamental rights and equal protection, 258–261
Poor people, boundaries of equality, 237

POOR PERSONS
Boundaries of equality, 236–244
Criminal defendants, free attorneys and free transcript for appeal, 237–239
Necessities, provision of, boundaries of equality, 239
Parental rights, termination of, boundaries of equality, 239, 241, 242

PREGNANCY
Gender discrimination
benefits denied to expectant fathers, 208, 209
disabilities, exclusions, 208

PROBATION OFFICERS
Boundaries of equality, 233

PROMOTIONS
Military service, gender discrimination, different time periods for men and women to receive, 195

PROPERTY OWNERS
Poor people, franchise limited to, boundaries of equality, 237

PROPERTY OWNERS—Cont'd

School district, voting rights, fundamental rights and equal protection, 260

Water district, voting rights, fundamental rights and equal protection, 263

PROPERTY TAX

Schools, this index

PUBLIC ASSISTANCE

Durational residency requirements for, boundaries of equality, 237

Noncitizens, 230–232

PUBLIC EMPLOYMENT

Civil Service Positions, this index

Noncitizens, 231, 233, 234

RACE–SPECIFIC CLASSIFICATIONS BENEFITING RACIAL MINORITIES

General discussion, 157, 158

Affirmative action

general discussion, 157, 158

modern law of, 166–174

racial integration and, 158–166

unanswered questions, 174–179

Compelling ends justifying race-specific measures, 175–177

Congruence, 158

Consistency, 157

Narrow tailoring approach, 177–179

Normative appraisal, 179–185

Skepticism, 157

Two unanswered questions, 174–179

RACE–SPECIFIC CLASSIFICATIONS WHICH ARE FACIALLY NEUTRAL

General discussion, 120–122

Jim Crow, struggle against, 128–135

Law schools for white students only, race-specific classifications which are facially neutral, 134

Modern examples of strict scrutiny for race specific but facially neutral statutes, 146–156

Railroads, this index

Reapportionment actually reflecting racial composition of state as a whole, 147–149

Residence in block where majority of houses occupied by African Americans, whites prohibited from occupying, 131

Separate but equal, 122–128

RACE–SPECIFIC STATUTES DISADVANTAGING RACIAL MINORITIES

General discussion, 74–76
Actual status of race based classifications, 79–85
Heightened scrutiny for race-specific classifications, 76–79
Minimal judicial scrutiny, 86

RAILROAD RETIREMENT

Low level scrutiny, impact of changes, 53

RAILROADS

Race-specific classifications which are facially neutral
    separate but equal accommodations for white and colored
        races, 122–128
    sleeping, dining, and chair cars only for whites, 130, 131

RAPE

Statutory rape, gender discrimination, only men prosecuted, 194,
    209–212

RATIONAL BASIS REVIEW

Nonrace-specific classifications which disadvantage racial minorities, 96–103

RATIONAL EQUALITY

General discussion, 5–7

REAPPORTIONMENT

Nonrace-specific classifications which disadvantage racial minorities, 104
Race-specific classifications which are facially neutral, actually
    reflecting racial composition of state as a whole, 147–149
Vote dilution, fundamental rights and equal protection, 264–277

RECOUNT OF VOTES

Fundamental rights and equal protection, 273–276

RESIDENCE

Block where majority of houses occupied by African Americans,
    whites prohibited from occupying residences in, 131
Noncitizens, residency rights, 234
Public assistance, durational residency requirements for, 237
School boards, initiative prohibiting requiring students to attend
    schools not nearest their residence, 152–156

RETARDED PERSONS
Group homes for, low level scrutiny, 55, 56

SAMENESS AND DIFFERENCE
Equality, 3–5

SCHOOLS
Higher education financial assistance, noncitizens prohibited from receiving, 231
Medical schools, race-specific classifications benefiting racial minorities, affirmative action, modern law of, 167, 168
Military academy, only men permitted to enroll in, gender discrimination, 195, 201–207
Poor areas, funding school districts, boundaries of equality, 239
Property ownership, school district, voting rights, fundamental rights and equal protection, 260
Property tax
　funding of public education, end of substantive equal protection, 285–289
　race-specific classifications which are facially neutral, school district not operating black school, 130
Race-specific classifications benefiting racial minorities
　medical schools, affirmative action, 167, 168
　Segregated Education In Public Elementary and High Schools, this index
Race-specific classifications which are facially neutral
　graduate school, special seat in class and dining room, 134
　Hasidic Jews, special school district for, 125
　initiative prohibiting school boards from requiring students to attend schools not nearest their residence, 152–156
　law school for white students only, 133, 134
　property tax assessment, school district not operating black school, 130
Segregated Education In Public Elementary and High Schools, this index
Teachers, this index

SEGREGATED EDUCATION IN PUBLIC ELEMENTARY AND HIGH SCHOOLS
　General discussion, 135–139
Classifications which benefit racial minorities, 158–162
Enforcement and implementation, 139–146

SELECTIVE SERVICE
Gender discrimination, only men required to register, 194, 195

SEPARATE BUT EQUAL
Race-specific classifications which are facially neutral, 122–128

SEX DISCRIMINATION
Gender Discrimination, this index

SKEPTICISM
Race-specific classifications benefiting racial minorities, 157

SOCIAL SECURITY
Gender Discrimination, this index

SODOMY STATUTE
Homosexuals, 220, 221

STANDARD OF REVIEW
Low level scrutiny, choosing standard of review, 46–52

STATUTORY RAPE
Gender discrimination, only men prosecuted, 194, 209–212

STERILIZATION OF HABITUAL CRIMINALS
Fundamental rights and equal protection, 248–257

SUBSTANTIVE EQUAL PROTECTION
End of, fundamental rights and equal protection, 285–290

SUMMARY
Overview of equal protection clause, 36–38

SWIMMING POOL
Municipal swimming pool, closing rather than desegregating, nonrace-specific classifications which disadvantage racial minorities, 117, 118

TEACHERS
Noncitizens, teachers in public schools, 233
Refusal to rehire, nonrace-specific classifications which disadvantage racial minorities, 118

TRANSCRIPTS
Criminal defendants, free transcripts on appeal, 237–239

TRAVEL
Fundamental rights and equal protection, 279–284

UNDERINCLUSION
Low level scrutiny, 67–73

VETERAN PREFERENCES
Civil service positions, nonrace-specific classifications which disadvantage racial minorities, 110–112

VISITATION RIGHTS
Noncitizens, 234

VOTING RIGHTS
Fundamental rights and equal protection
general discussion, 257–264
recount of votes, 273–276
vote dilution, 264–277
water district, land ownership, 263
Poll Tax, this index
Property Owners, this index
Reapportionment, this index
Recount of votes, fundamental rights and equal protection, 273–276
Vote dilution, fundamental rights and equal protection, 264–277

WATER DISTRICT
Land ownership, voting rights, 263

WELFARE
Public Assistance, this index

†